As Precious
as Blood

As
Precious
as Blood

The Western Slope in Colorado's Water Wars, 1900-1970

Steven C. Schulte

UNIVERSITY PRESS OF COLORADO
Boulder

© 2016 by University Press of Colorado

Published by University Press of Colorado
5589 Arapahoe Avenue, Suite 206C
Boulder, Colorado 80303

 The University Press of Colorado is a proud member of
Association of American University Presses.

The University Press of Colorado is a cooperative publishing enterprise supported, in part,
by Adams State University, Colorado State University, Fort Lewis College, Metropolitan State
University of Denver, Regis University, University of Colorado, University of Northern Colorado,
Utah State University, and Western State Colorado University.

∞ This paper meets the requirements of the ANSI/NISO Z39.48–1992 (Permanence of Paper).

ISBN: 978-1-60732-499-7 (cloth)
ISBN: 978-1-60732-500-0 (ebook)

Library of Congress Cataloging-in-Publication Data

Names: Schulte, Steven C., 1955– author.
Title: As precious as blood : the Western Slope in Colorado's water wars, 1900–1970 / Dr. Steven
   C. Schulte.
Description: Boulder : University Press of Colorado, [2016] | Includes bibliographical references.
Identifiers: LCCN 2016019926 | ISBN 9781607324997 (cloth) | ISBN 9781607325000 (ebook)
Subjects: LCSH: Water rights—Colorado—Western Slope—History.
Classification: LCC HD1694.C6 S38 2016 | DDC 333.91009788/40904—dc23
LC record available at https://lccn.loc.gov/2016019926

Cover photograph by Roy Tennant, FreeLargePhotos.com.

To Tracy—through thick and thin

Contents

Preface

All of the great values of this territory have
ultimately to be measured in acre-feet.

Wallace Stegner quoting John Wesley Powell, in Beyond the Hundredth Meridian[1]

As Precious as Blood explores the ideas, strategies, and motives that animated Colorado's Western Slope's attempts to maintain an adequate water
supply. Western Colorado, settled by Anglo-Americans a generation after
Colorado's better-known mining frontier, was slow to build its necessary
water infrastructure. Suffering from a combination of distance from sources
of capital, small population, and little political power, the Western Slope of
Colorado attempted to maintain its water supply in the face of challenges
from Colorado's Eastern Slope and nearby states.

Like a flowing stream, the current that connects Colorado politics across
the generations is devotion to the lifeblood of reclamation. From the 1930s to
the 1970s, Colorado engaged in a series of battles that collectively could be
called Colorado's twentieth-century water wars. The conflict catalyst in its

DOI: 10.5876/9781607325000.c000

simplest form may be reduced to this: the majority of Colorado's precipitation arises high in the mountainous region west of the Continental Divide, in an area referred to as the Western Slope. However, the vast majority of the state's population resides on the Eastern Slope, or Front Range, of Colorado, along what is referred to today as the Interstate-25 corridor stretching from Fort Collins in the north to Pueblo in the south.

From the beginning of human settlement in the lands that would become Colorado, the region shaped, bent, and broke civilizations according to the nature of their relationship to water supplies. From the Ancestral Puebloans to the Plains Indians to the Latino pioneers in the San Luis Valley, each culture wrestled with correlating its cultural horizons to a workable relationship with available water. With the start of the Colorado gold rush in 1858–59, it quickly became apparent that water would play the key role in determining the region's future. Within a few years, laws were enacted to control and distribute water that bore little resemblance to water laws and institutions in the eastern United States. The West's imposing geography spawned an array of new laws dealing with natural resources, land distribution, and, above all, water. Water laws, however, would be fundamentally a product of the region's abiding aridity. As author Wallace Stegner phrased it, "aridity and aridity alone" united the American West across state boundaries.[2] Water availability determined settlement patterns and in turn molded political values. Western water and land reformer John Wesley Powell perhaps said it best while addressing the Montana Constitutional Convention in 1889: "All of the great values in this territory have ultimately to be measured in acre-feet."[3]

Noted water law scholar Charles Wilkinson observed that Colorado has always been "the crucible" for western water law and policy.[4] The state's high elevation and its role as the "mother" of many of the West's river systems explain its predominant role as water law innovator. With so many streams originating in the state and flowing across neighboring state lines, Colorado's water history is a tangled web of legal contention. Colorado's Western Slope, the region west of the Continental Divide, contributes the most water to the state's total and to the entire Colorado River system. Most estimates believe the high Rocky Mountains west of the Divide produce at least 70 percent of the Colorado River's total flow. The Colorado is a stream that is literally the "river of life" for more than 35 million people in seven western states. Yet western Colorado, though growing, remains relatively sparsely populated;

FIGURE 0.1. Upper Colorado River Basin. The map shows the principal federal water projects in Colorado and the Upper Colorado River Basin. *Courtesy*, Upper Colorado River Commission.

thus the region is under constant pressure to cede additional water to more populous and politically powerful regions like Colorado's Front Range. This issue is the source of much of the political friction that is the primary object of this study.

As Precious as Blood explains several important questions that animate Colorado's water history, including how water emerged as the most pressing issue in Colorado history and why western Colorado began to equate trans-mountain diversions with a diminishment of its regional future. The strategies devised and implemented by Western Slope water officials are also explored and explained in some detail.

Western Colorado's historical fears over its ability to sustain an adequate water supply stemmed from recognition that it lacked the political power to engage the more populated and politically potent Front Range on this issue. This is evident in the struggles of the Western Slope to receive what it considered equitable treatment from the Colorado Water Conservation Board in the mid-1950s during the apex of Colorado's water wars. While western Colorado has exhibited an overall steady population increase, it has paled in comparison to the growth along the Front Range corridor where over two-thirds of the state's population lives in the twenty-first century. This population trend translated into political power that favored eastern Colorado at every level of government, from municipal to federal. From 1914 to 1964 underpopulated western Colorado, with fewer than 200,000 people, maintained its own congressional representative. In 1964 the US Supreme Court mandated that states re-draw their congressional districts to reflect its "one man, one vote" decision. After 1972, the Western Slope no longer had a stand-alone representative as portions of eastern Colorado were added to the Fourth Congressional District. Reapportionment at the Colorado General Assembly level also hit the Western Slope hard, further undermining western Colorado's political resources.[5]

For most of the twentieth century, western Colorado successfully combated the more populous Front Range to maintain a degree of equity in water allocation. The Western Slope utilized many tactics to hold on to its water. A series of well-placed congressional representatives (from Edward T. Taylor to Wayne Aspinall) gave the region more power than its sparse population might have warranted. Effective tactics to delay Front Range water development efforts took many forms over the first two-thirds of the

FIGURE 0.2. Aerial view of the Colorado River country on Colorado's Western Slope, near Grand Junction. The Colorado River, its river of life, snakes through this harsh, arid country above DeBeque Canyon. *Courtesy*, Roy Tennant and FreeLargePhotos.com.

twentieth century. Above all, groups like the Colorado River Water Conservation District fostered regional solidarity against efforts by eastern Colorado to tap the waters of western Colorado. By remaining vigilant and fighting almost every trans-mountain diversion proposal, the region avoided the fate of becoming another California–Owens Valley, which saw much of its local water appropriated for the growth of the greater Los Angeles area.

Scholars have attempted to explain the centrality of water to the American West through numerous lenses. Many favor an assessment based on the environmental damage done to regions that live on intensive reclamation efforts. Others see water control undermining normal democratic impulses. Historian Donald Worster has argued that the emphasis on the American West's water development has not only compromised the fragile environment but committed the region to an "aggressive capitalism" that has led to a "tragedy of unparalleled proportions." For Worster, the commitment to manipulate the West's limited water supply transformed the region into a "coercive, monolithic, and hierarchical system, ruled by a power elite, based on the ownership of capital and expertise."[6]

While the environmental costs of a hydraulic civilization are clear, *As Precious as Blood* is chronologically situated largely in an era before a general awareness of the costs of water development to the natural world became a standard assumption. The conclusion of the book discusses the arrival of environmental critiques of the American West's overall commitment to develop nearly every available drop of water. This is also a story that could be told, and told well, from an environmental perspective. Yet I have chosen to focus on the changing relationship between the two Colorados—one from the populated Eastern Slope corridor and the other from the slower-developing, underpopulated western half. Yet to say that the Western Slope always lost out would be incorrect. Western Colorado accepted incorporation within Colorado's water structure while fashioning its own institutions, arguments, and legal precedents to maintain some sovereignty over the waters originating west of the Continental Divide. The most significant casualties of Colorado's early- to mid-twentieth-century water wars have been intrastate trust and cooperation. It would take Colorado until the 1960s to build better working relationships between its Eastern and Western Slopes. However, even after that point, distrust rather than cooperation has been more the norm.

NOTES

1. Wallace Stegner, *Beyond the Hundredth Meridian: John Wesley Powell and the Second Opening of the West* (Boston: Houghton Mifflin, 1954), 315.

2. Quoted in Susan Rhoades Neel, "A Place of Extremes: Nature, History, and the American West," in Clyde Milner II, ed., *A New Significance: Re-Envisioning the History of the American West* (New York: Oxford University Press), 111.

3. Quoted in Stegner, *Beyond the Hundredth Meridian*, 315.

4. Charles F. Wilkinson, "To Settle a New Land: An Historical Essay on Water Law and Policy in the American West and Colorado," in David H. Getches, ed., *Water and the American West—Essays in Honor of Raphael J. Moses* (Boulder: Natural Resources Law Center, University of Colorado, 1988), 2.

5. http://fciruli.blogspot.com/2011/03/front-range-counties-to-dominate.html; Thomas J. Noel, Paul F. Mahoney, and Richard E. Stevens, *Historical Atlas of Colorado* (Norman: University of Oklahoma Press, 1993), map 47.

6. Norris Hundley Jr., "Water and the West in the Historical Imagination," *Western Historical Quarterly* 27, no. 1 (Spring 1996): 15; Donald Worster, *Rivers of Empire: Water, Aridity, and the Growth of the American West* (New York: Pantheon Books, 1985), 7, 276.

Acknowledgments

I am especially pleased to acknowledge those who contributed to the book's completion. As a historian who loves doing primary source research, I am in debt to the staffs of several institutions who provided the materials I needed to do this work. At the top of this list is the indefatigable archivist at the University of Colorado–Boulder Archives David Hays, who always entertained me with both vital research materials and stimulating lunchtime conversation. Aimee Brown, the former archivist at Colorado Mesa University, not only provided materials crucial to this project but helped inspire me through her enthusiasm for research. Colorado Mesa University archivist Jim Dildine has continued to make the university archives a hospitable place to conduct research. I thank Jim for his help with many of the book's photo illustrations. The staff of the Colorado River Water Conservation District in Glenwood Springs was also very helpful, especially Meredith Spyker. I would also like to acknowledge the personnel at the Denver Public Library, University of Denver Archives, and History Colorado for their assistance. I owe a particular debt to Professor John Redifer, who served as chair of the

Colorado Mesa University Department of Social and Behavioral Sciences for many of the years I researched and wrote this study. John connected me with the Colorado Water Conservation Board, which awarded me a small research grant that enabled me to spend valuable time in the Colorado Front Range archives referred to above. John's encouragement has been important in this study's outcome. A grant from Colorado Mesa University's Professional Development Fund help fund some of the book's illustrations.

Finally, I would be remiss if I did not acknowledge the support of my family throughout this long process. My wife, Tracy, son, Anders, and daughters, Inge and Kirstin, made my hours and days much more pleasant. Grandchildren Sophia, Liam, and Brian have transformed many vacations and visits into magnificent adventures for this "papa." My late father, Robert Schulte, was always supportive of his historian son. Last but not least, I acknowledge the unconditional love given by our amazing dog, Abby, and family cats Olaf, Clio, Annie, and Felix. Thanks to all of you humans and those of you who think you are human.

Abbreviations

CMUASC	Colorado Mesa University Archives and Special Collections, Grand Junction
CSHS	Colorado State Historical Society, Denver; presently known as History Colorado
CRWCD	Colorado River Water Conservation District, Glenwood Springs
CWCB	Colorado Water Conservation Board
DPL	Denver Public Library, Denver
JFKPL	John F. Kennedy Presidential Library, Boston, MA
LBJPL	Lyndon Baines Johnson Presidential Library, Austin, TX
LC	Library of Congress, Washington, DC
MOW	Museum of the West, Grand Junction, CO; also known as the Museum of Western Colorado
NA	National Archives, Washington, DC
SCASUL	Special Collections, Arizona State University Library
SCUAL	Special Collections, University of Arizona Library
UDA	University of Denver Archives

As Precious
as Blood

1

Colorado's Water

A Problem Rooted in Geography and History

Water conservation [in Colorado] is necessary because the supplies
are limited in amount. One limitation is by nature. We live in an arid
region where precipitation is deficient and where artificial application
of water is necessary for the reclamation and occupation of the
region. The same arid conditions that create demands for water, at
the same time produce limited supplies of water. Out of this relation
between the demand and supply grows the value of water and the
value of a right to use water in Colorado; values that are unknown
and non-existent in Eastern, Southern and other humid states.

—C. L. Patterson, Colorado state water engineer,
"Conservation of Water in Colorado"[1]

Colorado is a hydrological enigma. The state contains the headwaters of
some of the American West's largest river systems, yet it is perpetually thirsty.
It has the highest average elevation of the lower forty-eight states, yet it fights
to maintain its mountain-driven precipitation within its ample borders. The

DOI: 10.5876/9781607325000.c001

state is an innovator in the legal realm of western water law, yet it lives in perpetual fear of losing its waters to downstream and out-of-state users. Finally, the lion's share of its population resides far from where most of the precipitation originates. These quandaries represent some of the intellectual hurdles blocking the path of comprehending the nuances of Colorado's water history. These knotty problems have also conditioned the political culture of the state, creating an intense rivalry between political leaders on the populous eastern side and the water-rich Western Slope.

ARRIVAL OF ANGLO-AMERICANS

Long before the first Anglo-American settlers arrived in the land that would be called Colorado, waves of Native Americans, from the Ancestral Puebloans to the Cheyenne, Arapaho, Comanche, Kiowa, Apache, and Sioux, struggled with the region's abiding aridity. The first Anglo-American settlers in Colorado did not build a water right system from nothing. Yet when a water distribution system was constructed, according to William deBuys, they "erected a hydraulic civilization in one of the most intimidating environments in the continent."[2] Over time, Coloradans would freely borrow from, embroider, and revise existing legal doctrines and the common traditions of the diverse settlers. Native American, Spanish, and Mexican practices influenced early Anglo-American arid land legal doctrines in Colorado. The practices of the Utah Mormons, who had been vigorously irrigating their Great Basin kingdom since the late 1840s, played a role. The scattered body of legal rulings and on-the-ground practices that emanated from the California Gold Rush also provided important precedents for Colorado irrigators. These diverse influences and the experiences of pioneer settlers on the eastern plains from the late 1850s to the 1870s shaped the territory and the state's early water laws, as well as the practical needs of the first miners who flocked to the region.[3]

Colorado's water system began its distinctive developmental path with the great gold rush of 1858–59. As miners gouged the earth for riches, water became the miner's greatest asset other than the precious metal itself. When water was absent as a result of upstream mining diversions or seasonal shortfalls, most mining techniques became almost impossible to perform. Water abetted nearly all of the early mining processes and, if applied properly, could accomplish the work of many individual laborers. As early as 1860, miners used hydraulic techniques: water, forced under pressure, washed gravel into the increasingly larger sluices. Most mining processes demanded a reliable source of flowing water. Needing water to power mining technology, miners redirected the water flow to where it could be put to beneficial use. Hydraulic mining became crucial to mining success. Water was forced into large hoses, and the accumulated pressure led to a hard stream that could tear away mining-region hillsides. Tons of earth could be worked in this manner. As mining became more industrial, it required even more water than it had in its simpler early phases. Not surprising, the mining regions of California and, later, Colorado developed clear-cut rules for water use: "first in time, first in right." Life in the mining camps depended on a steady supply of water, and the rule of priority or what would be called prior appropriation supplied this order. In a short number of years, Colorado's mountain streams were tapped, re-routed, and made to serve the interests of the hordes of miners flocking to the mining districts.[4]

The real groundwork for the territory's and the state's water history occurred following the US Civil War when farmers, ranchers, and local political authorities realized that eastern Colorado's agricultural potential was severely limited by moisture scarcity. Agricultural products were in great demand because of the territory's fast-growing population. Estimates of the territorial population in 1870 ranged from the census total of 40,000 to statehood boosters who believed the count was closer to 100,000. Denver had grown from a dismal outpost of about 4,700 in both the 1860 and 1870 censuses to a booming 32,000 in 1880. The 1870s saw tremendous growth along the Front Range as railroads arrived and competed with one another to serve the young territory. The growing urban areas provided a lucrative market for agricultural products. While small-scale agricultural irrigation diversions had been built near Bent's Fort along the Arkansas River and in the Pueblo area prior to the Civil War, the population boom of the early 1870s correlated with a significant development early in Colorado's irrigated heritage—the establishment of Union Colony (later Greeley) in 1871. While some eastern plains farmers who occupied lands adjoining small streams and rivers had diverted small amounts of water to nearby fields, few early Coloradans had yet moved large amounts of water away from the streams to non-contiguous fields. This would change within a few years. Soon, irrigated farming would drive eastern Colorado's economy. By the time statehood had been achieved in 1876, the new state of Colorado struggled to codify its water regulations and would remain preoccupied with this activity for decades. By 1890, Colorado was competing closely with California for having the most irrigated acres in the nation.[5]

The humid-region farming techniques used in the eastern United States did not serve Colorado's agricultural industry. Farmers who depended on rainfall and natural moisture had a chance to survive in eastern Colorado during the occasional "wet" years. However, more often than not, a lack of adequate seasonal moisture quickly led to agricultural failure in a region where the annual precipitation was less than twenty inches per year. In many sectors of Colorado's eastern plains, precipitation averaged closer to twelve inches to fifteen inches per year. Farmers who later ventured to Colorado's Western Slope often experienced less than ten inches of moisture per year in the lower valleys like the Grand, where Grand Junction would be located in the early 1880s. As one early Colorado farmer advised, "It is better to abandon all [eastern US farming] notions and begin anew."[6]

Colorado began crafting its unique water laws early in its territorial history. The first mining camps made explicit references to water rights in their mining district law codes. Many, but not all, mining district laws made reference to priority of claim to have the best water right. Others did not, noting that water "should be divided proportionally among the users." The first territorial legislature enacted water legislation, allowing irrigators to withdraw water from streams to be carried to non-adjoining lands. Several years later, Colorado's Territorial Supreme Court, under its influential chief justice Moses Hallett, held that water could be diverted from streams and ditches built across both private and public lands if it was put to beneficial use. Hallett wrote that in a "dry and thirsty land it is necessary to divert the waters of the streams from their natural channels." Another Colorado Supreme Court justice added prophetically that Colorado water law is founded on "the force of necessity arising from local peculiarities of climate."[7]

Other Colorado and federal political acts reinforced the conclusions of Hallett and the Colorado Supreme Court. The federal Mining Acts of 1866 and 1872 and the Desert Land Act of 1877 collectively encouraged the American West's territories and states to develop their own water law systems. States could, in effect, "establish their own water laws and create property rights to unappropriated water on and off the federal lands." Colorado's water law system became codified in its 1876 constitution. Soon widely known as the Colorado Doctrine, the state's water laws would influence the policies adopted by many neighboring states. According to legal scholar David Schorr, the Colorado Doctrine of Prior Appropriation emerged from a variety of factors but above all from California and Colorado miners' water laws, combined with mid-nineteenth-century considerations of economic justice. Nineteenth-century Supreme Court justice Stephen Johnson Field stated that mining water laws "were so framed as to secure to all comers, within practicable limits, absolute equality of right and privilege in working the mines." The Colorado Doctrine offered widespread access to water for those who could prove they were using the water beneficially. Water scarcity led to the prioritization of water access on the basis of first use. Overall, Schorr believes this system helped avoid monopolization of this scarce resource by large-scale and corporate interests.[8]

As early as 1864, the Colorado Territorial Assembly asserted that stream waters could not be diverted from the original channel "to the detriment of any user who had a priority of right."[9] This continued a trend dating back to Jefferson Territory's (Colorado's short-lived territorial predecessor) policy of limiting appropriations and resolving conflicts among irrigators by "reference to the priority of appropriation."[10] Colorado's 1876 constitution also reflected almost a decade of struggle over water law definition, including intense conflict between the young cities of Greeley and Fort Collins. The Union Colony, or Greeley, constructed its irrigation canals first, while Fort Collins based its bid for water supremacy on its Cache la Poudre River location, upstream from Greeley. Nathan Meeker, one of the Greeley colony's founders, wrote an editorial in the *Greeley Tribune* calling for recognition of the Colorado Doctrine of Prior Appropriation, which he linked to the pioneering miners of California and Colorado. Until prior appropriation was recognized, Meeker wrote, "capital investment in irrigation would not be secure." The results of the Greeley versus Fort Collins conflict and other festering water matters were addressed in the Colorado State Constitution of 1876, which encouraged the development of irrigation systems. Section 6 declares that the right to divert the "unappropriated waters of any natural stream to beneficial uses shall never be denied." However, "priority of appropriation shall give the better right as between those using the water for the same purpose." Section 6 also awards preference to agriculture over what it terms "manufacturing uses."[11]

The Colorado State Constitution encouraged the more populous and politically powerful Front Range to embed its arguments for trans-mountain diversion in Article 16, Section 5. If a party could afford to construct a diversion work, water was free for the taking. The 1882 Colorado Supreme Court decision in *Coffin v. Left Hand Ditch Company* encouraged this activity. In this case the court determined that prior appropriation water rights, not riparian rights, would guide the young state. The court also recognized that water often needed to be carried across public or private lands to be put to beneficial use far from the original stream itself. The Front Range often had the financial wherewithal to construct the diversions. In the decades ahead, the Western Slope would try to develop arguments that would help the region reserve water for future potential uses, such as an oil shale industry. Anticipating such arguments, early Colorado water legal expert L. Ward Bannister declared, "There is nothing in this doctrine of potential use. It is against our constitution. We could not have it unless we have the constitution amended."[12]

ANGLO-AMERICAN SETTLEMENT ON COLORADO'S WESTERN SLOPE

While Colorado became known as a difficult place to make a living, the Western Slope had a unique set of circumstances that made it an even more precarious place to reside. High mountains, rugged terrain, distance from cities and markets, and an uneven and unreliable moisture cycle all compounded the challenges facing the area's first Euro-American settlers. The Western Slope, according to most accepted definitions, is the half of the state on the western side of the Continental Divide that "follows a snaking, confusing line" from the Wyoming border in the north to the New Mexico border in the south. Colorado's vast western half holds the nation's tallest mountain sentinels, the Colorado Rockies, reinforcing the Western Slope's sense of isolation and uniqueness.[13]

The first permanent white settlers, miners in the San Juan Mountain range, discovered that moisture ran in uneven cycles. Stream water was abundant for a short time in the spring and early summer, then trailed off and often disappeared altogether by late summer or fall. Even snowfall was somewhat of an illusion, as it tended to fall as a dry powder, lacking the moisture content of snow in the Midwest and the eastern half of the United States. Anglo-American miners had wandered and explored the Western Slope for years. Rumors of gold and silver brought enough miners to spark tensions between the Ute Indians and Anglo-American miners. In 1868 the federal government negotiated a treaty designating about one-third of today's Colorado as a Ute Indian reservation. The loss of some Ute land to the federal government only seemed to invite more miners and explorers to the Western Slope. By 1873 the increasing Anglo population demanded further Ute land cessions. The Brunot Agreement was ratified by the US Congress in 1874. This small but lucrative land cession (3.5 million acres) conferred legal title to thousands of acres already under Anglo-American control. It specifically clarified title to mining claims and to several communities supporting mining activity. Durango was founded in the southwest corner of the state in 1880 and quickly grew to several thousand citizens. The rich silver districts of Ouray and Silverton were also included in the dimensions of the Brunot Agreement.[14]

The mass removal of Ute Indians from the Western Slope flung open the door to a growing Anglo-American population. Following the so-called Meeker Massacre of 1879, the Utes were removed to reservations in Utah or sent to two small reservations in Colorado's southwest corner. A frantic rush for Ute land ensued, and in 1881 the Uncompahgre River Valley was opened to general settlement. The Western Slope had opened for business. Within a few years a land boom led to the founding of Grand Junction, Delta, and Montrose. The arrival of railroads like the Denver and Rio Grande in the 1880s gave the isolated region a sense of permanence and connection with the outside world. By 1899, Grand Junction envisioned itself as "the commercial capital of all [of] Western Colorado." The mining-based economy of the Western Slope grew in cycles, fits, and starts. Yet a permanent Anglo-American population continued to arrive.[15]

In its early years of Anglo-American settlement, the Western Slope remained largely unknown to eastern Colorado's population. Strong political ties between the two halves of the state would remain illusory for many decades. When Denver and Rocky Mountain Front Range citizens considered the western half of Colorado, they pictured a distant and strange land isolated from civilization and populated by barbaric whites and blood-thirsty Indians. The *Denver Tribune* said the Western Slope "is a region that is apparently about as valuable as would be a representative section of the Desert of Sahara." Nineteenth-century author and Colorado booster Frank Fossett described the Western Slope as "a terra incognita to Coloradans." Descriptions of the region's desolation and desert character seemed to creep into most late-nineteenth-century assessments of the state's western fringe.[16]

Western Slope land promoters busied themselves with building their small towns and communities. Leaders in the Uncompahgre and Grand Valleys discovered that they lacked one crucial ingredient for permanence and growth: a reliable water supply. According to Felix L. Sparks, who became a great advocate of twentieth-century Colorado water planning, "much Western Slope land is as fertile as a stray alley cat." Sparks did not mention that most of the easily obtained sources of water had been tapped by 1900. As early as 1900, 226,000 acres of the Western Slope were already under irrigation. Uncompahgre Valley promoters dreamed of diverting the nearby but inaccessible Gunnison River to supplement the water available from the small and irregularly flowing Uncompahgre River. Six miles of imposing mountain rock separated the Gunnison, which roared through the Black Canyon, from the fertile but dry Uncompahgre Valley. An ever-optimistic official of the Denver and Rio Grande Railroad predicted that with additional water, Montrose County could support a "population of two million people."[17]

Initially conceived as a private commercial venture, the Uncompahgre Project's costs and technical requirements quickly overwhelmed the capabilities of the private sector. The state of Colorado, which took control of the project in 1901, was soon similarly financially and technically challenged. Significant progress and project completion awaited the federal government's direct involvement in 1905. With federal financial and engineering assistance through the newly created US Reclamation Service (later the US Bureau of Reclamation), the Gunnison Tunnel was completed in 1909. Within a few years, Uncompahgre Valley land prices skyrocketed and impressive crop yields followed suit. In 1909 the potato crop yield brought $225,000 in profits. In 1910, with Gunnison Tunnel water, the yield surpassed $1 million.[18]

Similarly, the Grand Valley Project was one of the first six projects undertaken after passage of the Reclamation Project of 1902. In that year, western Colorado's Grand Valley lands that had not been surveyed were withdrawn from consideration as part of the proposed project. Reclamation Service surveys soon began investigating possible canal alignments. In 1903, local financial interests hoped to translate the federal government's reports into a privately financed water project. As a result, the government suspended further work on the Grand Valley Project. In 1907 the Reclamation Service again took over the sputtering private venture. After a series of lengthy delays, the project began to be built in 1912. The heart of the project was a fourteen-foot "roller dam" that provides water to four canals that stretch over ninety miles of the region.[19] Official US Bureau of Reclamation histories term this project "one of the most successful reclamation projects constructed," with water furnished to 33,368 acres of land along the Colorado River in the vicinity of Grand Junction. Future Colorado congressman Wayne N. Aspinall, who arrived in the Palisade area of the Grand Valley as a young child in the first decade of the twentieth century, literally grew up with the construction of the Grand Valley Project. Undoubtedly, his staunch advocacy of large-scale reclamation was, at least in part, conditioned by his observations of this reclamation effort.[20]

A pattern was thus established early on for large-scale water development on the Western Slope. Private enterprise would often try first and fail. State control would follow, with little more success than the private ventures. Finally, after the Reclamation Act of 1902, the federal government was in a position to either complete unfinished projects or design and build new ones. Yet the transformation of the Western Slope's image from a remote and isolated desert outpost to a fruitful land with unbounded economic potential was slow in developing. Local economic boosters tried to court private capital to invest in the region's land and water systems. This money often originated in distant East Coast regions and had strings attached: the need to make a fast profit for restless investors.[21] From the late nineteenth century to the World War I era, a self-conscious identification developed among Anglo-American Western Slope dwellers born of "boosterism, isolation, environment, and a common ambivalence" toward Front Range population and economic centers. This ambivalence remained and guided the interaction between Colorado's two halves for the first half of the twentieth century.[22]

ARRIVAL OF FEDERAL RECLAMATION IN THE CENTENNIAL STATE

Historian Donald Worster called the Reclamation Act of 1902 "the most important single piece of legislation in the history of the West, overshadowing

FIGURE I.I. The Grand Valley Diversion Dam or as it is known locally, the Roller Dam. Built between 1913 and 1916, the dam is on the Colorado River about eight miles northeast of Palisade, Colorado, in DeBeque Canyon. This concrete weir is 14 feet high and 546 feet long. Flow over its crest is controlled by six roller gates, the first and largest of their kind installed in the United States. It is a central feature of the US Bureau of Reclamation's Grand Valley Project. *Courtesy*, US Bureau of Reclamation.

even the Homestead Act" in ultimate significance. The Reclamation or Newlands Act (named for one of its principal US Senate sponsors, Francis Newlands [D-NV]) became law for many reasons, including the western states' increasing power in Congress and the personal interest of President Theodore Roosevelt. In the two-year period 1889 through 1890, the number of western states doubled, with the addition of six new states. The region did not contain many people, but in the US Senate its power had suddenly become considerable. In 1889 the head of the US Geological Survey, John Wesley Powell, was in the process of conducting an irrigation survey, locating future reservoir sites. The prophetic Powell hoped to convince Congress that future sales of western land could only occur if a reliable supply of water was available. Speaking to the Montana Constitutional Convention in 1889, Powell reminded delegates that eastern water laws and institutions did not match western environmental conditions. "All of the great values in this territory," he lectured, "have ultimately to be measured in acre-feet." Powell suggested that the new western states divide themselves into hydrographic basins rather than along traditional county lines, which often bore little resemblance to important geographic features like river systems.[23]

While federal reclamation policy did not follow Powell's suggestions, it promised development of water on a scale that would soon dwarf the many smaller private and state efforts of the late nineteenth century. The Newlands Act called for federally constructed irrigation projects, with funding provided through the sale of public lands linked to the new water projects. The act made an immediate difference in the Western Slope's future. During the previous twenty years, western Colorado's water development had sputtered along as a series of private ventures. In the years ahead, municipal water development, inspired by Populist and Progressive reform ideas of citizen control and abetted by the federal government's presence through the Reclamation Act, would increase the amount of water available to Western Slope settlers. Reclamation Act water, along with a determination to build municipal water systems, often with mountain collection points, also helped to stabilize the economy of towns like Grand Junction.[24]

In many respects, the federal reclamation program breathed new life into the region's economic backbone: agriculture. This observation is borne out by an examination of Mesa County land values, which skyrocketed following the arrival of federal reclamation in the valley. As one early-twentieth-century Palisade, Colorado, booster publication remarked, raw land, valued at $100 an acre, "under irrigation can easily be made [to be] worth over $1000 [an acre] in four years." While this might be a slight exaggeration, by 1910 irrigated fruit orchard lands near Palisade were usually valued between $200 and $300 per acre. By comparison, high, dry, non-irrigated acreage near the Mesa County town of Collbran was worth between $3 and $5 per acre. Mesa County's vaunted agricultural economy assumed an air of permanence with the arrival of the federal reclamation program.[25]

Coloradans both encouraged and celebrated the flurry of federal reclamation activity that characterized the early-twentieth-century Western Slope. Yet many citizens were of a divided mind about it: they were pleased with

the fruits of massive federal expenditures but wary that a loss of local political control over the state's water could accompany the national reclamation investment. In other words, federal political control and power might
follow national taxpayers' money into the American West. Section 8 of the
Reclamation Act required the federal government to honor state water laws,
a development that "pandered to home rule and institutionalized fragmen-
tation." In short, Section 8 undermined the goal of centralized irrigation
planning.[26] Overall, the Reclamation Act may have caused more haze than
clarity in addressing the state-federal water relationship. Earlier drafts of
the Reclamation Act had met with the disapproval of many western members of Congress because they attempted to confer rights to unappropriated
waters to the federal government, anticipating later reserved right doctrines.
However, in its final version Section 8 essentially reaffirmed the uneasy status
quo: "Nothing in this act shall be construed as affecting or intended to affect
or in any way [to] interfere with the laws of any State or Territory relating to
the control, appropriation, use of or distribution of water used in irrigation,
but State and Territorial laws shall govern and control . . . the waters rendered
available by the works constructed under the provisions of this act."[27]

Colorado and most other western states had spent almost fifty years developing their own frameworks for water law. Yet the sudden infusion of federal
money into the reclamation superstructure had the potential to undermine
western state water control. Colorado had sparred with federal authorities
for several decades over the matter, and events would heat up often in the
next several decades. Eastern and western Colorado joined together to battle
federal water initiatives.

In 1908 the venerable Colorado senator Henry M. Teller clearly articulated
Colorado's fears over federal water intentions. Soon, a new generation of
Colorado politicians joined Teller to argue that if water were taken away, "it
is equivalent to taking away your life." In a phrase almost every Colorado
politician would try to patent as his own, Teller argued that water "was, is,
and will be the lifeblood of the West." Teller denied that the US government
had any control over water in Colorado. "We hold that water belongs to the
state and we mean to keep it," Teller asserted in 1908. In upcoming years,
Colorado water commissioner Delphus E. Carpenter and Congressman
Edward T. Taylor inherited Teller's mantle in defending the state's water sovereignty against perceived federal encroachment.[28]

In his study of the Colorado River Compact, Norris Hundley Jr. argues that the western states wanted to take the federal largesse without "incurring federal control" of water. The cash-strapped young western states did not have the economic resources to construct and take charge of the necessary hydraulic infrastructure. Yet the states needed the water to chart an economic path to the future. Thus, a delicate political balancing act was perfected in Colorado and other western states—to claim as much federal reclamation money as possible while preserving the "integrity of state government" to control water policy. The American West entered the twentieth century moving politically closer to Washington yet still determined to discourage the federal government's attempts to establish authority over the unappropriated waters in the region. A real fear existed that doctrines like prior appropriation would face either destruction or severe modification if the wishes of some federal water officials carried the day.[29]

Advocates of federal water authority hoped the US Supreme Court might come to their aid in undermining state water-control powers. Prior to the monumental *Kansas v. Colorado* decision, Colorado water users believed they had a right to waters originating within their borders. With confidence born of this faith, in 1901 the Colorado General Assembly responded to demands for more legal control of water by passing the District Irrigation Law, which meshed perfectly with the Reclamation Act of 1902. Local districts could build canals and reservoirs, issue bonds, raise capital, and levy taxes to pay construction and maintenance debts. At the same time, the Colorado General Assembly created the Office of State Engineer, whose concern would be the distribution of water within the guidelines of state law. It is fair to say that Colorado entered the twentieth century with the full intention of putting to use all of the water it could find within its borders.[30]

In 1907 the US Supreme Court dashed the expansive hopes of many Coloradans in the decision *Kansas v. Colorado*. Kansas had accused Colorado of appropriating more than its share of Arkansas River water. Originating high in Colorado's Rockies, the river crosses Colorado's eastern plains and flows through Kansas, Oklahoma, and Arkansas on its long journey to the Mississippi River. As early as the 1890s, Kansas farmers had accused Colorado of undermining their irrigation operations by taking too much water from the Arkansas River. By 1900 more than 100 Arkansas River Valley ditch systems irrigated over 300,000 acres across eastern Colorado. Colorado farmers and industrial interests such as Colorado Fuel and Iron had used the prior appropriation doctrine to claim nearly all the surface water in the Arkansas River Valley. In 1901 Kansas filed suit against Colorado, insisting that its rights to water in the Arkansas River were depleted by Colorado's diversions. Colorado's attorneys argued that the state had rights to all waters within its boundaries. The heated tone of the interstate squabble gave credence to the arguments of federal-control proponents in the national government. An increasing number of federal bureaucrats believed it would take the wisdom and power of the federal government to resolve such a vital national issue and to referee an outcome acceptable to all parties.[31]

The Court's decision, as is often the case, failed to fully satisfy the three parties involved: Kansas, Colorado, and the federal government. The majority opinion, written by Justice David J. Brewer, took the Court in new regulatory directions in its interactions with the American West's waters. Reserving the right to determine the outcome of interstate water quarrels in the future, the Court announced the "doctrine of equitable apportionment," which did not undermine either the riparian or prior appropriation doctrines practiced in Kansas and Colorado, respectively, but seemed to say that each state had a right to water in the rivers within its boundaries. While the Court did not doubt that some harm was done to Kansas agriculture by Colorado's upstream diversions, it also argued that Colorado had built unquestionably beneficial irrigation projects.[32]

The aftermath of *Kansas v. Colorado* left an unsettled feeling in Colorado. Colorado had tried and failed to use what was called in legal circles "the Harmon Doctrine," claiming jurisdiction over all waters originating within the state's borders. The Court's assertion of the standard of "equitable apportionment" undermined Colorado's hopes and best-crafted arguments. Colorado could no longer "with impunity develop its water resources." The *Kansas* decision had served notice that if the state did damage to neighboring states by monopolizing waters flowing across borders, it would find itself answering to the Court again.[33]

The Supreme Court decision may have opened the door for itself to play an expanded federal referee role if states could not find agreement among themselves. Yet the federal government, notably the Department of the Interior, by choosing to become involved in the case, had been hoping for more satisfaction from the Supreme Court. The solicitor general had argued that the US Constitution "implied" that Congress had the sole authority to resolve interstate conflicts over waters. According to Justice Brewer's opinion, this role would be the Supreme Court's, not Congress's. The Reclamation Service would need to abide by each state's water law structure. Instead of moving toward a reading of western water law that would lead to more uniformity under federal direction, *Kansas v. Colorado* "strengthened the champions of state sovereignty."[34] At the time the Supreme Court decided *Kansas v. Colorado,* the leading booster organization for western irrigation interests, the National Irrigation Congress, distributed a questionnaire to water experts across the West. Federal water rights advocate Morris Bien devised the questionnaire. Among his questions was the predictable: who should control western interstate streams, the states or the federal government? Twenty-eight of forty-seven respondents supported state control over all streams, while only thirteen favored federal control of both interstate and intrastate waters; the remaining six had no opinion. Federal water-control advocates seemed to be steadily losing headway across the arid American West.[35]

Anti-federal feelings boiled up and peaked during a June 1907 Public Lands Convention held in Denver. Federal forest reserve withdrawals had dramatically increased since federal-control advocate Theodore Roosevelt ascended to the presidency in 1901. Questions over the impact of federal land withdrawals on state water laws abounded. The Denver conference passed a series of resolutions on a variety of natural resources topics. State water rights received more than their share of attention. Resolution number 4 declared that the peoples of the states had "free and unhampered use of all waters within forest reservations" for the "beneficial use" of irrigation, municipal water supply, and the development of power sites at no cost to states and local towns. Resolution 8 emphasized the importance of state control of waters, affirming the right of western states "to control the appropriation, use, and distribution for irrigation of the waters of all public non-navigable streams within their respective borders, and to be granted the right of way to build canals, ditches, and reservoirs across public forest lands." The Denver Public Lands Convention mainly acted as a sounding board for fears over growing federal power to control the terms of access to public lands and their resources.[36]

TAYLOR AND CARPENTER: FIGHTING CONSERVATION INITIATIVES

Fears of federal involvement in Colorado's and the West's water policies did not abate during the Progressive era. Senator Henry M. Teller had led the charge against federal encroachment on Colorado lands and resources for many years. However, Teller retired from the US Senate in 1908, leaving a void in Colorado's defense against federal encroachment on state land and water rights. Over the next decades, two new defenders of state prerogative in water matters would emerge: Congressman Edward T. Taylor and Colorado state senator and water commissioner Delphus E. Carpenter.

Born in Michigan, Taylor moved to the raucous mountain mining boom-town Leadville, where he served as high school principal in 1881–82 and county school superintendent until 1884. After studying law at the University of Michigan, he moved to Glenwood Springs in 1887, where he set up a law practice specializing in water litigation and was elected district attorney of the Ninth Judicial District. In 1896 Taylor was elected to the Colorado State Senate, and in 1908 he moved on to the US House of Representatives as Colorado's at-large member. In 1915 he became the US congressman from western Colorado's massive fourth district, comprising most of the Western Slope. At the time of his election in 1908, Taylor had already earned a repu-tation as a water law expert. As he recalled in an autobiographical fragment written in 1940: "On becoming district attorney [for the state's northwestern district] in 1887, the first thing I was confronted with was a lot of criminal prosecutions for murders and fights and conflicts of all kinds mainly over water rights. Upon investigation I immediately discovered that no one had any legal rights; no decrees, no records, nor anything but notices posted on trees or something of that kind concerning water rights."[37]

Over the next two years, Taylor published legal notices, held hearings, and traveled widely through Mesa, Garfield, Eagle, and Rio Blanco Counties to secure the facts about citizen water claims, including who had priority rights. "He personally took the evidence and prepared over 1000 decrees" for water rights in the state. Taylor's prepared decrees received approval by the district court in May 1889. In a *Denver Post* article written by legendary newspaper-man Damon Runyon, Taylor was referred to as early as 1908 as the "father of Water rights on the Western Slope."[38]

Early in his congressional career, Taylor also became an adamant foe of federal conservation efforts. Taylor viewed the Theodore Roosevelt and Taft administration's efforts to apply the 1891 Forest Reserve Act to vast parts of the West as a dangerous centralization of power and a detriment to the sovereignty of western states. Western people, courtesy of the conservation program, were being treated as "second-class citizens." A 1910 bill opposed by Taylor, HR 24070, would have authorized the president to make withdrawals from public lands and nullify existing land, mining, and water laws. Taylor argued that if this law passed, western states would lose their "absolute, constitutional, legal and equitable right to use and control the water within their borders." Taylor expressed particular concern over the potential impact of national forests on state water rights. "I give you fair warning that we will not surrender the waters of the West under any theoretical conservation pretext," he asserted. "The water belongs to us [western states] subject to the doctrine of prior appropriation and beneficial use under our constitution."[39]

Taylor constantly ruminated on potential threats to his large congressional district's water supply. Toward this end, he began agitating early in his political career for a name change to the river that now bears the state's name, from Grand to Colorado. On western maps prior to 1921, the Green River flowed from Wyoming and joined the Grand (whose origins are on Colorado's Western Slope) in southern Utah, forming the Colorado. The name change issue, Taylor claimed in 1907, "is entirely original with me." The change, he believed, would especially benefit the valleys through which the river flowed. "As a matter of state pride, we should make the change," he argued. Taylor also believed the state of Colorado and his congressional district could better formulate water claim arguments if the river's headwaters could be thought to have originated within the Centennial State's borders. Taylor prodded the Colorado General Assembly to endorse the name change, and in 1921 the US Congress passed the bill to ratify it officially.[40]

Taylor argued that the state of Colorado also had special rights to the river because "eight great streams from the western 20 counties" in his congressional district "furnish 70 percent" of the river's flow. Colorado, in short, had by far the "largest claim of any state" to the river's water because it furnished the greatest amount of the annual flow. This argument was imitated and used time and time again by Taylor and his successors, including Congressman Wayne N. Aspinall. Taylor buttressed his claims to Colorado's water rights by referring to the river as "the Nile of America." The Colorado, Taylor asserted with some exaggeration, is the only great river in the world "entirely within an arid region." For this reason, it is "intrinsically the most valuable stream in all the world."[41]

Delphus E. Carpenter would join Taylor in trying to define and protect Colorado's water rights in the early decades of the twentieth century. Born in 1877 near Greeley, Carpenter literally grew up with Colorado's agricultural history as the son of an irrigation farmer. After graduating from law school at the University of Denver (1899) and serving as a state senator, Carpenter built a career as Colorado's acknowledged defender of its water rights against neighboring states. Carpenter also believed, like Taylor, that the federal government's dangerous designs could be seen in recent developments, including the establishment of the Reclamation Service, the nationalization of vast amounts of forestlands, and the increased presence of the federal government in the daily lives of early-twentieth-century Americans. Carpenter, as his biographer Daniel Tyler tells the story, "viewed the government's attempt to control any aspect of natural resources as an abomination, a violation of states' rights." The new Reclamation Service "attached itself to the coattails of the conservation movement." The implication of a federally regulated western economy, to Coloradans like Edward T. Taylor and Delph Carpenter, above all meant the potential loss of water and water rights; thus, the state's ability to shape its own economic future would be jeopardized.[42]

After serving a term in the Colorado State Senate (1909–13), Carpenter embarked on his life's calling: to defend the state's water from the designs of other Colorado River states and to construct an innovative way of settling water disputes between aggrieved states. *Kansas v. Colorado* had waved a red flag in front of Carpenter. The US Supreme Court case had settled little between the states, and, for Carpenter, it had ominously raised the possibility of federal intervention in future interstate disputes. In addition, the protracted litigation had cost both states' taxpayers great amounts of money. In 1911 Wyoming filed suit against Colorado and two Colorado corporations when they attempted to divert portions of the Laramie River through a tunnel into the Cache la Poudre watershed. The water was to be put to use by Colorado land developers near Greeley. Wyoming, which used large amounts of Laramie River water downstream, would be threatened with the loss of more than 100,000 acre-feet.[43]

While the US Supreme Court accepted the case, the litigation "dragged on interminably." The Supreme Court finally decided in 1922 that Wyoming was entitled to a prior appropriation right to the Laramie River, since both states recognized the Doctrine of Prior Appropriation. Colorado would be able to divert a much more limited amount of water through the Laramie-Poudre Tunnel. As a result of this decision, Delph Carpenter grew more convinced than ever of the need to negotiate a multi-state water compact. *Wyoming v. Colorado* also influenced both Upper Colorado River states like Colorado and downstream states like California to consider bargaining for a Colorado River Compact.[44]

Without a doubt, however, heading into the World War I era, perhaps the greatest legal threat to Colorado's water emanated from Southern California, which had shown little hesitation in pulling out all the stops to increase its water supplies.[45] In 1913 Los Angeles opened its new aqueduct, which transported water 233 miles from its Owens Valley source to the burgeoning West Coast metropolis. By the early 1920s, California was using millions of acre-feet each year from the Colorado River. Colorado and other Upper Basin states understood that new tactics would have to be used to slow California's quest for more Colorado River water. Carpenter, however, had grown hesitant over what he had found so unsatisfactory in *Wyoming v. Colorado*—protracted and expensive legal recourse. Carpenter's fears over these matters, and California's proven record of acting decisively to assert its water prerogatives, inspired the Greeley attorney to begin building a consensus for an interstate water compact. The seeds of the movement for an agreement or compact among the seven states dependent on the Colorado River's waters had been planted.[46]

EARLY-TWENTIETH-CENTURY FRONT RANGE WATER INITIATIVES

As Colorado moved into the twentieth century, it could reflect positively on the groundwork it had established to protect its water supplies since gaining statehood. The Doctrine of Prior Appropriation had undergone tremendous articulation and legal testing. A rudimentary state water bureaucracy, including the Office of State Engineer, was in place and functioning. The state of Colorado had learned a hard lesson from the *Kansas* case—it would not be able to access all the waters originating in its high mountains. Perhaps as significant, the era of *Kansas v. Colorado* and *Wyoming v. Colorado* also marked the beginning of the state's intramural struggle for water. Long before 1900, the Front Range had cast a thirsty eye on the waters of the Western Slope, where most of the state's watershed is located. The first Western Slope diversion started in 1860 when a small ditch was built at Hoosier Pass allowing waters from a Blue River tributary to flow eastward to a mining operation. Two ditches were constructed, known as the East and West Hoosier Ditches. Though they carried a minute volume of water, they nonetheless served as important precedents for further diversions.[47]

As early as 1889, water users in the South Platte Valley began investigating the feasibility of accessing Western Slope waters to supplement their dwindling water supplies. The Colorado legislature authorized the expenditure of $25,000 to survey a possible canal to bring water from the Western Slope to the Front Range by way of a diversion to South Boulder Creek. While the original idea was ruled "infeasible" by the state engineer, for several more decades engineers and water users from eastern Colorado debated the possibility of tapping the Grand River headwaters for a major trans-mountain diversion to the Front Range. In the meantime, the growing urban oasis of Denver began searching for ways to enhance its water supply. In the last decades of the nineteenth century, the Queen City had several private water providers competing with one another for subscribers and sources of water. None of the companies could slake the growing city's thirst. Finally, in 1894 the Denver Union Water Company, headed by Walter Cheesman and David Moffat, received a twenty-year monopoly to provide the city's water. The company expanded the city's range of service and built Cheesman Dam, the world's highest dam at the time of its construction. A steady water supply meant population and economic growth for Denver. From 1900 to 1910, its population grew about 5 percent a year, from 130,000 to 215,000.[48]

Because of such growth and projections for an even larger population, Denver and the Front Range began an urgent search for additional water in the early twentieth century. Soon, Denver would be doing exactly what cities like Los Angeles and San Francisco were doing at the same time—tapping often distant sources of water at the expense of underpopulated and politically weak rural regions. The Denver Union Water Company sent engineering parties to the mountain regions of the Western Slope to prospect for sources of water to divert to the Front Range. By 1916 more than 20,000 acre-feet of water were being diverted annually from the Western to the Eastern Slope. The largest of these relatively small diversions included the Grand

River Ditch, which transferred 11,400 acre-feet of water from high in what in 1915 became Rocky Mountain National Park to the South Platte River system. Completed in 1892, the Grand Ditch, as it was then known, "set a precedent for later out of basin water transfers." Its location within the borders of Rocky Mountain National Park made it a controversial rearrangement of the park's natural features. However, its construction occurred before the park's creation and before citizens on the Western Slope became seriously concerned with such diversions. A clause in the park's authorization legislation allowed the Reclamation Service to "enter upon and utilize for flowage or other purposes any area within said park which may be necessary for the development and maintenance of government reclamation projects." Congressman Edward T. Taylor, sponsor of the park's authorization bill in the US House of Representatives, made sure the bill allowed access to some of the precipitation originating high on its picturesque and snowy mountain peaks.[49]

In their search for additional water to carry from the Western Slope, Denver and the Front Range region were armed with a large population, political clout, engineering expertise, and the Colorado State Constitution. As Article 16, Section 5, declares: "The water of every natural stream . . . within the state of Colorado is hereby declared to be the property of the public, and the same is dedicated to the use of the people of the state, subject to appropriation as hereinafter provided." While large trans-mountain diversions remained in the future, the Front Range understood that its limited water supply equated to dismal growth prospects.[50] Notable early Colorado mining engineer George J. Bancroft illustrated Denver's covetous attitude toward Western Slope water in a 1913 *Rocky Mountain News* article: "Armed with the majesty of the law, Denver stands prepared to take what it pleases." Bancroft and other Colorado water experts asserted that the Platte River system could provide for Denver's hydraulic needs only for a short time. The Western Slope, according to Bancroft, was a region of tremendous surplus water and "scant arable lands." The mountainous and desert region of western Colorado has "a world of water and a moon[scape] of land, while the Eastern Slope has a world of land and a moon[scape] of water." As for the legal politics of diversion, Bancroft asserted that the Front Range's ability to put the surplus water to beneficial use would be its trump card. All Western Slope protests against diversion "drop like a *portcullis* at the King's command when the city desires the water."[51]

In 1909, California trailed Colorado in overall irrigated acreage, but that would soon change. Between 1910 and 1920, California underwent a "spurt of development." The 1920 Federal Census revealed that California irrigated more than 4 million total acres and had taken the nation's lead in total irrigated acres. Colorado ranked second, followed by Idaho, Montana, Utah, Wyoming, and Oregon. California's surge resulted from several reasons, including the completion or near-completion of several massive and audacious water diversion projects such as the Los Angeles aqueduct, which brought ample amounts of fresh Owens Valley water to fuel the growth of Los Angeles and the surrounding region. The rural citizenry in the Owens Valley had proven powerless against the money and political influence of the growing Los Angeles region. Northern California was also building a spectacular project.[52]

By 1916 Joseph Lippincott, who had played a major role in Los Angeles's grab of Owens Valley water, was traversing the Continental Divide in Colorado on behalf of the Denver Union Water Company. Lippincott was making recommendations for possible trans-mountain diversions to enhance Denver's water supply. The very real fear that California would reach out and grab the Colorado River proved a motivating force behind Greeley, Colorado, attorney Delphus Carpenter's idea to negotiate a Colorado River Compact to ensure a measure of water security for all states dependent on the river.[53]

COLORADO, 1860–1920: "TRUE WEALTH" IN A DRY LAND

The first sixty years of Colorado history had confirmed what western author Wallace Stegner argued in his magnificent biography of John Wesley Powell. "Water," he wrote, "is the true wealth in a dry land; without it, land is worthless or nearly so." Moving Colorado toward prosperity in the twentieth century would require an all-out commitment to rearrange its streams and rivers for the benefit of its growing population. Historian Peter Iverson argued that Arizona's political history "may be seen . . . in the choices that have been made about water." By 1920, Colorado had started to make decisions about water that, in turn, would shape its political culture.[54]

Colorado had a divided mind about its water situation heading into the 1920s. It had made great strides toward constructing a hydraulic civilization in the midst of the deserts and mountains of the nation's highest state by enacting laws to encourage its citizens to put every drop of water to use. On the other hand, Colorado feared that it would not have enough water supplies to guarantee its future. The Front Range corridor of eastern Colorado was growing rapidly, and the extent of its growth, many believed, would be dictated by how much water it could commandeer. By 1920, eastern Colorado had reached the end of the water supplies it could easily access. As for western Colorado, it had been settled by an Anglo-American population more than a generation later than the Eastern Slope. The western half of Colorado did not participate in or influence the debate over Colorado's water allocation until the twentieth century. However, by 1920 some Western Slope officials had begun to connect economic growth aspirations with the region's need to retain a sufficient water supply. As in the case of Los Angeles and the Owens Valley, when Denver began to look across the mountains to obtain a water supply, a large and politically powerful force had the potential to exploit western Colorado's water resources and stifle the economic future of the Western Slope. This struggle would play out in the years ahead.[55]

NOTES

1. C. L. Patterson, "Conservation of Water in Colorado," Box 170, folder 8, Frank Delaney Papers, University of Colorado–Boulder Archives (hereafter UCBA).

2. William deBuys, *A Great Aridness: Climate Change and the Future of the American Southwest* (New York: Oxford University Press, 2011), 16.

3. See the discussions in Donald J. Pisani, *To Reclaim a Divided West: Water, Law, and Public Policy, 1848–1902* (Albuquerque: University of New Mexico Press, 1992), and Donald Worster, *Rivers of Empire: Water, Aridity, and the Growth of the American West* (New York: Pantheon Books, 1985).

4. Worster, *Rivers of Empire*, 89; Charles E. Wilkinson, *Crossing the Next Meridian: Land, Water, and the Future of the West* (Washington, DC: Island, 1992), 232; Duane A. Smith, *Rocky Mountain West: Colorado, Wyoming, and Montana* (Albuquerque: University of New Mexico Press, 1992), 10–11.

5. Denver population figures are from Stephen J. Leonard and Thomas J. Noel, *Denver: Mining Camp to Metropolis* (Niwot: University Press of Colorado, 1990), 12, 30, 41; Carl Ubbelohde, Maxine Benson, and Duane A. Smith, *A Colorado History*, 9th ed. (Boulder: Pruett, 2006), 141, 149; Pisani, *To Reclaim a Divided West*, 208–9.

6. Ubbelohde, Benson, and Smith, *Colorado History*, 188.

7. David Schorr, *The Colorado Doctrine: Water Rights, Corporations, and Distributive Justice on the American Frontier* (New Haven, CT: Yale University Press, 2012), 13–15 (first quotation); John D.W. Guice, *The Rocky Mountain Bench: The Territorial Supreme Courts of Colorado, Montana, and Wyoming, 1861–1890* (New Haven, CT: Yale University Press, 1972), 96–111, 123 (third quotation); Gregory J. Hobbs Jr., *Citizens Guide to Colorado Water Law* (Denver: Colorado Foundation for Water Education, 2004), 5, 28.

8. Schorr, *Colorado Doctrine*, 29.

9. G. E. Radosevich, K. C. Nobe, D. Allardice, and C. Kirkwood, *Evolution and Administration of Colorado Water Law: 1876–1976* (Fort Collins, CO: Water Resources Publications, 1976), ix, 32, 68.

10. Schorr, *Colorado Doctrine*, 33.

11. Daniel Tyler, *Silver Fox of the Rockies: Delphus E. Carpenter and Western Water Compacts* (Norman: University of Oklahoma Press, 2003), 50–53. Discussion of Meeker's editorial was reconstructed from Tyler, *Silver Fox*, 50–53; Meeker quoted in Dick Stenzel, "An Irrigated Legacy: The Union Colony," in *Citizen's Guide to Colorado's Water Heritage* (Denver: Colorado Foundation for Water Education, 2004), 22; Constitution of the State of Colorado, accessed March 8, 2011, www.michie.com /colorado/lpext.dll?f=templates&fn=main-h.htm&cp=.

12. Duane Vandenbusche and Duane A. Smith, *A Land Alone: Colorado's Western Slope* (Boulder: Pruett, 1981), 1; Hobbs, *Citizens Guide to Colorado Water Law*, 28; Bannister quoted in "The United Water Program for Colorado—Panel Discussions—1955," Box 44, folder 25, Pughe Papers, UCBA. Schorr, *Colorado Doctrine*, 32–64, offers thoughts on early territorial water laws and how water is treated in the Colorado State Constitution. See *Coffin v. Left Hand Ditch Company*, 6 Colo. 443 (1882).

13. Vandenbusche and Smith, *A Land Alone*, 1.

14. Ibid., 16–28, 55; Ubbelohde, Benson, and Smith, *Colorado History*, 42–50; Peter R. Decker, *Old Fences, New Neighbors* (Golden, CO: Fulcrum, 1998), 13–15; Robert W. Delaney, *The Ute Mountain Utes* (Albuquerque: University of New Mexico Press, 1988), 45–46; William Wyckoff, *Creating Colorado: The Making of a Western American Landscape* (New Haven, CT: Yale University Press, 1999), 223–25.

15. Vandenbusche and Smith, *A Land Alone*, 181; Denver and Rio Grande promotional literature quoted in Wyckoff, *Creating Colorado*, 234–35; Ubbelohde, Benson, and Smith, *Colorado History*, 183–85.

16. *Denver Tribune* and Fossett quoted in Wyckoff, *Creating Colorado*, 221; Ubbelohde, Benson, and Smith, *Colorado History*, 149–50; Duane A. Smith, "A Land unto Itself: The Western Slope," *Colorado Magazine* 55 (1978): 181–204.

17. Sparks quoted in Vandenbusche and Smith, *A Land Alone*, 184; railroad official quoted in Wyckoff, *Creating Colorado*, 232–33.

18. "Taft Opens Tunnel That Will Make the Desert Bloom," screamed the *Denver Post* headline at the time. See *Empire Magazine* (*Denver Post*), May 22, 1977; *Denver Post*, May 26, 1966; *Daily Sentinel* (Grand Junction, CO), January 18, 1949.

19. The major canals included the Government High Line Canal, completed in 1917, and the Orchard Mesa Power Canal, completed in 1924, bringing much-needed water to the higher lands of East Orchard Mesa. See William Joe Simonds, *Grand Valley Project* (Washington, DC: Bureau of Reclamation, 1994), 4–7. The unique roller structure, the largest of its type in the world, was placed on the National Register of Historic Places in 1991.

20. "Grand Valley Project," accessed June 14, 2015, http://www.usbr.gov/projects/Project.jsp?proj_Name=Grand+Valley+Project. Interestingly, future Bureau of Reclamation commissioner (1937–42) John Page learned his trade on the Grand Valley Project as a junior engineer, office engineer, and eventually project manager in 1925. See ibid., 22–23.

21. Pisani, *To Reclaim a Divided West*, 208–22, tells the story of the failure of early pre-federal efforts at reclamation in Colorado. Douglas Kupel, *Fuel for Growth: Water and Arizona's Urban Environment* (Tucson: University of Arizona Press, 2003), 23–24, shows the same pattern of private ventures giving way to territorial efforts and finally the arrival of federal reclamation in Arizona.

22. Wyckoff, *Creating Colorado*, 220.

23. Worster, *Rivers of Empire*, 130–31; Donald J. Pisani, ed., *Water, Land, and Law in the West: The Limits of Public Policy, 1850–1920* (Lawrence: University of Kansas Press, 1996), xiv; Wallace Stegner, *Beyond the Hundredth Meridian: John Wesley Powell and the Second Opening of the West* (Boston: Houghton Mifflin, 1954), 315.

24. Worster, *Rivers of Empire*, 160–69; Donald J. Pisani, *Water and American Government: The Reclamation Bureau, National Water Policy, and the West, 1902–1935* (Berkeley: University of California Press, 2002), xi–xvii.

25. This discussion is based on an examination of the *Mesa County Directory* for the years 1912–25. See also Bradley F. Raley, "Irrigation, Land Speculation, and the History of Grand Junction, Colorado" (paper presented at the Western History Association Meeting, Lincoln, NE, October 17, 1996), 6–8; quotation in Steven C. Schulte, *Wayne Aspinall and the Shaping of the American West* (Boulder: University Press of Colorado, 2002), 13.

26. Pisani, *To Reclaim a Divided West*, 325.

27. Donald J. Pisani, "State versus Nation: Federal Reclamation and Water Rights in the West: The Progressive Era," in Donald J. Pisani, ed., *Water, Land, and Law in*

the West: The Limits of Public Policy, 1850–1920 (Lawrence: University of Kansas Press, 1996), 42–43.

28. Ibid.; Duane A. Smith, Henry M. Teller: Colorado's Grand Old Man (Boulder: University Press of Colorado, 2002), 229–30; Ed Quillen, "The War on the West," High Country News Online, February 15, 2011, accessed February 20, 2014, http://www.hcn.org/articles/the-latest-war-on-the-west.

29. Norris Hundley Jr., Water and the West: The Colorado River Compact and the Politics of Water in the American West, 2nd ed. (Berkeley: University of California Press, 2009 [1975]), xi–xiv.

30. Ubbelohde, Benson, and Smith, Colorado History, 252–53; Pisani, "State versus Nation," 45; Gregory J. Hobbs Jr., "Colorado Water Law: An Historical Overview," Water Law Review 1, no. 1 (Fall 1997): 73. See Kansas v. Colorado, 185 U.S. 125 (1902).

31. James Earl Sherow, Watering the Valley: Development along the High Plains Arkansas River, 1870–1950 (Lawrence: University of Kansas Press, 1990), 79, 103–7.

32. Michael Broadhead, David J. Brewer: The Life of a Supreme Court Justice, 1837–1919 (Carbondale: Southern Illinois University Press, 1994), 162–63; Sherow, Watering the Valley, 116; James E. Sherow, "The Contest for the Nile of America, Kansas v. Colorado (1907)," Great Plains Quarterly 10 (1990): 57.

33. The Harmon Doctrine dated from 1895 when US attorney general Judson Harmon argued that the national government possesses "sole and absolute jurisdiction within its territory." In Kansas v. Colorado, Colorado's lawyers tried and failed to compare Colorado's control of water to this form of absolute sovereignty the nation possesses. See Sherow, Watering the Valley, 108.

34. Broadhead, Brewer, 163; Sherow, "Nile of America," 58. See also Pisani, "State versus Nation," 47–48, where he points out that Department of the Interior attorney Morris Bien, who continued as the head of the Reclamation Service's legal staff until 1924, never relinquished his belief in federal sovereignty over water matters.

35. Pisani, Water and the Federal Government, 41–42.

36. Proceedings of the Public Lands Convention, Held in Denver, Colorado June 18–20, 1907 by the States and Territories Containing the Public Lands of the United States and Lying West of the Missouri River. Copied and published by authority of the convention, Fred C. Johnson, secretary, Denver, CO, accessed February 10, 2013, http://memory.loc.gov/cgi-bin/query/r?ammem/consrvbib:@OR(@field(AU-THOR+@3(Public+land+convention,+Denver,+1907++)+@field(OTHER+@3 (Public+land+convention,+Denver,+1907++), 9–11; Michael G. McCarthy, Hour of Trial: The Conservation Conflict in Colorado and the West (Norman: University of Oklahoma Press, 1977), 218–22.

37. Daily Press (Montrose, CO), January 30, 1940.

38. Ibid., January 30, 1940; *Bingham (UT) Bullet*, January 23, 1907, undated articles in unnumbered scrapbook, Edward T. Taylor Papers, UCBA.

39. Carl Abbott, *Colorado: A History of the Centennial State* (Boulder: Colorado Associated University Press, 1976), 116; Taylor quoted in *Congressional Record*, February 1, April 20, 1910, in Box 1, folder 19, Edward T. Taylor Papers, Colorado State Historical Society, Denver (hereafter CSHS).

40. *Bingham (UT) Bullet*, January 23, 1907; Philip L. Fradkin, *A River No More: The Colorado River and the West*, expanded and updated ed. (Berkeley: University of California Press, 1996), 35; House Joint Resolution 32, 67th Congress, 1st session, US House of Representatives, in Box 1, folder 22, Edward T. Taylor Papers, CSHS.

41. Edward Taylor, in *Congressional Record*, 69th Congress, 2nd session, US House of Representatives, February 25, 1927.

42. Tyler, *Silver Fox of the Rockies*, 16–19; Pisani, *Water and American Government*, xii–xiii.

43. Tyler, *Silver Fox of the Rockies*, 15–16; G. E. Radosevich et al., *Evolution and Administration of Colorado Water Law: 1876–1976* (Fort Collins, CO: Water Resources Publications, 1976), 224–25; Frank Gibbard, "*Wyoming v. Colorado*: A 'Watershed' Decision," *Colorado Lawyer* 34, no. 3 (2005): 37.

44. Tyler, *Silver Fox of the Rockies*, 16, 107; Gibbard, "*Wyoming v. Colorado*," 37; *Wyoming v. Colorado*, 259 U.S. 419 (1922).

45. Tyler, *Silver Fox of the Rockies*, 18–19, 114–15.

46. Ibid., 17–19. For the story of the Los Angeles aqueduct and its impact on the rural Owens Valley, see Abraham Hoffman, *Vision or Villainy: Origins of the Owens Valley–Los Angeles Water Controversy* (College Station: Texas A&M Press, 1981); William L. Kahrl, *Water and Power: The Conflict over Los Angeles' Water Supply in the Owens Valley* (Berkeley: University of California Press, 1982).

47. John N. Winchester, "A Historical View: Transmountain Diversion Development in Colorado," Hydrosphere Resource Consultants, Inc., accessed February 29, 2012, https://dspace.library.colostate.edu/bitstream/handle/10217/46354/116_Pro ceedings%202001%20USCID%20Water%20Management%20-%20Transbasin%20 Water%20Transfers%20Winchester.pdf?sequence=15&isAllowed=y.

48. Daniel Tyler, *The Last Water Hole in the West: The Colorado–Big Thompson Project and the Northern Colorado Water Conservancy District* (Niwot: University Press of Colorado, 1992), 29–33; Stephen J. Leonard and Thomas J. Noel, *Denver: From Mining Camp to Metropolis* (Niwot: University Press of Colorado, 1990), 49–52; Neil S. Grigg, "A History of Colorado Water by the Decades," *Colorado Water* 27, no. 2 (March-April 2010): 13; Patricia Nelson Limerick with Jason Hanson, *A Ditch in Time: The City, the West, and Water* (Golden, CO: Fulcrum, 2012), 65–69.

49. Tyler, *Last Water Hole*, 32–33; Hundley, *Water and the West*, 97; Fradkin, *A River No More*, 45–47. Fradkin points out that Taylor's clause allowed for the later Colorado–Big Thompson Project's 13.1-mile tunnel to be built. In addition, more than thirty water rights were issued prior to the park's establishment, which led to the building of several small dams, constructed around 1900.

50. Colorado Constitution, Article XVI, Section 5.

51. *Rocky Mountain News* (Denver), December 22, 1913. A *portcullis* is a heavy iron grating that was lowered by chains to bar the gateway to a medieval castle or fortified town.

52. For an overview of both the Los Angeles–Owens Valley and San Francisco–Hetch Hetchy stories, see Norris Hundley Jr., *The Great Thirst: Californians and Water, 1770s–1990s* (Berkeley: University of California Press, 1992), 119–200; Worster, *Rivers of Empire*, 213–14. The Los Angeles–Owens Valley story is told in many places, including Kahrl, *Water and Power*, and Hoffman, *Visions or Villainy*.

53. Hundley, *Great Thirst*. It was Lippincott, (while working for the Bureau of Reclamation on a possible federal water project for the Owens Valley) who decided to recommend that his superiors curtail the project to allow Los Angeles to access a significant portion of the valley's water. Lippincott ended up working as an engineer for Los Angeles during the aqueduct project. Robert Righter calls Lippincott a "water engineer of questionable ethics." See Robert W. Righter, *The Battle over Hetch Hetchy: America's Most Controversial Dam and the Birth of Modern Environmentalism* (New York: Oxford University Press, 2005), 28. Righter's book is the most reliable guide to the Hetch Hetchy controversy. A Colorado perspective on the event is Limerick and Hanson, *A Ditch in Time*, 53–55.

54. Stegner, *Beyond the Hundredth Meridian*, 226; Kahrl, *Water and Power*, 1; Peter Iverson, "The Cultural Politics of Water in Arizona," in Richard Lowitt, ed., *Politics in the Postwar American West* (Norman: University of Oklahoma Press, 1995).

55. John Walton, *Western Times and Water Wars: State, Culture, and Rebellion in California* (Berkeley: University of California Press, 1993), 12, 193–94.

2

Colorado's Water Wars Begin, 1920-1940

[The waters of the Colorado River] are worth a thousand times
more to the Colorado River Basin than all its minerals and everything
else. It's the only great river in the world entirely within an arid
region and is intrinsically the most valuable stream on the planet.

Edward T. Taylor to Harold Ickes, April 2, 1935[1]

THE COLORADO RIVER COMPACT

The 1920s began with the negotiation of the monumental Colorado River
Compact, regarded as the foundation of the body of law that regulates the
river. With its origins high in the Colorado Rockies on the Western Slope,
the river flows across western Colorado, enters Utah, joins with the Green
and other tributaries, and traverses the Grand Canyon on its way to the Gulf
of California. In 1922 the seven states of the Colorado River Basin gathered at
the behest of Secretary of Commerce Herbert Hoover to divide the waters
of the Colorado River system. Under western water law, the strongest rights

DOI: 10.5876/9781607325000.c002

accrued to those who put the water to beneficial use at the earliest point in time. Every year, California was putting more water to use irrigating its growing agricultural empire. If California could get water structures built such as the Los Angeles aqueduct, few doubted that the state could also tap the Colorado River in the near future. To complicate matters, at least in the eyes of other Colorado River Basin states, California contributed the least amount of water to the river. Colorado contributed far and away the most water, a fact that both haunted and animated the state's politicians. While the exact figures varied by year, most Colorado politicians over the course of the twentieth century routinely claimed that between 65 percent and 75 percent of the river's entire flows originated high in the state's mountains.[2]

In 1920 the League of the Southwest, an association of regional business, political, and cultural leaders, met in Denver in conjunction with the Western States Reclamation Association to consider the future of the Colorado River.[3] At the league's Denver meeting, a consulting engineer for the newly created Denver Water Board[4] (DWB), George M. Bull, delivered a keynote address that likely sent shivers down the backs of league delegates from Colorado's Western Slope. The *Denver Post* reported on Bull's address under the bold headline "Western Governors Will Make Great Mountain Stream a Slave of Seven States." Bull made it clear that he equated Colorado's water needs with Denver's future water requirements—they were one and the same. In asserting the need to develop the Grand River (renamed Colorado in 1922), Bull noted that only 20,000 acre-feet were being diverted from the Western Slope to the Eastern Slope but proclaimed that the "final development" of the river would see more than 300,000 acre-feet of western Colorado's water diverted to the Denver–South Platte Basin. Future estimates revised this number upward significantly over the next decade. Bull insisted that this would be an inevitable development in the aftermath of an agreement to divide the river among the seven basin states.[5]

The solution to the problem of California's combined thirst and political might was to find a means to guarantee an amount of water for the future needs of the Upper Colorado River Basin. The form this guarantee would take was a product of the genius of Greeley, Colorado, water attorney Delphus (Delph) E. Carpenter. Between 1920 and 1922, Carpenter had proposed to Hoover and western state water officials that the seven basin states negotiate a compact to determine each state's river share. A compact might have the added benefit of limiting future interstate legal proceedings and the cost and time those proceedings would take. Carpenter also feared that if the western states did not put their water affairs in order, the federal government might step in, take control, and weaken "state autonomy on all the rivers." Carpenter also hoped to limit California to a certain maximum amount of water.[6]

Congressional enabling legislation created a Colorado River Compact Commission. Each of the seven Colorado River states sent a designated commissioner to Washington, DC, to begin the negotiations. At the first hearing in the nation's capital on January 26, 1922, Colorado commissioner Delph Carpenter argued that the "prime object" of the commission was to avoid or minimize future litigation among the states. The commission hoped to avoid provoking "an assertion of rights" by the federal government, which might jeopardize the main task of the gathering—to settle various claims to the river before the US Congress appropriated funding for dam and diversion structures. During most of 1922, the commission wrangled among itself with public hearings held in Phoenix, Los Angeles, Salt Lake City, Cheyenne, Wyoming, and Grand Junction, Colorado.[7]

The Grand Junction hearing on March 29, 1922, was the only hearing held on the Colorado River itself. On the eve of the meeting, the Grand Junction *Daily Sentinel* expressed the feelings of many Western Slope residents by bluntly stating that the Upper Colorado River states needed to devise "some way to keep water from running down hill" to California and the other Lower Colorado River states. Western Slope residents in attendance told commission chair Herbert Hoover and the other commissioners that the water rights of Colorado's Western Slope should not be abridged merely because California was moving more quickly to develop its resources. Addressing the meeting, Delph Carpenter pointed to another troublesome matter that would occupy Western Slope water officials in the decades ahead. Carpenter boldly predicted that the Grand Junction hearings would end in discord unless "every . . . objection by Grand Junction people against possible future tunnel diversions [to the Eastern Slope] can be eliminated." Carpenter was correct. The populous Eastern Slope had started to covet the abundant water supply of the Western Slope. In fact, at the time of the Colorado River Compact hearings, the Denver Board of Water Commissioners had started to formulate and implement an ambitious plan to claim waters on the west side of the Continental Divide.[8]

The Colorado River Compact negotiations highlighted a number of issues that soon soured relations between Colorado's two slopes. Foremost was the question of the legality of inter-basin transfers of water. Could the signatory states legally transfer water out of the Colorado River Basin? This question weighed heavily on the minds of representatives from all of the states, with Denver officials lobbying hard for the legality of such transfers. Utah's water interests also hoped to be able to move more water from rural areas to the growing Salt Lake Valley. Lower Basin state representatives hoped to use opposition to such transfers as a bargaining chip to gain some of their own compact concessions. At different times during the 1922 negotiations, eastern Colorado's water interests gave widely varying figures about the amount of water the region hoped to siphon from the Western Slope. During the initial Washington, DC, hearings in January 1922, Delph Carpenter estimated future Western Slope to Eastern Slope water transfers at 310,000 acre-feet. Two months later, at commission hearings in Denver, a deputy state engineer raised the figure to 500,000 acre-feet, while L. Ward Bannister, a noted Denver water attorney and law professor, believed future Front Range needs would be 500,000 acre-feet for agriculture and a larger unspecified figure for Denver's urban needs. Still another association of farmers from the Arkansas River Valley, perhaps anticipating the Fryingpan-Arkansas Project, claimed the right to take as much from the Colorado River as can "feasibly be diverted across the continental divide." The DWB's engineering consultant George Bull, in testimony prepared for the Colorado River Compact Commission's Denver hearings, pointed out that Denver could exponentially increase its water supply by diverting water from the Fraser, Williams Fork, and Blue Rivers. Bull estimated that 350,000 acre-feet could be brought to Denver from these sources. He also revealed that Denver had filed with the Colorado state engineer intentions to divert water from the Fraser and Williams Fork. "Filings will also be made for appropriations from the Blue River this coming summer," Bull announced.[9]

The public and private wrangling over the Colorado River's future continued until November 1922, when the commissioners gathered at Bishop's Lodge outside Santa Fe, New Mexico. There, the Colorado River Compact was drafted, apportioning the river between two groupings of states—the Upper Basin, comprising Wyoming, Colorado, Utah, and New Mexico, and the Lower Basin, composed of Arizona, Nevada, and California. Each basin was to receive 7.5 million of the river's estimated annual flow of 17.5 million acre-feet. More specifically, the Lower Basin states would receive 75 million acre-feet on a ten-year average. An additional 1.5 million acre-feet was reserved for the still undetermined water claims of Mexico. The final 1.0 million acre-feet was given to the Lower Basin states when they threatened to leave the negotiations. After finishing its work, the commission sent the document back to the seven states for ratification by their respective legislatures.[10]

Article 11 of the Colorado River Compact required that the negotiated pact would only become binding and obligatory "when it shall have been approved by the Legislatures of each of the signatory States and by the Congress of the United States." The compact came before the Colorado General Assembly during its 1923 legislative session.[11] Most of Colorado's public officials seemed ready to ratify the compact. The strongest concerns and opposition emanated from the Western Slope, a region that seemed to be waking up to the possibility that its future water supply might become endangered. The Colorado Assembly held more than thirty hearings in addition to several conferences and public meetings to discuss the proposed compact. The western half of the state's fears centered on Articles 3(b) and 8. Article 3(b) stated that Lower Basin states were to receive 1 million acre-feet of water in addition to an allotment of 7.5 million acre-feet. Western Slope water officials believed both articles could be misconstrued to the detriment of Colorado and other Upper Basin states. Western Colorado's water community believed these articles were required to minimize the chances of losing more water to the downstream states.[12]

To quiet western Colorado's compact critics and to smooth the pathway for state ratification, Delph Carpenter drafted a "Supplemental Report" to the Colorado Assembly addressing the Western Slope's concerns. In a telegram to Hoover detailing the Western Slope "uprising," Carpenter argued that "Article VIII is not intended to authorize, constitute, or result in any apportionment of water to the lower basin beyond that made in paragraphs (a) or (b) in Article III." Hoover's response strongly concurred with the Coloradans' views. After examining the "Supplemental Report," most Western Slope residents dropped their opposition to state ratification. With a strong response that addressed western Colorado's concerns, Carpenter had led the way for the Colorado Assembly to unanimously approve the Colorado River Compact in late March 1923.[13]

What the Upper Basin states achieved with the compact were assurances that water would be available when the region was ready to begin constructing its water infrastructure. The compact's flaws have been discussed in many places and need not be revisited here.[14] The issues for Colorado and the Upper Basin in the decades ahead would be twofold. How would the Upper Basin divide its 7.5 million acre-feet among the states? Finally, and as significant, would be the question of Colorado's internal divisions. How would Colorado divide its share of the river? Would most of the water remain in its basin of origin on the Western Slope? What mechanisms and institutions would the state of Colorado devise to apportion water within its borders? This story would begin to take definitive shape in the aftermath of the 1922 Santa Fe conference.

A "BULL" IN THE MOUNTAINS

The Denver Board of Water Commissioners emerged as the most active force for Colorado water development in the 1920s and 1930s. The public successor to the private Denver Union Water Company, in 1918 the DWB became the organization that allowed Denver to obtain the water it needed to assure its status as a major city. Its goal was not much different than that of the Los Angeles Water Department—to "coordinate and centralize the expansion of the city's water supplies."[15]

By the first decade of the twentieth century, the Denver Union Water Company envisioned tapping the headwaters of the Grand River (Colorado River) on the Western Slope to enhance the city's water supplies.[16] In 1914 the Public Utilities Commission of Denver, acting for the Denver Union Water Company, employed engineer R. I. Meeker to investigate the sources of a possible water supply for Denver on the Western Slope. Two years later the Public Utilities Commission engaged the famed California water engineer Joseph B. Lippincott to conduct another survey of the headwaters of the Colorado River region with the Fraser, Williams Fork, and Blue Rivers as possible water sources.[17]

Lippincott, as a city of Los Angeles water engineer, had helped that city acquire land and water rights in the Owens River Valley. In words that sounded strangely like those later uttered by Denver water engineer George M. Bull, Lippincott had remarked at the time that "the future development and prosperity [of the Los Angeles area] will be measured largely by the available water supply." Lippincott had also been involved in finalizing the water rights of the city of San Francisco to the Hetch Hetchy Valley, which would result in the submersion of the picturesque Yosemite Park Valley for San Francisco's water supply. In Colorado, Lippincott's findings and recommendations added gravity to Denver's ultimate water claims. In 1916 another engineering study conducted by San Francisco water engineers Van Sant and Houghton essentially confirmed the recommendations of the two earlier studies.[18]

Consulting water engineer George M. Bull alleged that the Denver Union Water Company had built an "inadequate water system for growing the city." The Denver Union Water Company had done little planning for the city's future, had an obsolete system of works, and operated its plant inefficiently. Above all, it controlled an inadequate water supply to sustain future growth. The new DWB took several crucial actions over the next few years. In addition to a program of renovation and new facility construction within the city, it started a program to "prepare plans and cost estimates of an additional supply of water." Key to the plans was securing the services of Bull in May 1920 to enlarge the city's water supply. An experienced engineer, Bull had carried out engineering projects all over the nation after enlisting as a volunteer engineer during the Spanish-American War in 1898. His first contact with the Denver area occurred as an employee of the New York engineering firm J. G. White Company, which included the legendary reclamation advocate (and future commissioner of the Bureau of Reclamation) Elwood Mead as one of its consulting engineers. Bull later said that during the 1920s he was "engaged by [Denver] to make an extensive study of the need and location of water supply systems to be built by the city."[19]

Bull understood the huge task expected of him—to act on the new board's behalf, survey the headwaters of the Colorado River system, and file claims in that region for his employer. DWB manager W. F. R. Mills announced the city's intention to claim water from the Colorado River's headwaters in a 1921 letter to Colorado's state engineer, Addison J. McCune. The letter revealed the impressive progress the DWB had made toward developing a master water-supply plan. In phrasing that would be repeated often, Mills wrote that Denver needed a larger water supply if it were "to maintain its pre-eminence as a manufacturing and distributing center." The city's meager South Platte water supply needed augmentation with waters "from the Western Slope by diversion from the Blue River, Williams Fork, and Fraser River." Mills also minimized the impact that trans-basin diversion would have on the Western Slope. The area's power and irrigation needs would barely be compromised; the Western Slope was not putting its water to extensive use. In fact, at the time, "there are 2,695,500 acre-feet passing out of the State of Colorado." As for the concept of trans-basin diversion, Mills assured McCune that it is "not a novel or an untried endeavor lacking in precedent." Southern California's diversion of more than 2 million acre-feet from the Owens Valley to the growing Los Angeles area was cited as an example of the beneficial and lawful nature of such a diversion. Denver's municipal water needs, by comparison, would be much less.[20]

Mills and the Denver Water Board directed Bull to undertake a survey in the summer of 1921 to finish the work done previously by Meeker, Lippincott, and Van Sant and Houghton. Beginning on July 4, 1921, Bull led an engineering survey party into the high mountains west of Denver to make a survey "upon which Denver's transmountain water rights are basically dependent." Bull completed the Fraser and Williams Fork portions of his survey in the summer of 1921. The Fraser River Project received top priority because it could utilize the pilot bore of the Denver and Salt Lake Railroad's Moffat Railroad Tunnel as a six-mile conduit to bring water through the Continental Divide. The pilot bore was a parallel tunnel used to bring workers and supplies to the main tunnel as it was being constructed.[21] Williams Fork also remained a priority project, but it would have to wait for greater economic prosperity and the crucial support of federal New Deal programs before its water would flow toward the east.

In 1922 another George Bull–led engineering party embarked on a trip to the mountains, this time in the vicinity of the headwaters of the Blue River. Bull filed amended maps in the Office of the State Engineer in 1923 and again in 1927. He returned again in 1926 to "resurvey the Blue." When Denver tried to claim an early date for its Blue River water rights during its conflict with the Western Slope and the Northern Colorado District in the mid-1950s, it attempted to establish its rights as the year 1914 (as a result of the work of both the Meeker and Lippincott expeditions) or, failing that, 1921, the year Bull visited the Fraser and Williams Fork Rivers.[22]

By the mid-1920s, Denver had started to discuss what would be done with all the water it planned to divert from the Williams Fork, Fraser, and Blue Rivers. In late 1926 Bull recommended that the city build additional South

FIGURE 2.1. Enormous snowbanks on the Western Slope near Berthoud Pass. Water engineer George M. Bull noted that "the abundance of snow on the Western Slope, shown here, indicates the large quantities of water available by transmountain diversion." *Courtesy*, University of Colorado–Boulder Archives.

Platte reservoirs "to control the entire flow of the South Platte" to accomplish a multiplicity of tasks, including storing spring runoff waters, adding generating power, and storing Western Slope diversions. Denver had already foreseen the possibility of building a large reservoir at Two Forks, on the North Fork of the Platte; Bull believed the city would "eventually construct the Two Forks Reservoir" and in the meantime could study it from an engineering perspective and do the needed legal and preliminary construction work to "perfect the City's rights for its ultimate construction when needed."[23]

By the end of the 1920s, Denver was still receiving its entire municipal water supply from the South Platte River and its tributaries. However, the South Platte had reached the end of its ability to sustain Denver's growth. The three projected Western Slope projects (Fraser, Williams Fork, and Blue) would mean a combined annual gross diversion to Denver of about 354,000 acre-feet of Western Slope water. In a 1929 summary of "Colorado River Appropriations" made by DWB president C. C. Schrepferman, the president discussed Denver's water needs in apocalyptic terms with Delph Carpenter, Colorado's interstate stream's commissioner: "If Denver were unable to get its water from [the Western Slope] it could not hope to maintain its position as a metropolitan center." For this reason, Denver had begun to act on a comprehensive water plan with Western Slope water sources as its lynchpin.[24]

Schrepferman offered insights into what strategy Denver would follow in its water development in the decades ahead. Denver could not consider its water supply "from a standpoint of what it needs" in the next ten or twenty years; it must accumulate a surplus in anticipation of great predicated growth, and the "headwaters of the Colorado River are the only supply that it can possibly safeguard to satisfy the growth it must look forward to." At this point, Western Slope political officials were only dimly aware of the extent of Denver's plans. When Denver and the Front Range's water plans became fully known in the years ahead, Western Slope politicians and civic leaders began formulating a defense of their water supply.[25]

THE DEPRESSION YEARS: ACCELERATION OF WATER PLANNING

The Centennial State floundered like most western states in the face of Depression-era challenges. Ironically, however, the terrible dislocation and despair bred a determination to begin systematic statewide water planning for Colorado. While the Colorado River Compact had assuaged some anxiety over both the question of water availability and California's hydraulic intentions, many Coloradans continued to believe cooperation with federal agencies like the Bureau of Reclamation would not lead to positive results for the state. Before the onset of the Great Depression, Colorado's state-level water planning remained virtually nonexistent. Water planning was at best a local affair, with municipalities filing claims and grabbing what water they could.

By the 1930s Denver and the Front Range's increased water-planning efforts could no longer escape the public's notice on the Western Slope. In 1922 the Busk-Ivanhoe Tunnel, an abandoned Colorado Midland Railroad right-of-way, began carrying water to the Front Range from the Roaring Fork River to the Arkansas River. The DWB's engineering expeditions and Colorado

River headwaters claims were also known and starting to be feared by the Western Slope. Yet for all the Eastern Slope's diversion plans and ambitions for more, little water actually flowed from the Western Slope to the Front Range. During most of the early decades of the twentieth century, the state rallied as a whole to oppose the possibility of water loss to other states. Most Coloradans reasoned that the state needed to guard against the ambitions of California, Utah, and Arizona. After all, the Colorado River Compact safeguarded Upper Basin rights for a later day when sparsely populated states like Colorado could amass the water needs and political clout to begin large-scale reclamation construction. No one could predict when this would occur.[26]

By the time Colorado began to wrestle with the impacts of the Great Depression, the Western Slope was starting to slowly realize that it may have a nearby competitor for its precious water supply. This rival lay within the state's borders—the Front Range and Denver region, where an estimated two-thirds of the state's population and the bulk of the political clout resided. By this time the Western Slope's water leaders could compare what could potentially happen to the Western Slope with the tragic and well-known story of the Owens Valley in California, a tale that described what could occur "when a rich and powerful area goes after the water in an arid country." Supporters of the Owens Valley Project had argued that Los Angeles was doomed to secondary-city status without the water and the project. It was hard to refute the raw yet bizarre logic of the head of the Los Angeles Department of Water and Power, William Mulholland: "If we don't get the water, we won't need it."[27]

Did Denver's ambitious water acquisition plans reveal the making of another Los Angeles–Owens Valley scenario? The Western Slope's leading water attorney of the era, Glenwood Springs's Frank Delaney, believed so. Other Western Slope water attorneys and politicians evaluated the situation as Delaney did. Delaney remarked, "A moment's consideration of what happened in the Owens Valley in California is the most forcible application of the dangers inherent in any transmountain diversion project." Delaney concluded that Western Slope water users would do well to study the lessons to be learned from the Owens Valley, particularly how it changed "from a rich and prosperous farming community to an arid, worthless region."[28]

Delaney envisioned "evil possibilities" in the application of New Deal relief funds for trans-mountain diversions. While he was undoubtedly referring to the Grand Lake Project as it was known early on (before being named the Colorado–Big Thompson Project), he believed that with political power and "unlimited funds," the Front Range could purchase senior water rights, ask for a legal change in the point of water diversion, and wear down the resistance "of our sparsely populated communities" on the Western Slope. The result would be "constant turmoil and uncertainty." Delaney, who more than anyone else would engineer the Western Slope's defense of its water rights over the next thirty years, could not have predicted the future course of events more clearly.[29]

Another of the Western Slope's leading water strategists in the first half of the twentieth century, Grand Junction attorney Silmon Smith, always believed the Western Slope was at a great disadvantage in scrambling to protect its water resources. The Western Slope was settled "from 40 to 60 years later than other sections of Colorado and neighboring states." Because the Western Slope was settled by Anglo-Americans more recently than Front Range cities had been, it needed to guard its "most vital resource, water" to assure its opportunity to grow. By the 1930s the development of Western Slope oil shale reserves had been envisioned as a resource of great promise. However, its extraction would require large amounts of water. Smith, along with Delaney and others, would help form organizations in the 1930s and beyond to protect the western half of the state's water supply. One of western Colorado's leading attorneys since the early twentieth century, Smith, like Delaney, would be an indefatigable advocate of Western Slope water rights in the decades ahead.[30]

Yet as late as the 1930s, Colorado's overall state water-planning efforts lagged behind those of most neighboring states. No stable state-level bureaucracy existed to facilitate water management. It was not until the late 1930s that a water organization structure would be built at the state level. At the same time, the Colorado General Assembly would pass legislation allowing for the organization of large water conservancy districts. These organizations encouraged Coloradans to link with federal agencies and the US Congress to construct large-scale water projects.[31] Yet because of Colorado's late organizational start, controversy "between the peoples of the two slopes of the Continental Divide" muddled and confused early state efforts at building reclamation projects.[32]

FIGURE 2.2. George M. Bull at his desk. Bull, a career water engineer, conducted some of the first surveys to file for Denver's water rights on Western Slope streams. During the New Deal years, Bull headed the Denver Regional Office of the PWA and in that capacity promoted water project planning. *Courtesy*, University of Colorado–Boulder Archives.

NEW DEAL RECLAMATION IN COLORADO

President Franklin Delano Roosevelt said he wanted to be remembered "as the greatest conservationist and developer of all time." The New Deal agency that proved to be an early catalyst for Colorado's water planning was the

FIGURE 2.3. Frank Delaney, a Glenwood Spring water attorney, was a leading western Colorado water strategist before and after the organization of the Colorado River Water Conservation District in 1937. He served as its counsel until the mid-1950s. *Courtesy*, Colorado River Water Conservation District.

Public Works Administration (PWA). Its intent was to "prime the pump" of the economy by pouring money into the region through public works projects. Established in 1933 under Title II of the National Industrial Recovery Act (NIRA), the PWA, under the leadership of Secretary of the Interior Harold Ickes, had the authority to initiate its own projects as a construction agency, make financial allotments to other federal agencies, and make loans to states and other public bodies to stimulate non-federal construction. George M. Bull, who had scoured the mountains claiming unclaimed water on behalf of the DWB, was named state engineer for the PWA. Naturally, Bull encouraged use of the PWA to plan large-scale water projects in Colorado. Not surprisingly, Bull's efforts proved especially beneficial to Colorado's Front Range region.[33]

Bull maintained close ties with his old employer, the Denver Water Board, while in the employ of the federal government. Bull's many studies of potential water supplies on the Western Slope became the basis of the PWA's plans to further enhance Denver's water supply. In his first year as a PWA engineer,

FIGURE 2.4. Celebration of the opening of the Moffat Tunnel, June 1936. The tunnel brought Western Slope water to the Denver area. Pictured (*left to right*) are M. C. Hinderliider, Denver mayor Benjamin T. Stapleton, H. S. Crocker, George M. Bull, Stanley Wallbank, and Richard Wensley. *Courtesy,* University of Colorado–Boulder Archives.

Bull proposed tapping the NIRA to facilitate Colorado's water development. Bull asserted that 1.5 million to 2 million acre-feet of water in the Colorado River system flowed out of the state: "The greater part of this supply is now in excess of that required for future development on the Western Slope." The engineer believed that at least 600,000 acre-feet could be diverted each year through the Continental Divide into the South Platte and Arkansas River drainage areas. Bull also cautioned that such an ambitious program might require the construction of several replacement reservoirs on the Western Slope to assure that region of the state would have a water supply. Finally, Bull asserted what had already become a DWB mantra: the capital city's future appeared bleak without the addition of more water supplies from the Fraser, Williams Fork, and Blue Rivers. While Bull endorsed using New Deal "reconstruction" funds to enhance Denver's water supply, he also indicated that the possibility existed to construct the Grand Lake Project for northern Colorado.[34]

Bull's ambitious agenda received support from the Denver-based Colorado Engineering Council, which had published a report reiterating what had become standard arguments favoring massive diversions from the Western Slope. "It is fairly obvious," the report intoned, "that Western Colorado will never use more than a small portion of the total water produced on the western slope." Even with massive diversions, the council did not envision any damage to the western half of the state. The engineers went on record arguing that 100,000 acre-feet could be brought to the Arkansas River Valley and "perhaps" another 500,000 to the South Platte region. The group concurred with George Bull's dream of tapping into the massive public works program associated with Roosevelt's New Deal to garner low-cost reclamation loans.[35]

The *Denver Post* touted the plans of the DWB, noting that new PWA director Bull had asked for about $137 million in water projects for the state, with many projects slated to divert water to the Eastern Slope. Bull had been busy during the summer of 1933 gathering specific project recommendations by calling on local water leaders like Weld County attorney and Grand Lake diversion advocate Thomas Nixon. In his recommendations, Bull had touted the projects he had embraced while in the employ of the Denver Water Board: diversion projects from the Williams Fork, the Fraser River–Moffat Tunnel, and the Blue River were all included in the package of projects he had sent to Washington, DC.[36]

Denver's first successful PWA request asked for federal funding to complete the Moffat Railroad Tunnel's unused 6.4-mile pioneer bore to bring Fraser River and Williams Fork water from the Western Slope to Denver. The Moffat Tunnel Project had been contemplated for as long as the larger railroad tunnel had been planned. With the railroad tunnel operating by 1927, Denver could turn full attention to use of the pioneer bore. The tunnel needed to be enlarged and lined before it could convey water. Water flowed through the tunnel in 1936, and the project was in full operation by 1938 at a cost of $9.5 million. Soon, 43,000 acre-feet of water were running from the Western Slope to the Eastern Slope in what was, up to that time, the largest diversion of water in Colorado history. While more water would be flowing uphill and through the mountains toward the Front Range's growing population, the Moffat Tunnel Project relieved Denver of immediate water concerns and gave it the stability and confidence to reach for more western Colorado water.[37]

Western Slope water officials Frank Delaney, Silmon Smith, Dan Hughes, and others had argued against Denver's need for the Moffat Tunnel diversions. Western Slope critics predicted that Denver would simply be leasing the water to farmers near Denver until the city needed it, sounding a Western Slope argument that would be repeated many times in the decades ahead. At about the same time, the ever-thirsty Arkansas River Valley added another diversion from the Western Slope by accessing the Roaring Fork River through the Twin Lakes Tunnel. A $1.2 million loan from the Reconstruction Finance Corporation financed this project. The completion of the Twin Lakes Tunnel only added to speculation that more railroad or mining tunnels could be adapted to the cause of trans-basin diversion to the Front Range.[38]

Western Slope congressman Edward Taylor had opposed the Twin Lakes diversion. The Grand Junction *Daily Sentinel* referred to Taylor and western Colorado as coming to a "late awakening" of the dangers of this diversion plan. Taylor seemed to be rehearsing arguments he would use with more regularity over the next several years as the threat of Front Range diversions became magnified. In a protest letter, Taylor acquainted Secretary of the Interior Harold Ickes with his considerable expertise and long background in Colorado water rights before arguing that the Twin Lakes Canal Company's action "was an unwarranted invasion upon the water users on the Western Slope of Colorado." Taylor tried to argue that trans-basin diversions should be prohibited until the amount of water allocated to each state had been allotted by an interstate compact. In other words, the Upper Colorado River Basin states needed to divide their 7.5 million acre-feet among themselves first. Taylor did not question the legality of trans-mountain diversions, noting that both the Colorado River Compact and state legal decisions allowed the procedure. However, diversions should only be allowed on the condition that they "shall not injuriously affect the rights of the people from which [they are] taken."[39]

CHALLENGING THE BIG THOMPSON DIVERSION

In 1933, South Platte Valley water users began to act on their old dream of accessing Western Slope water. With George Bull's encouragement, northern Colorado boosters, politicians, and farmers were openly discussing plans to build a trans-mountain diversion to bring Western Slope waters to the Big

Thompson River from Grand Lake and the Colorado River.[40] In late September 1933, Bull's office convened a meeting to establish a priority list for Colorado's PWA projects. Representatives from both slopes attended the meeting, and a spirit of harmony seemed to temporarily prevail among the state's water users who were animated by the prospect that Washington, DC's, considerable economic power was coming to their aid. Congressman Edward T. Taylor introduced a resolution that was adopted, stating: "Every transmountain diversion project out of the Colorado River Basin . . . shall include as an essential part of such project the construction of a compensatory reservoir on the Western Slope of sufficient capacity to hold an amount of water equal to the amount to be annually diverted by the transmountain diversion."[41]

This would soon be known in Colorado water history as the "acre-foot for acre-foot provision" and would become a staple in the arsenal of Western Slope partisans in water wars with the Eastern Slope. Taylor believed this meeting and, more important, the passage of the resolution resulted in the state accepting the acre-foot for acre-foot provision as official policy. He was sadly mistaken. His fervent belief clouded progress toward statewide cooperation for several more years. The September 1933 meeting and Taylor's resolution were referred to often by Western Slope officials in upcoming decades.

In June 1933, western Colorado water interests had formed the Western Colorado Protective Association (WCPA) to advocate against the designs of Front Range water interests. Organized "for the purpose of protecting the water of western Colorado against loss through transmountain diversion on the East and the demands of California and Arizona on the West," the WCPA member counties levied small assessments on themselves to compensate officers for travel to statewide conferences, employ consulting experts, and defray day-to-day expenses to carry on the group's water protection program. The WCPA represented the rise of a regional consciousness about the vulnerable nature of the Western Slope's water supply. The association also signaled the fracturing of a degree of statewide consensus that had existed among Colorado water interests up to this time, as well as recognition that Denver and other Front Range interests had designs on the water resources of the western half of the state. The WCPA jumped into the Twin Lakes diversion fray in 1933, negotiating an agreement with the Twin Lakes Canal Company that it would refrain from diverting water at any time of the year "when it is needed by the water users in this Western Slope territory." The

WCPA took the reasonable position that it could not object to diversions if the water is not needed "by our own people."[42]

It became apparent to the WCPA's founders early on that "this water diversion question" would confront the Western Slope for an indefinite period. Grand Junction businessman David W. (D. W.) Aupperle, president of the new organization, noted that simply protesting and not being open to the negotiation of substitute plans would fail to prevent what he believed were inevitable incursions on the Western Slope's water supply.[43] As a result, the WCPA had suggested to Western Slope native and Colorado governor Edwin ("Big Ed") Johnson that the PWA construct reservoirs on the Western Slope as replacement storage for waters diverted to the Eastern Slope. The WCPA indicated its willingness to cooperate with the Front Range, but only if replacement storage could be built on the Western Slope. Optimistically, the organization hoped federal and state relief programs could be a way for Colorado's "East and West to get together on common grounds."[44]

While it was becoming clear to many in Colorado that the state lacked unity in its water planning, others believed this situation could be corrected by creating a political body with some responsibility to foster consensus among the state's regions. An important step toward statewide water planning was the creation of the Colorado State Planning Commission (CSPC). On January 15, 1934, Governor Johnson established the commission by executive order to abet the development of the state and help it take advantage of the many federal New Deal programs. The CSPC hoped to plan large-scale infrastructure projects such as highways, public buildings, and water projects and to link Colorado's plans with sources of federal funding.[45]

Both inspired and frightened by the actions of the other Colorado River states, in early June 1935 Colorado launched a water conservation offensive at a meeting of more than 200 businessmen and state officials who gathered in the chambers of the Colorado House of Representatives. Presiding over the meeting was John T. Barnett, chair of the CSPC. Noting that Colorado lacked a statewide water policy, Barnett argued that more central coordination was needed to foster the state's water resources. The lack of central direction had led to inaction or a policy of defensive reaction when nearby states had moved to access water originating in Colorado. Barnett remarked that "this meeting should have been held a generation ago." Several neighboring states already had state-level water-planning agencies. As a result, the water summit meeting ended with a call for Colorado to "look out for itself" by establishing central water-planning agencies or be prepared to lose the water that flowed over the state's borders.[46]

Colorado's earliest statewide water-planning efforts took shape through the actions of the CSPC, which created a Water Resources Advisory Committee. The committee met in Denver on June 13–15, 1935. Known thereafter as the Committee of 17, the delegates passed resolutions that would shape the state's water deliberations for years to come. Seven members each hailed from the Western and Eastern Slopes, while three came from the San Luis Valley. Glenwood Springs attorney Frank Delaney accepted membership on the CSPC to offer protection for Western Slope water. No action was more important at the meeting than the passage of Resolution Number 1, hereafter known as the Delaney Resolution. This proposal had first been articulated by Congressman Taylor in an early 1935 discussion between western and eastern Colorado water users over the proposed Grand Lake Project. The Delaney Resolution outlined western Colorado's requirements for cooperation on water issues in the decades ahead. The resolution stated that "to protect and insure the growth of Western Colorado, every plan for transmountain Diversion projects shall incorporate and include as an integral part of the cost thereof to be borne by the proponents compensatory storage equal to the amount to be diverted."[47] In other words, for every acre-foot of water diverted to the Eastern Slope, an equal amount of new storage would need to be built on the Western Slope, with the cost borne by the importing region.

The Delaney Resolution also contained a provision that became a staple in the arsenal of Western Slope water defenders in the years ahead. Delaney called for a "detailed survey" of industrial and agricultural uses for western Colorado's irrigation water to help the region plan for its future. The request's legal basis was Section 15 of the 1928 Boulder Canyon Project Act, which directed the secretary of the interior to "make an investigation . . . on the feasibility of projects for irrigation" in the Upper Basin states. Delaney maintained that no major trans-mountain project would be started until a comprehensive survey was done "to include all necessary data to show the effect of the proposed diversion upon existing Western Slope rights and probable future development of the Western Slope areas affected." Finally, the comprehensive study would locate the sites for compensatory storage reservoirs. This water protection tactic had also been suggested by Taylor in the January 1935 discussion of the Grand Lake Project.[48]

The June 1935 meeting of the Committee of 17 received extensive newspaper coverage, coming as it did at a time of severe statewide drought coupled with the hope that federal involvement in water project planning would lead to major water projects. A spirited discussion over trans-basin diversion, doubtlessly inspired by the Delaney Resolution, proved to be the highlight of the meeting. Its ultimate approval by the Committee of 17 gave a momentary but deceptive appearance of statewide harmony on the diversion question. The Delaney Resolution was debated during a four-hour closed-door executive session pitting Delaney against Denver Water Board attorney Malcolm Lindsey. The main argument over what would become the Delaney Resolution centered on the Western Slope attorney's insistence that trans-mountain diversions should be prohibited until "it is assured [that] sufficient water [exists] to meet all vested rights and future development" on the Western Slope.[49]

The Committee of 17 agreed to a listing and ranking of water projects to be considered by the federal government and financed through the mechanisms of the Public Works Administration. Over $100 million in Colorado water project financing requests had been submitted to the federal government, with many proposals asking for a loan of 55 percent of total costs. A handful also hoped to obtain a grant for 100 percent of the costs. For most of June 14, the Committee of 17 heard Western Slope objections to any projects involving trans-mountain diversion, at least until "satisfactory adjustments [were] provided for compensatory storage as well as surveys."[50]

Edward Foster, on behalf of the CSPC, recommended that the committee's resolutions be favorably adopted. He also recommended that the PWA construct the water projects. The Committee of 17 had substantially whittled the original $100 million down to $33.6 million. The Western Slope was slated to receive only $6 million in construction funding, the Arkansas Valley about $10 million, the South Platte region $11 million, and the San Luis Valley $7 million. The committee recommended the immediate construction of Denver's Moffat Tunnel extension and Williams Fork diversion. A $100,000 appropriation was also included to survey the Blue River Transmountain Project. The South Platte Valley received top priority for the Grand Lake Transmountain Diversion Project ($5 million) and $150,000 for its survey. The Western Slope also received priority for two reservoirs on the La Plata River, forerunners of the later Animas–La Plata Project, in addition to a reservoir on the Dolores River. Other prioritized Western Slope requests included a reservoir on the North Fork of the Gunnison, a Mancos River Reservoir, and four reservoirs on the Yampa River. Not to be outdone, southern Colorado requested funding ($150,000) to survey the feasibility of diverting Western Slope water to the Arkansas River. The number of trans-mountain diversions on the list shocked and alarmed Western Slope water officials. In what would soon occupy center stage in Colorado's first water war, the Grand Lake Project (later renamed the Colorado–Big Thompson Project) received the highest amount of recommended funding ($5 million).[51]

While only a few of the Committee of 17's project requests were funded in the next several years by Franklin Delano Roosevelt's New Deal administration, it succeeded in presenting a startlingly accurate blueprint for Colorado's water future. New Deal funding sources began building the Moffat Tunnel, Williams Fork, and Grand Lake (Colorado–Big Thompson) Projects and several smaller projects. The Blue River proposal, which the Denver Water Board had worked on for more than twenty years, would continue to be fought over and modified until the mid-1950s. Some of the proposed Yampa River reservoirs would become points of contention as part of the proposed Colorado River Storage Project in the 1950s, notably at Echo Park. Animas–La Plata, West Divide, and Dolores would ultimately be included in the 1968 Colorado River Basin Project (better known as the Central Arizona Project) Act. Finally, southern Colorado's bid to investigate and survey the possibility of bringing Western Slope water to the Arkansas River Valley signified the beginning of another round of battles in the state's water wars involving the Gunnison-Arkansas Project, later known as the Fryingpan-Arkansas Project.[52]

Both slopes believed they had emerged from the deliberations of the Committee of 17 in a strong position. Grand Junction's *Daily Sentinel* observed that Western Slope delegates to the Committee of 17 believed the Delaney Resolution had successfully protected the estimated annual 12 million acre-feet of water arising on Colorado's Western Slope. Perhaps overstating the sectional harmony that seemed to be prevailing, the *Rocky Mountain News* believed that by mandating compensatory dams, western Colorado "will actually benefit from transmountain diversions. Colorado seems at last to have overcome the jealousies and antagonisms which came from its topographical divisions."[53] Yet within a year, a full-scale water war would erupt between the Eastern and Western Slopes. The apparent harmony within the state was short-lived.

A COLORADO WATER WAR ERUPTS

The New Deal years brought many tangible economic benefits to Colorado. However, no 1930s era project did more to transform the state than the Colorado–Big Thompson Project (C-BT). A complex system of dams, reservoirs, and tunnels, the C-BT was signed into law by President Franklin Delano Roosevelt on December 28, 1937, the culmination of a two-year struggle between the state's Eastern and Western Slopes. Relations between the two halves of Colorado would never be the same following the massive reclamation project.

Advocates of the C-BT saw the activities of the CSPC and the New Deal as an opportunity to finally construct a water project that had been envisioned since the late nineteenth century. The C-BT had its origins in the dreams and "imaginative minds and watering mouths of eastern slope agriculturalists"; it represented one of the most dramatic "human signatures upon Colorado's twentieth century landscape." For decades, South Platte Valley railroads, big businesses like the Great Western Sugar Company, chambers of commerce, and newspapers had hoped to tap the rich water resources of the Western Slope. In 1934 these economic interest groups formed the Northern Colorado Water Users Association (NCWUA) to lobby for such a project. By the early days of the New Deal, Colorado's PWA's chief engineer was none other than the notable advocate for Front Range water development George M. Bull. On August 14, 1933, Bull telephoned Weld County attorney Thomas A. Nixon to see if Nixon knew how the state could spend some of the $200 million supposedly available to Bull's PWA for large-scale water projects. Within several days, a Grand Lake Committee had been formed in Greeley to advocate for the trans-mountain diversion project. With Bull's encouragement and favorable reports filed by water engineers who conducted field surveys over the next year, the project had begun to take shape.[54]

In January 1935, Western Colorado Protective Association (WCPA) delegates met with representatives of the NCWUA in Denver. Discussions ensued regarding the proposed project and the need for compensatory storage. At the Denver meeting, NCWUA delegates refused to accede to the idea of acre-foot for acre-foot compensation, citing both engineering and financial difficulties. Yet "they were willing to see that we would be amply protected," agreeing to build a smaller reservoir for the storage of 75,000 acre-feet on the Williams Fork and additional water storage elsewhere. The real reason for this meeting quickly became apparent to WCPA delegates: the NCWUA hoped to get the support of the WCPA for the proposed $150,000 Bureau of Reclamation survey needed to gain federal approval for the Grand Lake Project. Why was the cooperation of the WCPA so earnestly sought? "They realize," the WCPA minutes reported, "that only through our cooperation do they secure that of Congressman [Edward] Taylor." Taylor, who had seniority on the House Appropriations Committee, held the key to project approval and its ultimate funding.[55]

Taylor pioneered the use of what would become three staple Western Slope arguments used time and again over the next several decades: the acre-foot for acre-foot "rule," do not act on Eastern Slope diversion demands until an Upper Basin compact is negotiated, and do not allow serious diversion discussion to occur until the Bureau of Reclamation has surveyed the amount of water available and the economic needs for that water on the Western Slope. Many Eastern Slope water officials believed these arguments were simply stalling tactics, ways to avoid confronting the issue of trans-basin diversion. Taylor indicated that he would willingly use his power as second in line to the chair of the House Appropriations Committee and chair of the House Interior Appropriations Committee to not allow money for planning or construction of the project unless "provision is made for the construction of reservoirs on the Western Slope to conserve as much water for residents of that section of the state as will be permitted to be drawn off for use on the eastern side of the divide."[56]

In February 1936 the Colorado State Planning Commission under Director Edward Foster called for a conference in Grand Junction to try to reach a statewide consensus on issues relating to trans-mountain diversions. Foster framed his meeting call in somewhat apocalyptic terms—if Colorado did not develop its water resources, it would lose them to "alert and determined users in the other states. When [the water] is gone it will be gone forever . . . and that will mean also an end to the growth and prosperity" of Colorado's economy. In other words, Foster hoped the state could unify, reach a consensus on diversion, and move forward to develop all of its water resources. The

Grand Junction *Daily Sentinel*, anticipating the meeting, also issued pleas for state harmony but not at the expense of the Western Slope's water future.[57]

More than 200 delegates from across Colorado gathered in Grand Junction for a two-day meeting to establish a "definite water policy for [the] state," as the *Daily Sentinel* termed it. Meeting with the delegates was the Committee of 17, which had taken important steps in June 1935 to begin comprehensive statewide water planning. A large attendance was predicted because of the controversial nature of proposed trans-mountain diversions. Western Colorado, the *Daily Sentinel* observed, "[has] been aroused to the necessity of protecting its water interests."[58]

Overshadowing the proceedings was an "ultimatum to the Eastern Slope" sent from Washington, DC, by Western Slope congressman Edward T. Taylor. Taylor's telegram to Western Slope delegates traced the history of the acre-foot for acre-foot water storage replacement requirement, including the Delaney Resolution agreed to by the Committee of 17. Taylor's anger was inspired by his examination of Senate Appropriations Committee hearings on the Grand Lake Project, in which he did not find "one word about any compensating reservoirs." When Taylor made this discovery, he became determined to use his position as chair of the House Interior Appropriations Subcommittee to block the Grand Lake appropriation unless compensatory storage was included. As Taylor phrased it, "The boys [on the subcommittee] will stay by me." Taylor also complained that the Reclamation Service had not yet started a long-promised survey of Western Slope water needs and replacement reservoir sites. Thus, "no one can estimate what our necessities are at this time or what [the] effect of this Grand Lake Project will be." Employing the language of an Old West sheriff, Taylor promised that if the Eastern Slope proved unwilling to keep its agreement, "we may as well learn it now and come to a show down."[59]

The Grand Junction meeting got off to a fast, tense start with the reading of Taylor's telegram, a message that "suppli[ed] the fireworks" for the conference. Taylor asked Western Slope representatives to "stand pat for a 100 percent compensatory storage." Meeting again on the morning of February 28, the conference expected a resolution on trans-mountain diversion from the Committee of 17 that might set the stage for an East–West Slope compromise. Taylor's message, however, had inspired so much tension that the committee failed to reach an agreement. The presiding officer of the CSPC, John T. Barnett, adjourned the meeting *sine die*.[60] Taylor's message became the centerpiece of a discussion at the conference banquet the evening of February 27 that led to a flurry of arguments over compensatory storage. A resolution was introduced by Western Slope delegates to gain support for compensatory storage (to be built and maintained by the diversionists). At this point the discussion grew heated and "the lights failed in the La Court [Hotel] banquet room."[61]

For over an hour, delegates argued in a room lit only by a few flickering candles. The evening banquet session, while failing to reach a resolution on compensatory storage, did find agreement on several other issues that would help shape Colorado's water environment over the next few decades, including demands that the Bureau of Reclamation work with Colorado to shape and qualify long-planned reclamation projects, build an effective water conservancy district law that would "obviate defects" in state water laws, and elect members to the state legislature who understood the importance of irrigation and were prepared to take on "the biggest job before Colorado in the last fifty years."[62]

In the aftermath of the Grand Junction meeting, Chairman Barnett tried to put a good face on the gathering, saying that the meeting had made the state "more water conscious." Barnett also announced that he would stand behind the Committee of 17's Delaney Resolution, enacted in June 1935. The *Daily Sentinel* reporter noted that several Eastern Slope speakers expressed a willingness to abide by the terms of the Delaney Resolution. Some Western Slope observers also saw this meeting as an important step toward the unification of their water interests. "A new water consciousness has been created which is expected to result in further protection of the [Western] slope water interests," the *Daily Sentinel* observed. An editorial in the Grand Junction newspaper noted that the meeting had underscored the message that Colorado's failure to unite had held the state back for more than twenty-five years in the race to develop its water resources. Yet to expect western Colorado to cave in to the demands of the Front Range simply because "more waters arise on the west slope than on the east" did not seem fair without adequate compensation.[63]

THE BATTLE IS JOINED

In a strongly worded letter to David W. Aupperle of the WCPA, Taylor stated that "I am going to insist upon 'equal' storage reservoirs, or I'll kick the slats out of the whole business." Without acre-foot for acre-foot compensation, Taylor promised to delete the diversion project startup funding when it reached the House Appropriations Committee. On March 4, 1936, the congressman argued to the officers of the Western Colorado Protective Association that "adequate" reservoirs were meaningless because the Eastern Slope dominated the Office of the State Engineer while the Bureau of Reclamation "will insist we need no such structures." With Taylor insisting on exact amounts of replacement water, Grand Lake Project supporters preferred not to tie eastern Colorado to exact amounts. Colorado Democratic senator Alva B. Adams believed the term *adequate storage* gave the Western Slope better protection than did Taylor's insistence on "acre-foot for acre-foot." Of course, many citizens on the Western Slope paid little attention since Adams, a scion of Colorado's political dynasty, hailed from Pueblo on the Front Range.[64]

Taylor was aware (as was Senator Adams, who confirmed this in his letter to the *Daily Sentinel*) that his commanding position as chair of the House Interior Appropriations Subcommittee allowed him to have "complete control in this matter. He can have the Grand Lake project authorization eliminated or modified as he may desire." Taylor indicated in a letter to Silmon Smith on March 7, 1936, that he sought guidance from his constituents over how far to push this issue. He might be setting important precedents: "I feel we are making history in this matter and whether we successfully do it or not may be of great importance for years to come." The Garfield County, Colorado (Taylor's home county) Board of County Commissioners urged the congressman to maintain his uncompromising approach to the diversion issue. The commissioners asked Taylor to approve the diversion but to insist upon a "clear unambiguous clause . . . to the effect that compensatory storage must be provided through reservoirs to be constructed on the Western Slope at suitable locations and capacities equal to the amount of water to be diverted to the Eastern Slope."[65]

Taylor continued to believe that the September 1933 discussion and handshake agreement in PWA director Bull's office and the 1935 Delaney Resolution had resulted in a statewide acre-foot for acre-foot policy. While the battle over the Grand Lake Project was significant, Taylor hoped this struggle would guide future water developments in the state because "half [a] dozen pending transmountain diversion schemes" loomed on the near horizon.[66]

Taylor was part of a ten-member Congressional Conference Committee on Appropriations and was in a commanding position to either change the language in the Grand Lake Project authorization or undermine the project entirely. Taylor believed that if he killed the bill, an opportunity to enact important reclamation legislation for Colorado might not occur again for many years. As a result, Taylor suggested that it might be possible to authorize Grand Lake if a number of Western Slope projects such as La Plata, North Fork (Gunnison River), and Divide Creek were given the same high priority as Grand Lake. Taylor hoped that ten to fifteen small Western Slope projects for supplemental water supplies might be inserted and considered alongside the Grand Lake Project. It was his desire that this would be done every time the Western Slope faced a trans-mountain diversion threat. With so many other diversion schemes on the drawing board, "we have a running-fire fight on in front of us all the time."[67]

In late March 1936 the *Rocky Mountain News* reported that the Grand Lake Project and other water projects had been "temporarily defeated" in the US House appropriation process. Taylor's influence in the decision was clear and obvious to citizens on both sides of the Continental Divide. As Taylor said on the eve of killing the project, Front Range water advocates "are the biggest fools on earth if they do not agree to" his conditions. If they did not acquiesce, he was content to "let the matter ride over until the next session of Congress." Taylor remained particularly angry that Colorado senator Alva B. Adams and Senator Carl Hayden (D-AZ) had inserted the phrase "adequate" compensation instead of the "straight acre for acre basis" in the proposed bill.[68]

Taylor's fervent opposition to the Grand Lake Project stemmed from awareness that the diversion represented just one of several trans-mountain diversion proposals with which western Colorado would soon be forced to deal. Western slope officials believed the Denver Water Board, which had worked on the Fraser and Blue River diversions "without consulting with Western Slope people about actual conditions," had essentially demeaned and overlooked them. Front Range water officials seemed to view their access to the Western Slope's water bounty as an entitlement. The DWB had not even said as much as "with your cooperation we would like to share with you a portion of the water of the Western Slope." When Western Slope officials got word of Front Range plans and began to question them, they were dubbed "water hogs, obstructionists, and other pet names." But just below Grand Lake in elevation lay the Fraser River, which was being taken by Denver; below that was the Williams Fork, which Denver also hoped to harvest. Taylor continued, "Then there is the Blue River which is also under investigation." Other western Colorado rivers were being "robbed" through small diversions, notably the Eagle and Roaring Fork (Twin Lakes diversion). Finally, plans were being formulated in southeast Colorado to tap the Gunnison "down into her vitals."[69]

The attempt to ramrod the Grand Lake Project through the US Congress in 1936 represented a turning point in East–West Slope water relations; it was equivalent to an open declaration of war in the context of Colorado's twentieth-century water conflicts. At its annual meeting in 1936, the Western Colorado Protective Association offered full support for Taylor's 1936 actions. Not surprisingly, the *Daily Sentinel* also praised Taylor's actions. Other parts of the state did not view Taylor's actions as positively. Most Denver newspapers bitterly criticized Taylor as a stubborn obstacle to progress, a betrayer of state-wide interests who by selfish inaction was supporting the water aspirations of the Lower Colorado Basin states. Some critics, likely following a "divide and conquer" strategy, also asserted that many of Taylor's western Colorado constituents had deserted him because he had become a "dog in the manger."[70]

At the end of 1936, the Colorado–Big Thompson Project continued to be opposed by Congressman Taylor and the WCPA. Taylor made a special post-election trip to Washington, DC, attempting to "put enough pressure through various departments to influence the Budget Committee against" the project. Heading into 1937, there were some crucial differences in the unfolding story. Taylor's health had taken a turn for the worse in late 1936. By late December he recognized that he was against the "Northern Colorado people, the Denver attorneys and engineers, the Reclamation Bureau and the State Engineer." He had asked David W. Aupperle about the "best terms" for possible concessions. Taylor suggested a series of possible negotiating points, including insistence upon a "blanket priority right for all present and future western slope appropriations." He also asked about fixing a minimum Colorado River flow year-round. He suggested that 1,250 cubic feet per second be adjudicated to the Shoshone Power Plant, east of Glenwood Springs, but admitted ("to you, me and the lamp post") that that was about double the amount of water in the river much of the year. As another strategy, Taylor went back to the perennial idea of an irrigation survey of the four Upper

Basin states to determine how much water existed and what future applications for those waters might be. "I think we should stand pat" on completing the Upper Basin survey before allowing any large out-of-basin diversions, Taylor remarked. Finally, the congressman argued that much of the pressure for trans-basin diversion to the Front Range emanated from the public utility companies, which envisioned a financial bonanza from an increased water supply. As a result, he believed that no matter what the eventual deal looked like, the Western Slope should negotiate power production facilities into the resulting water projects.[71]

The year 1937 was one of the most formative years in Colorado water history, for many reasons. Congressman Taylor, recovering from illness and preparing to negotiate with the Eastern Slope over the Grand Lake diversion, saw his already tremendous political power bolstered on February 22, 1937. Having served as acting majority leader since 1935 (for the often ill Alabaman William R. Bankhead), Taylor became chair of the House Appropriations Committee when the chair, James P. Buchanan (D-TX), died. Taylor's increased power did not bode well for the C-BT project. The other issue that needed to be addressed, at least from the perspective of most Colorado water advocates, was the divide between the east and the west, which at times loomed higher than Colorado's Rockies. Observers both in the state and in Washington had argued that Colorado needed to demonstrate more unity before the Roosevelt administration would invest millions of dollars in its water projects. Toward that end, one of the goals of the Northern Colorado Water Users Association would be to work toward a more cooperative relationship with those elements on the Western Slope open to improved relations. At the state level there would soon be other movements that would lead toward greater statewide coordination of water policy.[72]

Toward Compromise

In January 1937 Wayne N. Aspinall (D-Palisade) was elected speaker of the house for the Thirty-First Colorado General Assembly. To line up the votes he needed for the speakership, Aspinall, from the small fruit-growing town of Palisade in the Grand Valley near Grand Junction, needed more than a handful of Eastern Slope votes. What was unusual about Aspinall's victory were his origins on the sparsely populated Western Slope. As House speaker, Aspinall believed he had a mandate to not only represent his Western Slope district but to pursue programs to promote broader intrastate cooperation, particularly on water issues. This position sometimes put Aspinall squarely against the less-compromising wishes of his two political mentors, Edward T. Taylor and Grand Junction *Daily Sentinel* publisher and editor Walter Walker. Walker told Aspinall, with perhaps an implied threat, that as the latter ascended to the House speaker's chair, the *Daily Sentinel* would continue "to uphold the position of the Western Slope against any program that will jeopardize the losing of any of our water resources."[73]

Taylor's role in the trans-mountain diversion controversy changed considerably during 1937. As chair of the House Appropriations Committee, the time he could give to local matters, even one as important as Western Slope water protection, had diminished. Furthermore, renewed hopes of compromise emanated from both sides of the Continental Divide. Taylor, the oldest member of the House of Representatives, suffered a series of illnesses in 1936–37. A new variable also entered into play in early 1937: the resignation of Western Colorado Protective Association president Aupperle. Combined, these factors paved the way toward a peaceful reconciliation in this hard-fought Colorado water war.

In a lengthy resignation letter, Aupperle proudly reflected that his group had not achieved all of its goals, but added, using a familiar analogy, "it has not exactly been a case where the tail has wagged the dog, but we have used the 'tail hold' which we have had to keep the dog [the Front Range] from running away with the water we need." Significantly, he also noted that negotiations with northern Colorado had resumed at the surprising insistence of Congressman Taylor, who wanted to have Western Slope representatives "contact the Eastern Slope to ascertain whether there was some practical solution and grounds of compromise which would . . . adequately protect our rights over here." Western Slope representatives included Delaney, Judge Clifford Stone of Gunnison County, Dan Hughes (Montrose County), and Mesa County's Silmon Smith and engineer Frank Merriell. After several years of intensive fighting, a "tentative agreement between the two slopes" had been reached at a meeting in Denver in mid-March 1937, according to Aupperle.[74]

On March 24, 1937, the WCPA Board of Directors presented the tentative agreement at a "mass meeting" held in Grand Junction. In many ways this meeting became the turning point toward the final reconciliation in the

Western Slope–northern Colorado water war. Those negotiations had suddenly become more complicated because of an awareness of recent filings by Denver in the Grand County Court for a water decree. In addition to the filings for water from the Williams Fork and Fraser Rivers, Denver had made more public revelations of its claims to the Blue River. All this was coming on top of other rumored diversion projects, including several emanating from the southeastern part of the state. A new complicating factor also began to cloud the picture—the appearance of legislative propositions before the Colorado General Assembly to set up a new, more powerful water-planning apparatus: not just a central state water policy organization but regional water associations that could interface with the Bureau of Reclamation on project construction and have taxation powers. The organization being set up by the Northern Colorado Water Users Association reflected the region's wealth, population, and determination to gain trans-mountain waters.[75]

At the mass meeting in Grand Junction in March 1937, Aupperle and the Western Colorado Protective Association revealed that they had moved toward a compromise and agreement with northern Colorado as a result of changing political circumstances. A federal survey of the Grand Lake Project had been completed; it was likely that the project would pass—if not this year, then within several years. The formation of a special conservancy district by Grand Lake Project supporters appeared especially dangerous to Aupperle and Frank Delaney. Northern Colorado attorneys had spent months drafting the bill, which was at that moment before the Colorado General Assembly. To make matters worse, "In all probability the Arkansas Valley and other sections of Colorado" might be organizing additional conservancy districts. Finally, Taylor's behavior seemed to send a message that he could not maintain the intensity he had brought to the fight in previous years. The Western Slope's negotiators indicated that they may need to move from their previous uncompromising "acre foot for acre foot" position.[76]

Virtually every community and district on the Western Slope gathered in Grand Junction to hear the details of the tentative agreement. Aupperle assured the meeting that he had been working both "with" Edward Taylor and "under him." Frank Delaney also addressed the group and indicated that if a new conservancy district law passed the Colorado General Assembly in 1937, "we could set up organizations . . . over here on the Western Slope" to cooperate with the Bureau of Reclamation and protect the region's water.

In short, do what the Western Colorado Protective Association had been doing, but coordinate the activities of all the counties with "tremendous and far-reaching powers of taxation and of exercise of eminent domain." The contemplated conservancy district would, in Delaney's words, protect the water interests of "ourselves and those who follow us in the future." The proposed Northern Colorado Water Conservancy District would have the power and financial wherewithal to construct the project without full federal funding. Delaney indicated that he had also drafted a bill for the Western Slope water district, and it was going to be introduced in the general assembly. Delaney's proposed district would be "set up as a counter-irritant to be used as a bulwark against attempted future infringements of our rights, as well as to serve a useful purpose in promoting our resources over here. It will set up organizations which will cooperate with the government and bring as much of this land into irrigation and use as much of the surplus water as can be used within a reasonable time."[77]

Finally, Delaney presented the much-anticipated "tentative agreement" to the Grand Junction meeting: "They get their project [Grand Lake, or Colorado–Big Thompson] with the right to divert 310,000 acre-feet of water. We get our reservoir for 152,000 acre-feet." The Western Slope's storage reservoir of 152,000 acre-feet "is to be on parity [in terms of priority] with the works they construct to take water from other streams."[78]

The diversion agreement provided for a storage reservoir near Granby, south of Grand Lake. A pumping plant would be built at the Granby Reservoir to move water into the Grand Lake extension. A thirteen-mile tunnel under Rocky Mountain National Park would transport water to the Front Range, where a system of reservoirs, ditches, and canals would distribute the water. The key provision Delaney mentioned was the Green Mountain Reservoir, to be built south of Kremmling, to store 152,000 acre-feet of water so that, according to the Bureau of Reclamation, "the diversion of water from the Colorado River watershed will not interfere with or encroach upon the present and future irrigation along the Colorado River and tributaries within the state."[79]

Delaney also anticipated the question many Western Slope residents were ready to bombard him with: why did the Western Slope appear to be "giving in" to northern Colorado at this time, especially after Taylor's determined defense of the region's water in 1936? Phrasing the matter delicately, Delaney remarked that the "only thing that stands between" the Grand Lake

Project's fast approval and the Western Slope not being protected at all was "the power and prestige that Mr. [Edward] Taylor possesses in Washington." With careful wording, Delaney added that "just as soon as there should be a *change of circumstances* [emphasis added], and you know the affairs of men are uncertain and so is life, as soon as that comes to pass, they [northern Colorado water users] are going to construct this project and take that water without giving us anything." In other words, while Taylor was still alive and in a powerful position, this tentative agreement may have been the best deal the Western Slope could make.[80]

Delaney had other arguments in support of the agreement. Stream flow would be stabilized, and wild annual fluctuations would cease to plague Western Slope irrigators. He also believed northern Colorado people were meeting with the Western Slope's representatives on a fairer basis than had been the case in the past. Above all, the Glenwood Springs attorney concluded that "this thing," the Grand Lake Project, "is coming because it is feasible and can't be stopped." Delaney made a strong plea to the mass meeting that it support the agreement and also respond favorably to the conservancy district proposal, which would enforce the agreement and safeguard the Western Slope's water rights in the years ahead.[81]

Despite Delaney's plea for cooperation, the mass meeting did not go as smoothly as the Western Slope's negotiating team had hoped. Charges that Grand County would be left high and dry by what was being referred to now as the Colorado–Big Thompson diversion echoed throughout the meeting. As a result, the 206 delegates to the meeting refused to sanction the compromise settlement. While the meeting did not embrace the compromise, it did not vote to condemn it either.[82] Grand County representatives saw nothing in the proposed settlement that protected their interests and demanded compensation for the land and resources they alleged would be "impaired by the damming up of the Colorado River headwaters."[83]

Negotiations continued between the two slopes. While the Western Slope negotiating committee did not gain approval at the March 24, 1937, mass meeting, it did gain legitimacy as a fully recognized arm of the Western Colorado Protective Association, empowered to continue negotiations. By April 10, 1937, two major objections voiced by Grand County's representatives had been resolved: northern Colorado water users had agreed to pay taxes on lands to be submerged by Grand Lake Project reservoirs and had consented to spend money to build small dams and ditches to provide irrigation for meadows that had previously been flood-irrigated. Grand County's only remaining complaint dealt with minimum stream flow for Colorado River fishermen. The Colorado–Big Thompson Project had gained crucial political momentum.[84]

The federal government added to a sense of inevitability for the C-BT while simultaneously fueling speculation that more trans-mountain diversion plans were on the horizon. On April 12, 1937, the National Resources Committee endorsed a $64 million long-term water conservation and development program for the state of Colorado. While the committee did not automatically enact the forty-nine western state projects recommended in the report, its well-publicized appearance gave momentum to supporters of federal reclamation projects. The Colorado–Big Thompson Project sat at the top of the list of projects slated for "immediate construction." Other Colorado trans-mountain diversion projects recommended in the report for immediate investigation or construction were the Blue River diversion, investigations seeking additional water for the Moffat Tunnel diversion, and a study of the diversion of the headwaters of the Gunnison and Fryingpan Rivers into the Arkansas River. The Blue River diversion and the various forms of what would be variously called the Gunnison-Arkansas or Fryingpan-Arkansas Project would provide some of the most explosive moments in upcoming years in Colorado's twentieth-century water wars.[85]

1937: ACCELERATION OF OFFICIAL COLORADO WATER PLANNING

Late in the 1937 Colorado General Assembly session, three laws passed that set the stage for the modern era of state water planning. These laws and the institutions they created allowed Colorado to respond to the realization that state and regional water planning had to move along at a more determined pace. The assembly passed the Colorado Water Conservancy District Act of 1937, which has spawned more than fifty water conservancy districts since that time. The largest and most notable was clearly the first, the Northern Colorado Water Conservancy District, the host agency for the Colorado–Big Thompson Project. The Water Conservancy District Act allowed for the creation of local entities that could enter into repayment contracts with the building agency, usually the Bureau of Reclamation. The districts had contracting, bonding, and taxing authority. The act also outlined procedures

for establishing a water conservancy district, starting with landowner peti-
tions submitted to the Colorado District Court. The court would then issue
a decree establishing the district, and within thirty days a district board of
directors must be appointed with backgrounds reflecting the "agricultural,
municipal, industrial, and other interests in the beneficial use of water within
the district." Board members had to be property owners within the boundaries of the district and be "knowledgeable in water matters."[86]

The Colorado Water Conservancy District Act had many provisions, but
inserted at the insistence of Western Slope water officials was the requirement that any facilities planned or designed by water districts to export water
from the natural basin of the Colorado River had to be operated in such a
manner as to not damage the basin of origin. In addition, the costs for compensatory storage or other mitigations would not be passed on to Colorado
River Basin water users. Instead, the district sponsoring the project would
need to factor in and pay the mitigation costs to the affected area of the
Western Slope. Other provisions protected Western Slope water rights from
eminent domain powers vested in the districts. Up until 1937, irrigation districts, spawned by the 1901 Irrigation District Law, were the preferred method
to organize local water management. The 1937 Colorado Water Conservancy
Act vested more power and authority for water management; especially
attractive for water policymakers were the taxation powers that allowed for
the repayment of federal water projects.[87]

The assembly also passed House Bill 6 on June 1, 1937, "An Act Relating to
the Waters in the State of Colorado, Providing for the Control, Protection
and Development Thereof . . ." This law created the Colorado Water
Conservation Board. Forged in the fires of Colorado's first full-scale water
war, it represented a perception that the state needed to take an emotional
step back from contention, unite if possible, and engage in long-range state
water planning. Members included the governor, attorney general, state
engineer, and a seven-member board overseen by an executive director.
Three members were to represent Western Slope counties, three came from
the Eastern Slope, while one represented the San Luis Valley.[88]

Finally, on June 8, 1937, Governor Teller Ammons signed an act creating the Colorado River Water Conservation District (CRWCD). Written
by western Colorado water attorney Frank Delaney, the law created the
legal successor organization to the largely ad hoc Western Colorado

Protective Association. The CRWCD, or "River District" in the language of its Western Slope constituents, originally comprised the region of Mesa, Garfield, Pitkin, Eagle, Delta, Gunnison, and Summit Counties. The act also created a board of directors, with the requirement that each of the member counties have one board member, appointed by the county commissioners of the county "in which he resides." Among its many powers, the CRWCD had the right to conduct surveys and investigations, to make filings for water rights and initiate appropriations for the use and benefit of the appropriators, and to perform all acts necessary or advisable to "secure an adequate supply of water . . . for irrigation, mining, manufacturing, and domestic purposes" within the district. In addition, the River District could contract with the US government and its agencies; exercise the power of eminent domain to acquire ditches, reservoirs, and other works; and file for water rights to maintain sufficient stream flow to preserve fish and fishing habitat for the benefit of the public. A few months later, Delaney became the attorney for the River District, a job he would hold for the next several decades.[89]

At the conclusion of the 1937 Colorado General Assembly session, a newspaper reporter concluded that at least in one realm—water conservation—the Thirty-First Colorado General Assembly had "done a good job." Reporter Noland Norgaard listed the session's outstanding new legislation as the creation of the Colorado Water Conservation Board, Representative Moses E. Smith's (D-Ault) Colorado Water Conservancy District Act, and Representative Clifford H. Stone's (D-Gunnison) Colorado River Water Conservation District. Governor Teller Ammons remarked that if the legislature had done nothing else, it could have "justified itself with the enactment of" the Colorado Water Conservation Board. In a presentation to the Grand Junction Forum Club, Grand Junction state senator Roy Chapman labeled this session of the legislature "the thinking 31st." Chapman believed the water bills would prove to be beneficial to the interests of the Western Slope and the state as a whole. It is apparent that the lessons of the long struggle over trans-mountain diversion had started to dawn on the state's water community. New and more sophisticated organizations were needed to lend both expertise and clout to regional and state water planning. The Colorado Water Conservation Board especially reflected the need to provide leadership and centralized water planning at the state level.[90]

FIGURE 2.5. Alva B. Adams Tunnel, west portal. This is the start of the tunnel, which conveys Western Slope water thirteen miles under the Continental Divide and Rocky Mountain National Park for distribution to Colorado's Front Range by way of the Colorado–Big Thompson Project. *Courtesy*, Northern Colorado Water Conservancy District. © 2012 Northern Colorado Water Conservancy District. All rights reserved.

COLORADO–BIG THOMPSON: FINISHING THE TASK

The passage of such vital legislation seemed to indicate that Colorado's water leaders were eagerly looking to the future. Yet the elusive task of gaining final East–West Slope approval of the giant C-BT diversion still remained.

FIGURE 2.6. Green Mountain Reservoir. Part of the Colorado–Big Thompson Project, Green Mountain Reservoir holds water for release into Western Slope streams as compensation for water conveyed to the Eastern Slope through the Alva B. Adams Tunnel. *Courtesy*, Northern Colorado Water Conservancy District. © 2012 Northern Colorado Water Conservancy District. All rights reserved.

The project could still face challenges from Congressman Taylor, and while the Roosevelt administration remained on record as favoring the project, it needed to be signed into law.

On May 31, 1937, representatives of the WCPA and a contingent of western Colorado county commissioners gathered in Grand Junction to attempt to reach agreement on the details of the latest C-BT diversion proposal. The WCPA Board of Directors, meeting with representatives from Grand County, voted unanimously to approve the settlement. The scene then shifted back to Washington, DC, where most of Colorado's congressional delegation, the commissioner of the Bureau of Reclamation, and representatives from the Eastern and Western Slopes met on June 6 to finalize the agreement. Silmon Smith, Clifford Stone, Frank Merriell, and Grand County representative Dr. C. H. Sudan represented western Colorado. Eastern Colorado representatives included Charles Hansen, Thomas Nixon, and Moses E. Smith. The *Daily Sentinel*'s Walter Walker editorialized that contentious water issues between Eastern and Western

Slope water interests would remain, even if the Colorado–Big Thompson Project finally reached a resolution.[91]

The *Daily Sentinel* headline on June 12, 1937, trumpeted the good news: "Water Fight Ended: Eastern and Western Slopes Now to Congress as a United Body to Ask for Water Funds." Negotiators from both slopes, still meeting in Washington, DC, had approved the agreement, as had, crucially, Congressman Edward T. Taylor. While there would still be hurdles for the Colorado–Big Thompson Project in the months ahead, it did seem to finally be on the pathway toward official authorization.[92] The CB-T would build two dams to store water in Granby and Shadow Mountain Reservoirs. From there, water flowed by gravity to Grand Lake, exiting through the thirteen-mile Alva V. Adams Tunnel under Rocky Mountain National Park and the Continental Divide, passing through a power plant at Estes Park, and flowing into the Big Thompson River to be fed into the farm ditches of northeastern Colorado through a system of Eastern Slope siphons, canals, and reservoirs. The Western Slope gained construction of the 152,000-acre-foot–capacity Green Mountain Reservoir.[93]

A key element in the state's apparent water harmony had been what well-known Denver newspaperman Alva A. Swain called the emergence of a "new political element" in the state. The water fight between the Eastern and Western Slopes had "retarded the growth of the entire state." The "new element" Swain referred to realized that if the water war continued, the whole state would suffer, and "California and the others states" would grab all the unappropriated water and put it to beneficial use. Swain believed that friendships formed during the Colorado General Assembly sessions in the 1930s had helped to foster unity and make progress in the legislative session that ended in the spring of 1937. The newspaperman heralded Wayne Aspinall, Clifford Stone, Byron Rogers, Frank Delaney, Governor Teller Ammons, and northern Colorado water planners Moses E. Smith, Thomas Nixon, and Charles Hansen as examples of the new "statesmen" who had brought "order out of [the] chaos" facing the state's water situation. Not only had this group opened the path for constructing C-BT, but the enactment of the Colorado River Conservation District, a new water conservancy district law, and the creation of the Colorado Water Conservation Board reflected the new spirit of cooperation.[94]

A crucial step toward enactment of the Colorado–Big Thompson Project was the writing of and agreement to what would be known as Senate Document 80 in June 1937. Senate Document 80 provided the operating guidelines for the C-BT and contained the Western Slope's requirements for the maintenance and operation of the project. Both at the time of the C-BT conflict and in subsequent decades, Senate Document 80 embodied provisions considered almost sacred by Western Slope water officials. Most significant from the Western Slope's perspective was Section 5, stipulating the conditions for operating the project "in a fair and efficient manner, equitable to all parties having interests therein" to maintain conditions of river flow for the benefit of Western Slope agricultural and industrial uses. Notable provisions included the Shoshone diversion dam's water right to maintain a flow of 1,250 cubic feet per second and 52,000 acre-feet of water in the newly constructed Green Mountain Reservoir for replacement water for the Western Slope.[95]

This water held an earlier priority date than waters that would be diverted to the Eastern Slope; the Western Slope's project water would be subject to a later call than the Eastern Slope's in the event that Colorado needed to provide additional water under the 1922 Colorado River Compact to satisfy the Upper Basin's obligations to the Lower Basin. Grand County received its guarantee of tax loss compensation ($100,000 total, paid in ten annual installments) and a guaranteed river flow to preserve the Colorado River "as a live stream" to facilitate irrigation and aquatic life.[96]

While Colorado's water picture had clearly become more harmonious, signs of potential troubles continued to fester. One of the principal features of the CB-T was the construction of a thirteen-mile tunnel *under* Rocky Mountain National Park. In the summer and fall of 1937, National Park Service officials actively opposed the construction of the project, arguing that it would damage the park's natural beauty. Yet the act that created the park in 1916 reserved the right for the Bureau of Reclamation to survey and construct an irrigation project within the park's boundaries.[97]

The fear that some last-minute issue might delay or block the C-BT subsided somewhat in early August 1937 when President Franklin Roosevelt signed a $900,000 appropriation bill to commence preliminary work on the long-awaited project. Colorado senators Alva Adams and Ed Johnson hailed the passage of the C-BT as "the most important thing in our state since the discovery of gold and the coming of the railroad." While most Reclamation Bureau officials believed the actual on-the-ground construction would commence in the early spring, important preliminary work was getting under way in the summer and fall of 1937. [98]

Even with $900,000 appropriated for construction planning, the C-BT had yet to be authorized by the US Congress. Senate Bill 2681 contained the authorization for the Colorado–Big Thompson Project. However, the bill inspired further debate over potential damage to the natural features of Rocky Mountain National Park. Secretary of the Interior Harold Ickes called a hearing in Washington, DC, on November 12 to air concerns over the possible consequences to the park. To the delight of Coloradans present at the hearing, Ickes declared in favor of the project despite having some personal misgivings. Every Colorado witness spoke in the project's favor, including Congressman Edward T. Taylor, indicating that the fragile agreements between eastern and western Colorado were still holding. Taylor, making his first public speech in six months (because of recurring illnesses), emphasized that there was no longer a difference of opinion dividing Coloradans on the C-BT.[99]

Colorado's first water war ended on December 27, 1937, when President Franklin Roosevelt signed the Colorado–Big Thompson Project into law. The first elements of the project to be built were the Green Mountain Dam, Reservoir, and power plant. In Colorado-Thompson historian Daniel Tyler's words, these features were the Western Slope's *"sine qua non* for participation in the C-BT." However, with another world war looming, immediate project funding would prove tenuous at best and often became almost impossible to obtain after America's direct participation in World War II. It took until 1947 for the first water to flow through the Alva B. Adams Tunnel to farms and towns on Colorado's Eastern Slope. Even then, the massive project was not fully operational until the late 1950s.[100]

From 1920 to 1940, the stage was set on both the Eastern and Western Slopes over how the state would apportion its share of the Colorado River. Denver and the Eastern Slope, driven by a growing population and equipped with strong political support, moved first. The Western Slope, led by stalwart Congressman Edward T. Taylor and a cadre of water rights advocates, realized it needed to draw a firm line and not allow the Front Range carte blanche where western Colorado's water was concerned; nothing less than the region's future development appeared to be at stake. As a result of hardening intrastate attitudes, Colorado's first water war raged across the mountains dividing the Eastern Slope from the Western Slope during the depths of the nation's Great Depression.

Notes

1. Edward T. Taylor to Harold Ickes, April 2, 1935, Box 11, folder 1, Silmon Smith Papers, Colorado State Historical Society, Denver (hereafter CSHS).

2. Steven C. Schulte, *Wayne Aspinall and the Shaping of the American West* (Boulder: University Press of Colorado, 2002), 13.

3. The League of the Southwest, formed in San Diego in 1917, was knit together by hopes of transforming the Colorado River Basin into a "unified, habitable, and productive community." Daniel Tyler, *Silver Fox of the Rockies: Delphus E. Carpenter and Western Water Compacts* (Norman: University of Oklahoma Press, 2003), 112.

4. It will also be referred to as the Denver Water Board and by the acronym DWB.

5. *Denver Post*, August 25, 1920. George M. Bull was born in Troy, New York, in 1873. A graduate of Rensselaer Polytechnic Institute, he worked on the reconfiguration of the Erie Canal in the late 1890s. He became a resident of Denver in 1910 and worked for private engineering companies until 1918, building irrigation projects throughout Colorado. He served in World War I as a lieutenant commander in the Civil Engineering Corps Naval Reserve. Following the war, he became a consulting engineer and began to work for the new Denver Board of Water Commissioners. In this capacity, Bull explored the headwaters region of the Colorado River. His recommendations for trans-basin diversion were largely implemented by the city of Denver. From 1933 to 1940, Bull headed many of the activities of the Public Works Administration in Colorado and other southwestern states. See *Guide to the George M. Bull Papers*, University of Colorado–Boulder Archives (hereafter UCBA).

6. Tyler, *Silver Fox of the Rockies*, chapters 3 and 4; Norris Hundley Jr., "The West against Itself: The Colorado River—an Institutional History," in Gary D. Weatherford and F. Lee Brown, eds., *New Courses for the Colorado River: Major Issues for the Next Century* (Albuquerque: University of New Mexico Press, 1986), 15–16.

7. *Minutes and Records of the Colorado River Commission Negotiating the Colorado River Compact of 1922*, January 26, 1922, 16–17, copy in the Colorado Mesa University Archives and Special Collections (hereafter CMUASC), Grand Junction; Norris Hundley Jr., *Water and the West: The Colorado River Compact and the Politics of Water in the American West*, 2nd ed. (Berkeley: University of California Press, 2009), 52–59; Hundley, "The West against Itself," 16–17; Donald Worster, *Rivers of Empire: Water, Aridity, and the Growth of the American West* (New York: Pantheon Books, 1985), 209.

8. *Daily Sentinel* (Grand Junction, CO), March 29, 1922; Carpenter quoted in Hundley, *Water and the West*, 158.

9. Hundley, *Water and the West*, 156; George M. Bull to the Colorado River Commission, March 31, 1922, Box 7, folder "Moffat Tunnel," George M. Bull Papers, UCBA.

10. Schulte, *Wayne Aspinall*, 14.

11. See the Colorado River Compact, Article 11, reprinted in Hundley, *Water and the West*, appendix, 337–43.

12. Ibid., 223–25; *Rocky Mountain News* (Denver), February 10, March 23, 1923; Tyler, *Silver Fox of the Rockies*, 209–13.

13. Tyler, *Silver Fox of the Rockies*, 209–13; Hundley, *Water and the West*, 224–25; *Rocky Mountain News*, March 23, 1923.

14. Schulte, *Wayne Aspinall*, 14; Marc Reisner, *Cadillac Desert: The American West and Its Disappearing Water*, rev. ed. (New York: Penguin Books, 1993), 124–25; Norris Hundley Jr., "Water and the West in the Historical Imagination," *Western Historical Quarterly* 27, no. 1 (Spring 1996): 13–14; Carl Abbott, "The Federal Presence," in Clyde A. Milner II, Carol O'Connor, and Martha A. Sandweiss, eds., *Oxford History of the American West* (New York: Oxford University Press, 1994), 475.

15. Robert Gottlieb and Peter Wiley, *Empires in the Sun: The Rise of the New American West* (New York: Putnam 1982), 126.

16. As early as 1907, Denver was considering a new water system, and "the need of securing water from the western slope" was suggested. See George M. Bull, Report of Consulting Board on Construction of Moffat Water Tunnel Development, September 18, 1931, Box 7, folder "Report on Consulting Board," George M. Bull Papers, UCBA.

17. R. I. Meeker's recommendations are in "A Trans-Mountain Supply from the Fraser, Williams Fork, or Blue Rivers for the City of Denver," 1914. Lippincott's report is "Preliminary Report for a New Water Supply for the City of Denver," August 1914. See discussions of these reports in the United States District Court for the District of Colorado, Civil Action no. 2782, *United States v. Northern Colorado Water Conservancy District*, Deposition of George M. Bull, July 6–7, 1954, Box 7, folder "Notes, Memos, Testimony, etc.," George M. Bull Papers, UCBA. For biographical information on Lippincott, see Inventory of the Joseph Barlow Lippincott Papers, Biographical Information, Online Archive of California, accessed October 16, 2013, http://oac.cdlib.org/. For interpretations of Lippincott's California activities, see Robert W. Righter, *The Battle over Hetch Hetchy: America's Most Controversial Dam and the Birth of Modern Environmentalism* (New York: Oxford University Press, 2005), 28, 50, 79; Robert Gottlieb, *A Life of Its Own: The Politics and Power of Water* (New York: Harcourt Brace Jovanovich, 1988), 44–45. Righter refers to Lippincott as "a water engineer of questionable ethics" who while in the employ of the US Geological Survey was also hired as a consultant by San

Francisco to assist with its Hetch Hetchy Valley water claims. As Gottlieb tells the story, Lippincott, then working for the Reclamation Service, was also secretly in the employ of the Board of Water Commissioners of the City of Los Angeles. Lippincott did not reveal his Los Angeles connection while representing himself as a Reclamation Service agent to Owens Valley farmers whose land tenure and water rights he actively undermined.

18. Righter, *Battle over Hetch Hetchy*, 28, 50, 79; William Mulholland, Lippincott, and Parker, "Report on Water Supply," in *Annual Report of the Board of Water Commissioners of the Domestic Water Works System of the City of Los Angeles for the Fiscal Year Ending November 30, 1902* (Los Angeles: Press of the Out West Company, 1902), 79.

19. Notes on Deposition of George M. Bull and Dwight D. Gross, July 6–7, 1954, Box 7, folder "Notes, Memos, Testimony, etc.," George M. Bull Papers, UCBA; Minutes, Denver Board of Water Commissioners, June 1, 1920, E. G. Plowman Papers, Box 1, folder 1, UCBA; Stephen J. Leonard and Thomas J. Noel, *Denver: From Mining Camp to Metropolis* (Niwot: University Press of Colorado, 1990), 138–39; Report of Consulting Board on Construction of Moffat Water Tunnel Development, September 18, 1931. Also see Patricia Limerick with Jason L. Hanson, *A Ditch in Time: The City, the West, and Water* (Golden, CO: Fulcrum Books, 2012), 101–28; George M. Bull, "Notes Covering the General Situation as to Water Supply and Use of Water that Confronted the Board of Water Commissioners at the Time of the Purchase of the Denver Union Water Plant," undated, Box 7, folder "Notes, Memos, Testimony, etc.," George M. Bull Papers, UCBA; loose biographical material on George M. Bull, Box 2, folder 18, George M. Bull Papers, UCBA; George M. Bull, Personal Record, undated, Box 7, unlabeled folder, George M. Bull Papers, UCBA.

20. W. F. R. Mills to Hon. Addison J. McCune, April 12, 1921, Box 7, unlabeled folder, George M. Bull Papers, UCBA.

21. Gottlieb and Wiley, *Empires in the Sun*, 126; Duane Vandenbusche and Duane A. Smith, *A Land Alone: Colorado's Western Slope* (Boulder: Pruett, 1981), 261–62; George M. Bull et al., "Report of Consulting Board on the Construction of Moffat Water Tunnel Development," September 18, 1932, Box 7, folder "Moffat Tunnel," George M. Bull Papers, UCBA.

22. In a key 1950s court case, *Denver v. Northern Colorado Water Conservation District*, 130 Colo. 375, 276 P.2d 992 (1954), Denver would try to gain legal recognition for an early water decree on the Blue River. The court discovered that Bull had not actually visited the Blue River Basin in 1921 as he had the Williams Fork and Fraser Basins. Perhaps as significant, the court found that the city of Denver had not made continuous efforts to act on its Blue River plans until 1946, when Denver finalized plans for a reservoir and diversion tunnel after changing its plans several times over the preceding years. Denver's Blue River water claims would be litigated in the

early 1950s. See *Denver v. Northern Colorado Water Conservation District*; Gottlieb and Wiley, *Empires in the Sun*, 126–27; Denver Water Board, Information Data and Fact Sheet on the Harold D. Roberts Transmountain Diversion Tunnel, Denver Public Library; Glenn G. Saunders, "Reflections on Sixty Years of Water Law Practice," Natural Resources Law Center, Occasional Papers Series (Boulder: University of Colorado School of Law, 1989), 15–16; Ivan C. Crawford, *Water Resources Planning in Colorado* (Denver: Colorado Water Conservation Board, 1957), 26–27.

23. George M. Bull, Memorandum Regarding Present and Possible Future Development of Storage Reservoirs above Platte Canyon to Care for the Complete Control of the River Supply, undated, Box 7, folder "Western Slope and Denver," George M. Bull Papers, UCBA.

24. C. C. Schrepferman to Delphus Carpenter, November 30, 1929, Box 7, unlabeled folder, George M. Bull Papers, UCBA.

25. Ibid.

26. William Wyckoff, *Creating Colorado: The Making of a Western American Landscape, 1860–1940* (New Haven, CT: Yale University Press, 1999), 283.

27. First quotation in Reisner, *Cadillac Desert*, 54–107, which tells the story in detail of Los Angeles's grab of Owens Valley's water. Also see Richard White, *It's Your Misfortune and None of My Own: A New History of the American West* (Norman: University of Oklahoma Press, 1991), 423–26 (Mulholland quotation).

28. Frank Delaney to N. H. Meeker, December 27, 1935, Box 33, folder "Western Colorado Protective Association," Frank Delaney Papers, UCBA.

29. Ibid.

30. Statement of Silmon Smith, Grand Junction, CO, HR 3384, 84th Congress, First Session, Colorado River Storage Project and Participation Projects, January 18, 1954, Box 2, folder 1, Silmon Smith Papers, CSHS. Smith was described in his Grand Junction *Daily Sentinel* as "one of western Colorado's builders." Born in Iowa, he moved to Grand Junction with his parents in 1892 as a six-year-old boy. He was always at the forefront of defending the water rights of the Western Slope. A tough negotiator, Smith represented western Colorado in many controversies with eastern Colorado, including the Colorado–Big Thompson and Blue River diversion issues. He died at age seventy-eight on November 24, 1964. See *Daily Sentinel*, November 26 and November 27, 1964. Also see Laurena Davis, *125 People, 125 Years: The Grand Junction Story* (Grand Junction: Museum of Western Colorado, 2007), 69.

31. Sandra K. Davis, "Water Politics in Colorado: Change, or Business as Usual?" in Richard Lowitt, ed., *Politics in the Postwar American West* (Norman: University of Oklahoma Press, 1995), 64.

32. Clifford Stone, "Some Problems and Programs in Connection with the Colorado River Basin," December 2, 1949, Box 5, folder 2, Silmon Smith Papers, CSHS.

33. Arthur Schlesinger Jr., *The Coming of the New Deal* (Boston: Houghton Mifflin, 1959), 281–84; William E. Leuchtenburg, *Franklin D. Roosevelt and the New Deal, 1932–40* (New York: Harper and Row, 1963), 70; Tyler, *Last Water Hole*, 34; James F. Wickens, *Colorado in the Great Depression* (New York: Garland, 1979), 180; Reisner, *Cadillac Desert*, 145.

34. George M. Bull, "Proposal for the Use of NIRA Funds in Colorado," n.d., ca. 1933, Box 2a, folder 14, George M. Bull Papers, UCBA.

35. Colorado Engineering Council, "Transmountain Diversions from the Colorado River and Tributaries in Colorado," Box 3, folder 3, E. G. Plowman Papers, UCBA.

36. *Denver Post*, September 6, 1933; Tyler, *Last Water Hole*, 34; Wickens, *Colorado in the Great Depression*, 181.

37. Tyler, *Last Water Hole*, 23–25; Leonard, *Trials and Triumphs*, 99–102; Carl Ubbelohde, Maxine Benson, and Duane A. Smith, *A Colorado History*, 9th ed. (Boulder: Pruett, 2006), 206; Wickens, *Colorado in the Great Depression*, 183–84; Vandenbusche and Smith, *A Land Alone*, 262; "Objections to the Proposed Decree for the Fraser River Diversion Project Filed on Behalf of the Western Colorado Protective Association," undated, Box 2, folder 11, Silmon Smith Papers, CSHS. On the Twin Lakes Tunnel, see *Denver Post*, January 31, 1935; *Rocky Mountain News*, February 5, June 2, 1935.

38. *Denver Post*, January 31, 1935; *Rocky Mountain News*, February 5, June 2, 1935.

39. Letter in the *Daily Sentinel*, May 25, 1933.

40. Tyler, *Last Water Hole*, 24–26, 34.

41. Ibid., 41–42.

42. Quotation in D. W. Aupperle to Directors of the Western Colorado Protective Association, June 23, 1933, Box 21, folder 1, Wayne N. Aspinall Papers, University of Denver Archives (hereafter UDA).

43. David W. Aupperle moved to Grand Junction from Iowa in 1904 seeking help to combat his tuberculosis. From the time of his arrival, Aupperle took a deep interest in the city's water supply. The Highline Canal and its power plant on Orchard Mesa bear his imprint. He was among the early advocates of federal reclamation activity on the Western Slope. A community leader, he was involved in many causes but was especially a leader of western Colorado's water community. He died in 1945. See Davis, *125 People, 125 Years*, 45; Alice Wright, "Those Were the Days," *Colorado West* (Sunday magazine of the Grand Junction *Daily Sentinel*), October 15, 1972, 4–8.

44. Aupperle to Directors, June 23, 1933; D. W. Aupperle to Governor Edwin C. Johnson, June 21, 1933, Box 21, folder 1, Wayne N. Aspinall Papers, UDA.

45. Wickens, *Colorado and the Great Depression*, 202–3.

46. Quoted in the *Denver Post*, June 3, 1935.

47. Crawford, *Water Resources Planning in Colorado*; *Daily Sentinel*, June 13, 1935.

48. Quoted in Crawford, *Water Resources Planning in Colorado*.

49. *Daily Sentinel*, June 13, 14, 15, 1935.

50. Ibid., June 15, 1935.

51. Ibid., June 15 and 16, 1935; Report of Water Resources Advisory Committee to the Colorado State Planning Commission, June 13–15, 1935, Box 21, folder 6, Wayne N. Aspinall Papers, UDA; Foster to Members of the Advisory Committee, December 13, 1935; George Corlett to John T. Barnett, June 15, 1935, folder "Larry Brown, Colorado River History," Colorado River Water Conservation District (hereafter CRWCD), Glenwood Springs.

52. *Daily Sentinel*, June 15, 1935.

53. Ibid., June 16 and 17, 1935; *Rocky Mountain News*, June 17, 1935.

54. Quotations in Wyckoff, *Creating Colorado*, 283; Tyler, *Last Water Hole*, 35–36.

55. Meeting of the Board of Directors, Western Colorado Protective Association, January 29, 1935, Box 33, folder 10, Frank Delaney Papers, UCBA.

56. Taylor characterized the acre-foot for acre-foot provision this way: "I think that for every acre-foot transferred to the Eastern Slope, an equal amount should be retained for the Western Slope, and this provision should be incorporated in the plans for any project." Edward T. Taylor to Frank Delaney, June 4, 1935, Box 196, folder 6, Frank Delaney Papers, UCBA; *Rocky Mountain News*, January 13, 1935.

57. Edward Foster to Frank Delaney, February 14, 1936, Box 196, folder 6, Frank Delaney Papers, UCBA; see the extensive coverage of the conference in the Grand Junction *Daily Sentinel* from February 24 to March 1, 1936.

58. *Daily Sentinel*, February 25 and 26, 1936.

59. *Daily Sentinel*, February 25, 1936; Edward T. Taylor telegram to Silmon Smith, February 29, 1936, Box 10, folder 2, Silmon Smith Papers, CSHS.

60. *Daily Sentinel*, February 26, 27, 28, 1936.

61. Ibid., February 28, 1936.

62. Ibid.

63. Ibid.

64. Edward T. Taylor to D. W. Aupperle, March 4, 1936, Box 10, folder 5, Silmon Smith Papers, SHSC; *Rocky Mountain News*, March 3, 1936. On March 5, 1936, the *Daily Sentinel* compared Taylor to the Roman hero Horatius "at the bridge," who defended the city from the Etruscans. Adams's letter to the editor of the *Daily Sentinel*, March 6, 1936; Board of Directors Minutes, Northern Colorado Water Users Association, November 7, 1936, Box 181, folder 10, Frank Delaney Papers, UCBA.

65. Tyler, *Last Water Hole*, 54–55; Alva Adams letter, March 6, 1936; Edward T. Taylor to Silmon Smith, March 7, 1936, Box 10, folder 5, Silmon Smith Papers, CSHS;

Garfield County Board of Commissioners to Edward T. Taylor, March 11, 1936, Box 33, folder 10, Frank Delaney Papers, UCBA.

66. Taylor to Smith, March 7, 1936.

67. Ibid.

68. *Rocky Mountain News*, May 21, 1936; Edward T. Taylor telegram to Silmon Smith, March 18, 1936, Box 10, folder 5, Silmon Smith Papers, CSHS; Tyler, *Last Water Hole*, 54–57.

69. Taylor telegram to Smith, March 18, 1936.

70. *Daily Sentinel*, March 28, May 27, 1936.

71. Board of Directors of the Northern Colorado Water Users Association Minutes, November 7, 1936, Box 181, folder 10, Frank Delaney Papers, UCBA; Edward T. Taylor to D. W. Aupperle, December 22, 1936, Box 10, folder 5, Silmon Smith Papers, CSHS.

72. Tyler, *Last Water Hole*, 56–57; *Denver Post*, May 19, 1935; *Daily Sentinel*, February 23, 1937.

73. Cited in Schulte, *Wayne Aspinall*, 23–24; *Rocky Mountain News*, January 6, 1937.

74. D. W. Aupperle to Board of County Commissioners, Mesa County, February 3, 1937, Box 10, folder 4, Silmon Smith Papers, CSHS; Western Colorado Protective Association Minutes, March 24, 1937, Box 33, folder 10, Frank Delaney Papers, UCBA; *Daily Sentinel*, March 21, 1937.

75. Western Colorado Protective Association Minutes, March 24, 1937.

76. *Daily Sentinel*, March 19, 1937; Western Colorado Protective Association Minutes, March 24, 1937.

77. Quoted in Western Colorado Protective Association Minutes, March 24, 1937; *Daily Sentinel*, March 24, 1937.

78. Western Colorado Protective Association Minutes, March 24, 1937.

79. *Daily Sentinel*, March 24, 1937.

80. Western Colorado Protective Association Minutes, March 24, 1937.

81. Delaney quoted in ibid.; *Daily Sentinel*, March 24, 1937.

82. *Daily Sentinel*, March 24 and 25, 1937; *Rocky Mountain News*, March 25, 1937.

83. *Daily Sentinel*, March 25, 1937.

84. Ibid., April 11, 1937; Tyler, *Last Water Hole*, 77–78.

85. *Daily Sentinel*, April 12, 1937.

86. Davis, "Water Politics in Colorado," 64–65; Ed Quillen, "Courts and Conservancy," *Colorado Central Magazine* (April 2001), accessed June 24, 2016, http://cozine.com/2001-April/courts-and-conservancy; Session Laws of Colorado, 1937, Water Conservation Districts (CRS 37-45-101).

87. Davis, "Water Politics in Colorado"; Quillen, "Courts and Conservancy."

88. Tyler, *Last Water Hole*, 78–79; *Daily Sentinel*, May 1, May 9, May 17, 1937.

89. Chapter 220, House Bill no. 504, "An Act to Provide for the Creation of a Water Conservation District, to Be Called 'The Colorado River Water Conservation District,'" June 7, 1937, folder "River District/WCPA Basin States, etc.," CRWCD; Limerick and Hanson, *A Ditch in Time*, 122–26; George Sibley, *Water Wranglers: The 75-Year History of the Colorado River District—a Story about the Embattled Colorado River and the Growth of the West* (Glenwood Springs: Colorado River District, 2012), 59–69; Frank Delaney to Clifford Stone, January 16, 1937; Delaney to Stone, February 16, 1937, both in folder "River District/WCPA/Basin States, etc.," CRWCD; Colorado River District History, http://www.coloradoriverdistrict.org.

90. *Daily Sentinel*, May 26, May 28, 1937.

91. Ibid., June 6, June 9, June 10, 1937.

92. Ibid., June 12, June 15, 1937; Tyler, *Last Water Hole*, 79–80.

93. Ubbelohde, Benson, and Smith, *Colorado History*, 306–9.

94. Alva A. Swain, "Under the Capitol Dome," newspaper column printed in the *Daily Sentinel*, June 26, 1937, copy in Box 56, folder "Water Board," Wayne N. Aspinall Papers, UDA.

95. Senate Document 80, 75th Congress, 1st Session, Colorado–Big Thompson Project, *Synopsis of Report on Colorado–Big Thompson Project, Plan of Development and Cost Estimate Prepared by the Bureau of Reclamation, Department of the Interior*, June 15, 1937 (Washington, DC: Government Printing Office, 1937), 1–5; Sibley, *Water Wranglers*, 67–69.

96. Senate Document 80, June 15, 1937.

97. *Rocky Mountain News*, July 19, 1937; Tyler, *Last Water Hole*, 84–88.

98. Adams and Johnson quoted in the *Daily Sentinel*, August 11, 1937; *Fort Lupton (CO) Press*, September 23, 1937; *Rocky Mountain News*, September 23, 1937.

99. *Rocky Mountain News*, November 13, 1937; Tyler, *Last Water Hole*, 86–88.

100. *Rocky Mountain News*, December 28, 1937; US Department of the Interior news release, December 16, 1962, Box 3, folder "Colorado–Big Thompson," William Nelson Papers, CMUASC; Schulte, *Wayne Aspinall*, 24–25; Ubbelohde, Benson, and Smith, *Colorado History*, 306–9; Tyler, *Last Water Hole*, 95.

3

Portents of Mid-Century Conflict, Pre-1940-1950

Some years ago the question of transmountain diversion came to the attention of the citizens of that State [Colorado] . . . Finally the matter was more or less settled on a principle which has been adopted by the Colorado Water Conservation Board. That principle is this: that no water shall be taken from the western half of the State for utilization in the eastern part of the State unless the present and prospective uses of water in the west half of the State are as near as possible fully protected.[1]

Clifford Stone, director of the Colorado Water
Conservation Board, May 6, 1938

WORLD WAR II AND THE RENEWAL OF EAST-WEST TENSIONS

From the late 1930s to 1950, Colorado entered an era of startling change in its water-planning environment. The newly formed Colorado Water Conservation Board (CWCB) began issuing plans for state water projects and emerged as a crucial intermediary between the state's water interest groups and the Bureau of Reclamation. Above all, World War II inaugurated

DOI: 10.5876/9781607325000.c003

an era of profound change for both the American West and Colorado. The West emerged from the conflict, in the words of historian Gerald D. Nash, "a transformed region." When the war began, many westerners who had experienced the severe economic dislocations of the 1930s feared that the region's economic expansion had come to a close. The economy seemed stagnant, and population growth had all but ceased. The frenzied development of the postwar era would prove that this viewpoint was incorrect.[2]

The war had initiated an "incredible burst of economic activity" across the region. Three of the nine fastest-growing states between 1940 and 1943 were in the American West. Colorado mirrored these trends. The beginnings of the Front Range urban corridor can be traced to this era. While much of the rural Western Slope had lost population, cities like Grand Junction exhibited strong growth. Federal activity, including the frenzied search for uranium, brought 2,000 more people to Grand Junction in the 1940s, swelling its 1950 population to 14,000.[3]

Colorado and the other states of the Upper Colorado River Basin regarded the undeveloped and unappropriated water within their borders as a key economic resource. Since the late 1920s, Western Slope communities had clamored for more water development. The 1930s activities of the Colorado State Planning Commission and some of the early water projects considered by the new Colorado Water Conservation Board only heightened the expectations of people across the Centennial State. As Mark W.T. Harvey notes in his history of the Echo Park water controversy, by the late 1930s the Upper Basin states "were urging the Bureau [of Reclamation] to pay attention to their own water demands." Not only did Colorado want to put the water to use within its borders, but the Upper Basin expressed frequent concern over the requirements of the Colorado River Compact that compelled the Upper Basin to allow 75 million acre-feet to flow to the Lower Basin every ten years. New water projects would be a catalyst for Colorado's economic growth while also enabling the Upper Basin states to meet the Colorado River Compact requirements.[4]

During the organizational meeting of the CWCB in July 1937, a discussion of the proposed Gunnison-Arkansas diversion occurred. The board approved a resolution pledging its cooperation with the US Bureau of Reclamation to conduct a survey of the proposed diversion to determine its feasibility and suggest protective measures for Western Slope water users.

CWCB counsel Clifford H. Stone emphasized that "protection for present and future development of Western Colorado must be included in any transmountain diversion."[5]

At the January 1938 quarterly meeting of the new Colorado River Water Conservation District (CRWCD), Stone addressed the gathering about the fast-moving plans of Arkansas Valley water users for a Gunnison-Arkansas (Colorado–Big Thompson [C-BT]) Project. A former Gunnison state legislator and a well-respected water attorney, Stone had co-sponsored much of the water legislation in the 1937 legislative session. As a representative of the CWCB, Stone appeared to reassure the CRWCD that the state water board was taking the position that the Senate Document 80 operating principles of the C-BT, which included protections for the basin of origin, "must be included in any transmountain diversion." Stone concluded: "It would seem that any effort to revive this controversy after this principle [of protecting the Western Slope's future needs] may have the effect of destroying what has already been accomplished." Yet despite his words of assurance to Western Slope water officials, Stone and advocates of a state water program were up against a profound Western Slope sense of "here we go again." Demands for both Denver's Blue River Project and the Gunnison-Arkansas diversions came fast on the heels of the exhausting C-BT controversy.[6]

In 1938 Clifford Stone was appointed director of the Colorado Water Conservation Board. Because of his western Colorado origins, Stone had earned the confidence of most Western Slope citizens. Evidence of Stone's intentions to safeguard Western Slope interests are numerous and continued until his death in 1952. Early on, he made it clear where he stood on the subject of future diversions. Stone spoke at a hearing in Washington, DC, on May 6, 1938, about the petition of the Moffat Tunnel Water and Development Company to "restore to the public domain lands withdrawn by the Department of the Interior in connection with the Colorado–Big Thompson Project." As he told the hearing:

> Some years ago the question of transmountain diversion came to the attention of the citizens of that State [Colorado]. Naturally the people in the western half of the State were apprehensive about taking water from that section for application in the eastern part. The controversy existed for some years. Finally the matter was more or less settled on a principle which has

been adopted by the Colorado Water Conservation Board. That principle is this: that no water shall be taken from the western half of the State for utilization in the eastern part of the State unless the present and prospective uses of water in the west half of the State are as near as possible fully protected.[7]

At the next meeting of the CWCB (May 20, 1938), Stone reported on his testimony at the hearing. Western Slope board member Wayne N. Aspinall of Palisade offered a motion asking the CWCB to ratify Stone's action by upholding the principle of the 1935 Delaney Resolution. Aspinall's action passed unanimously.[8] It is clear that Stone's leadership of the CWCB attempted to harmonize the interests of the entire state while protecting the politically vulnerable yet water-rich Western Slope.

Congressman Edward T. Taylor remained fully engaged in the brewing Gunnison-Arkansas controversy by encouraging Gunnison-area residents to fight for their water and stand against the rumored trans-mountain diversion. Taylor warned Gunnison County commissioners that he needed support that went beyond mere resolutions as he worked to deny federal funding for a Gunnison-Arkansas survey. In fact, it was Taylor who gave Gunnison newspaper editor and staunch anti-diversionist Henry F. Lake many of his ideas, suggesting that local Gunnison River–area people "spend some money" and hire the "best attorneys and best engineers available" and make a thorough study of the area's water needs to combat Eastern Slope plans. The Gunnison-Arkansas diversion, according to Taylor, was a "bold, brazen, buccaneering fight to deliberately steal the summer water of the Gunnison country."[9]

Later in 1938, with an eye toward the Arkansas River Valley, Taylor announced that all future diversions from the Western Slope would require plans that included compensatory water storage: "As long as I am Chairman of the [House] Appropriations Committee, not a drop of water would pass over the divide until we do get guarantees." To emphasize his intentions, in 1938 Taylor blocked a proposed $100,000 appropriation to survey the Gunnison-Arkansas Project because no such guarantee for compensatory storage was included in the project plans. Taylor and Frank Delaney advocated a different kind of study—a comprehensive survey of future western Colorado water needed to be conducted with an eye toward quantifying the water needed to support such activities as gas, oil, and, above all, oil shale development. Keeping streams alive was of vital concern to recreational

FIGURE 3.1. Edward T. Taylor, who served in the US Congress, representing western Colorado from 1909 until 1941. A strong advocate for Western Slope water and protecting it for future uses, he led the fight at the congressional level against the Colorado–Big Thompson Project until he could ensure that western Colorado would receive fair treatment in the authorizing legislation. *Courtesy*, Colorado Mesa University Archives and Special Collections, Grand Junction.

fishermen, especially in the Gunnison region, an area that already enjoyed a substantial tourist trade.[10]

According to one estimate, the Gunnison-Arkansas Project would have taken over "half the total water produced by the Gunnison River and its tributaries and seriously affected any future growth of the region." A 1946 Bureau of Reclamation study noted the severe impact the Gunnison-Arkansas Project would have on fishing and the local Gunnison Valley recreation economy. The same study examined the possibility of diverting waters of the Gunnison, Crystal, and Fryingpan Rivers to the Front Range, with the potential to divert a total of 800,000 acre-feet. Over the next several years, the determined opposition of Taylor and Gunnison-area water officials forced project planners to reconfigure the project on a smaller scale.[11]

THE DEATH OF EDWARD T. TAYLOR

Edward Taylor continued his fight for Western Slope water into the 1940s. He also played an important role in mentoring a future US congressman, Wayne Aspinall. Aspinall always admitted that he followed in Taylor's "political footsteps," admiring the congressman's commanding approach to western resource issues and his staunch defense of the Western Slope's water supply. Aspinall drew inspiration from Taylor during his own political rise and, in part, modeled his behavior as a congressman after that of the Glenwood Springs congressman. Taylor's unimpeachable political reputation was rooted in his ability to promote the economic growth of his huge, rural, mountainous Fourth Congressional District. Almost every adult in the district could say that he or she had met the legendary congressman. Always foremost in Taylor's mind were the defense and aggrandizement of the district's water resources, a lesson that was not lost on Aspinall. Aspinall recognized that one way to achieve political power would be to model his career upon Taylor's— to gain control over a powerful committee that could impact the fortunes of Western Colorado. This practical lesson in western politics was also not lost on Aspinall. In less than ten years, he would begin his meteoric rise to the chairmanship of the House Interior Committee, the legislative body that addressed almost every significant piece of legislation—including reclamation—affecting the American West.[12]

Despite a Republican resurgence in Colorado politics in the late 1930s, Democrat Edward Taylor remained firmly in control of his Fourth Congressional District seat. Grand Junction attorney Silmon Smith admitted that even though he was a diehard Republican, "I have hoped that Congressman Taylor would remain in his position forever. My better judgment tells me that his tenure is limited." Smith's prediction about Taylor's longevity came to pass sooner than he and other Western Slope admirers of Taylor cared to envision. Taylor's storied life and legislative career came to an end on September 4, 1941, following a heart attack he suffered in Denver.[13]

Newspaper obituaries and congressional eulogies struck many of the same notes in assessing Taylor's remarkable legacy. The *Rocky Mountain News* referred to Taylor as the "father of reclamation" and a "zealous champion of the West." Perhaps the most fitting remembrance of Taylor was offered later by Silmon Smith. In a 1948 letter to Grand Junction *Daily Sentinel* editor and publisher Walter Walker, Smith discussed the 1948 congressional election, which featured the Democratic state senator Wayne Aspinall challenging the incumbent Republican and successor to Edward T. Taylor, Robert Rockwell. Smith, as a Republican, might have been expected to tout Rockwell's candidacy. Not so. When water became intertwined in western Colorado's politics, political affiliation was often abandoned. Smith remarked, "It is not my purpose to become greatly excited over our representation in the Fourth Congressional District except to remark that length of tenure adds up to a Congressman's value if other things are equal. Only a few of us realized the importance of Congressman Taylor to this problem and I realized it fully while we were in Washington negotiating with Northeastern Colorado on the Big Thompson Project and Congressman Taylor was in the hospital, and the contents of our document and agreement depended so much each day on whether he was better or worse."[14]

DENVER'S PLANS FOR THE BLUE RIVER

America's entrance into World War II acted as a brake on water project construction. The Bureau of Reclamation lost both personnel and budgets as wartime defense took on a greater national priority. Construction projects like the Colorado–Big Thompson Project slowed to a crawl. Important building materials were delayed, redirected to high-priority defense needs, or became impossible to find. State water planning, however, continued, sometimes at a frenzied pace. As the war began to turn in the direction of an Allied victory by 1944, postwar domestic priorities began to be earnestly discussed. What water projects should be built? How would Colorado cooperate with neighboring states? Would the Western Slope be able to retain its water in the face of new political pressures to surrender more water to the more populous eastern regions of the state?

Even though World War II all but halted reclamation work, CWCB director Clifford Stone believed the state needed to move forward with planning and strategies to better position itself in the postwar era. Developing a comprehensive program took time, Stone asserted, and Colorado needed to be ready to claim its share of funding for postwar project investigations. The clearest demonstration of this axiom at the state level was a renewed bid by the Denver Water Board to lay the groundwork for obtaining water from the Blue River. As early as July 1940, the directors of the CRWCD discussed a new

Bureau of Reclamation report that assessed the proposed Blue River–South Platte Project. In words that likely chilled the bones of most Western Slope water officials, this project would, when completed, "divert all remaining water of [the] Blue River and Williams Fork River to Eastern Colorado."[15]

Prior to World War II, CRWCD counsel Frank Delaney predicted future friction over Denver's designs on the Blue River. Delaney's sources informed him that any more diversions on the Colorado or its tributaries in western Colorado would cause economic and political friction during times of low water flow. Diversions such as the proposed Blue River Project would endanger the operation of the C-BT. Delaney remarked that "few people have any conception of the length to which the City of Denver is going in the taking of our Western Colorado water."[16]

To calm mounting Western Slope fears over Denver's diversion plans, CWCB director Clifford Stone appeared before the Colorado River Water Conservation District Board in October 1940 to assure Western Slope water officials that the principles of the original 1935 Delaney Resolution would still be honored by the state water board. The Colorado–Big Thompson Project operated according to the principles of Senate Document 80, which remained the legislative embodiment of the compensatory storage idea. Stone insisted that all proposed water diversions would follow these guidelines since they were now "the settled policy of the Bureau of Reclamation as well as the policy of the Colorado Water Conservation Board." Stone noted that the CWCB regularly received criticism for insisting on compensatory storage, but under his leadership the board would not deviate from this policy. Stone had done more than almost anyone to broker the C-BT struggle. As long as he headed the CWCB, Western Slope water interests believed few projects could pass that might hurt them.[17]

While understandably wary of Denver's intentions, Delaney advised a "wait and see" approach. After Denver's water planning became more public, the Western Slope could better devise a counter-strategy. From his experience dealing with Denver water interests as a member of the Colorado State Planning Commission, Delaney knew that Denver's intentions to divert the Blue River were not "theoretical" but a "future certainty to them and their water planning efforts." Denver would enlarge the powers of its water board, use past filings and studies, and try to push the date of its earliest decrees as far back in time as legally possible.[18]

By 1943 the dimensions of Denver's aspirations for the Blue River had become public and apparent. Legal hearings had started in Summit County courts and would continue on and off for more than ten years. The interests opposed to Denver's water claims were the Colorado River Water Conservation District, the Northern Colorado Water Conservancy District, and the Bureau of Reclamation. The Denver Water Board's plans for the Blue River–South Platte Project threatened the potential operation of the Colorado–Big Thompson Project. The Blue River–South Platte Project had the potential to undermine the available water supply and operation of the Green Mountain Reservoir, which was being constructed to serve as a key power and replacement storage for waters diverted to the Front Range through the Alva B. Adams Tunnel. Central to this legal contest was the question of the date of Denver's water claim. The awarding of a 1914 priority date would endanger the operation of Green Mountain Reservoir, as well as threaten other Western Slope water rights.[19]

The CRWCD discussed the Blue River diversion extensively at its July 20, 1943, board of directors meeting. In an attempt to convince western Colorado officials about the legality of Denver's Blue River claims, Mills E. Bunger, a senior engineer for the Bureau of Reclamation, appeared before the CRWCD. Denver's diversion plans had changed rather radically several times over a twenty-year period. The original plans, made by the engineering consulting firm Van Sant Houghton Company, called for an annual diversion of 88,000 acre-feet without project storage in the Blue River or South Platte Basins. As a young man, Bunger had worked for the Van Sant Houghton survey when it explored the Blue River region in 1915. The Van Sant Houghton plan would gather project water from high elevations (10,300 feet or higher) and distribute the water through a system of tunnels and canals to the South Platte, above Cheesman Reservoir. No attempt was made to secure a conditional water decree for this project, and a water right filing was not made until 1923. No rights-of-way were ever secured across public lands for this version of the project.[20]

The next incarnation of the Blue River Plan by the Denver Water Board (DWB) constituted the plans formulated by the DWB's former chief engineer, George M. Bull. Bull's plan, based on his surveys in 1922 and 1923, represented a radical departure from Van Sant Houghton's approach. Water was to be taken only at Dillon and delivered at Grant on the North Fork of the South

Platte. Bull's ideas were ambitious—a much larger amount of water would be earmarked for diversion. Bull's plan was made public through a filing by the Denver Water Board on October 17, 1927. This filing also accounted for a large reservoir, later named Two Forks, to be constructed on the South Platte River. In the mid-1930s, while the city of Denver was busy constructing the Moffat Tunnel water system, the Bureau of Reclamation began investigating the feasibility of Denver tapping the Blue River. The bureau's first report on the Blue River plan, not issued publicly until 1940, discussed a version of the project that was yet another departure from previous plans.[21]

Bunger's appearance before the CRWCD was intended in part to convince Western Slope water leaders that Denver's plans for the Blue River were becoming more stable and less changeable, but the engineer still took the Western Slope directors through a dizzying series of possibilities about possible points of diversion, tunnel locations, and potential reservoir sites. As the CRWCD Board of Directors indicated in late 1943, "It was quite apparent . . . that from time to time so many changes had been made [to the Blue River Project] that there could not be said to be any connection between the first scheme proposed in 1923 and the one now presented" to the CWCB, the CRWCD, and the Summit County Colorado District Court. It was the consensus of western Colorado water officials that "no claim for the project . . . in the present adjudication should be properly dated back [to] the first surveys for the Dillon reservoir." Western Colorado asserted that more recent versions of the project bore little resemblance to early surveys conducted from 1914 through the 1920s. Denver's various plans would be the subject of a great deal of litigation and heated discussion between the Eastern and Western Slopes in the 1940s and 1950s before a final form of the project gained approval.[22]

With World War II over, in 1946 the Western Slope continued to monitor the Denver Water Board's planning for the Blue River diversion. As long as the Western Slope maintained strong representation on the CWCB, its interests would receive consideration and, perhaps, protection. The Western Slope had a strong avenging angel as long as Edward Taylor was alive. After his death, the same sentiments were often expressed about Clifford Stone's role as director of the state water board. Though Stone was always fair to Front Range water interests, his presence at the Colorado Water Conservation Board's helm helped balance the power the Eastern Slope often asserted over Colorado's water policy. As long as Stone continued in office, western Colorado water officials believed they could at least cope with the more powerful Front Range water interests.[23]

FROM UPPER BASIN COMPACT TO THE CRSP

With World War II winding down, Colorado officials began serious discussion of the state's future water program. Two major issues dominated the energies of Colorado's planning bureaucracies from 1945 to 1950: the need to divide the waters of the Upper Colorado River Basin and the Bureau of Reclamation's plans for a massive postwar reclamation construction program that by the late 1940s had evolved into the Colorado River Storage Project (CRSP).

In 1945, Governor Lester C. Hunt of Wyoming took the lead in asking the other Upper Colorado River Basin states to begin discussions concerning allocation of the Upper Basin's 7.5 million acre-foot share of the Colorado River. Initially, some Colorado water officials thought the most prudent policy was to continue to delay the accomplishment of this task. The basis of the delay strategy centered on the idea that Colorado was already in the strongest position of the four Upper Basin states and that official allocation could only result in losses for the state's share. The historical basis of this position was that Colorado contributed more than 70 percent of the river's water, so any legal division would result in a major loss of the state's overall contributions to the river system. With the state growing fast during and after the war, a strategy of delay might allow Colorado to claim that more water was being put to beneficial consumptive use. The state's official position as of March 1945 was that there was not sufficient data available to divide the Upper Colorado River Basin's water; each basin state should continue with its postwar project planning and only cease if, in the opinion of one of the other states, a particular state was "approaching . . . nearly the equitable share of water that under the [proposed] compact might eventually be apportioned to each state."[24]

In June 1946 the Bureau of Reclamation submitted a lengthy report to the Department of the Interior, provocatively titled *The Colorado River: A Natural Menace Becomes a Natural Resource*, for Colorado River reclamation planning. The study listed and described 134 potential reclamation projects the Upper Colorado River states had been planning for several decades. In Colorado, projects such as Echo Park, Split Mountain, Fruitland Mesa, Animas–La Plata,

Dolores, Collbran, West Divide, Silt, San Miguel, and others were included and discussed. The report amounted to a huge, basin-wide best-case-scenario water project "wish list." In a chapter on water utilization, the Bureau of Reclamation candidly admitted that construction of all the projects detailed in the report, "added to present water uses . . . would create a demand for more water than normally is available in the river system." Despite this and other shortcomings, the study represented an important blueprint for the CRSP that would begin to take shape legislatively over the next few years as the document was debated.[25]

Yet the report also appeared to threaten the waters of western Colorado. The study discussed the possibility of diverting waters from above the Gunnison Basin for export across the Continental Divide to supplement the flows of the Platte and Arkansas River Basins. However, the Reclamation Bureau's plans for the Upper Basin states, Denver's hopes to corral the Blue River, and southeastern Colorado's bid for the Gunnison-Arkansas Project would need to wait for the negotiation of an Upper Colorado River Basin Compact.[26]

The Upper Colorado River Basin Compact traced its legal origins to the Colorado River Compact of 1922, the Boulder Canyon Project Act of 1928, and the Boulder Canyon Project Adjustments Act passed in 1939. These laws addressed the Upper Basin's water situation by authorizing the Bureau of Reclamation to begin investigating the reclamation future of the entire Colorado River system. The Colorado River Compact of 1922 represented the most intensive interaction among the Colorado River Basin states. In its aftermath, gatherings of those states tended to occur through negotiations between two states that sometimes led to small, two-state compacts or through informal basin-wide meetings. Article 3 of the Colorado River Compact had left the division of waters among the states to future negotiations among the states of both the Upper and Lower Basins.[27]

The four Upper Colorado River Basin states had yet to divide their share of the Colorado River Compact water among themselves; only one major diversion project had been authorized in the Upper Basin—the Colorado–Big Thompson Project. Since the time of the Colorado River Compact, several interior secretaries had insisted that the Upper Basin states commence the process of dividing up that basin's share of the river. For most of that period, incomplete stream flow records and the region's perceived lack of need for additional water storage had discouraged further compact negotiation. Colorado had taken the position that water is, "more or less, allocated by its place of origin." This philosophy, tested and found wanting in legal cases like *Kansas v. Colorado* and *Wyoming v. Colorado*, nevertheless offered a degree of comfort to the Centennial State, the birthplace of many of the Intermountain West's most notable streams. With World War II over and a political movement toward a division of the Upper Basin's waters occurring, Colorado could no longer drag its feet on the issue of Upper Basin negotiations and allocations.[28]

In July 1947, Secretary of the Interior Julius Krug noted in the Bureau of Reclamation's report that "existing circumstances" precluded him from making specific project recommendations. The secretary's reluctance to recommend water projects was in part a result of the Upper Basin's need to divide its share of the compact waters. Further development of the river basin, "particularly large-scale development, is seriously handicapped, if not barred" by the Upper Basin's reluctance to divide its waters. In short, Krug argued that without a compact, the Upper Basin states would be unable to enjoy the federal government's reclamation largesse. Krug stated the obvious: the Upper Basin states had far too many projects on their wish lists and too little water available to build them. Dividing the waters among themselves would add a crucial element of realism to the planning process and, more important, allow construction to proceed. In Colorado, several projects had been investigated and found feasible, including Paonia, Pine River Extension, Animas–La Plata, Florida, Dolores, Silt, and Collbran. However, without an Upper Basin Compact, these projects would not advance beyond the planning stage.[29]

As early as the summer of 1946, the Upper Basin states initiated the first tentative steps toward dividing the Colorado River among themselves. Meeting in Salt Lake City on July 31, 1946, representatives of the states formed an Upper Colorado River Commission to negotiate an agreement. Former Bureau of Reclamation commissioner Harry W. Bashore represented the interests of the federal government during the proceedings. Water engineers from each state were tasked to supply information about state water availability and projected state needs.[30]

Over the next two years, the negotiations took several wild turns and twists as commissioners discussed and argued over matters in eight formal meetings and more than fifty sessions of the commission. Pressing issues included the standards to use to divide the Upper Basin's waters. Should it be divided by percentage of consumptive use of water? Should it be divided by the amount of water produced by each individual state? With that standard, Colorado would gain more than 70 percent of the Upper Basin's water. How should Native American water rights in New Mexico be considered—or should this question be addressed at all? Should restrictions be put in place prohibiting or limiting trans-mountain diversions out of the basin? An overriding concern dealt with meeting deliveries of water at Lees Ferry under the terms of the Colorado River Compact. While the Upper Basin had not had problems allowing 7.5 million acre-feet annually to flow to the Lower Basin, how would this requirement be met when the Upper Basin states began constructing their own water projects? Colorado commissioner Clifford H. Stone made a motion during the fifth meeting that the delivery of the requisite amount of water at Lees Ferry should be "spread over the Upper Basin on an equitable basis."[31] Stone's motion carried.

The Upper Colorado River Commission's deliberations climaxed in 1948 with a state-by-state division of the Upper Basin's 7.5 million acre-foot share of the river's annual flow. For more than two years the commission, state water engineers, and the federal representative were motivated by the realization that the Bureau of Reclamation would not budge on any more reclamation construction until the Upper Basin states settled pressing questions that concerned them.[32] Colorado's hopes for the major share of the Upper Basin's allotment continued to be kindled. When the negotiators had finished their job in 1948, Colorado received the right to 51.75 percent of the Upper Basin's share, which would translate to about 3.5 million acre-feet per year. Utah gained 23 percent, Wyoming 14 percent, and New Mexico settled for 11.25 percent. The compact had to be approved by each of the state's legislatures and then by the US Congress before reaching the president's desk.[33]

In early 1949 the Colorado General Assembly ratified the Upper Colorado River Basin Compact. During the compact's consideration before the House of Representatives, freshman congressman Wayne Aspinall entered the debate over its approval to refute arguments emanating from California's delegation implying that ratification could potentially damage all western states' water plans. Aspinall countered that the Upper Basin Compact would actually help California and the Lower Basin by imposing order on the plans of the Upper Basin states. A state-by-state water development free-for-all, Aspinall stated, would not benefit any state. During the compact hearings,

Aspinall gave his new colleagues a preview of his strong proprietary interest in the Western Slope's water supply by noting that his congressional district was the region in which "sixty-five percent of the water of the Colorado River arises." After Congress approved the agreement, President Harry Truman signed the Upper Colorado River Basin Compact on April 6, 1949. According to historian Mark W.T. Harvey, the compact "removed the central obstacle blocking the Bureau's plan for dams and thereby paved the way for the upper basin to use its half of the great river." Politicians and water planners from the Upper Basin states could now begin to write legislation that would ensure the region's economic growth in the decades ahead.[34]

THE EMERGENCE OF CONGRESSMAN WAYNE ASPINALL AND THE CRSP

As the Upper Colorado River Basin Compact was being negotiated, several political events were occurring that augured well for Colorado's hydraulic future. After years of positioning himself for a seat in the US Congress, Western Slope state senator Wayne Aspinall challenged Republican incumbent Robert Rockwell for Colorado's Fourth Congressional District seat. A fruit grower, schoolteacher, and attorney, Aspinall was intimately acquainted with the life-or-death significance of irrigation. He had been well taught by two political teachers: Walter Walker, publisher of the Grand Junction *Daily Sentinel*, and the legendary Edward T. Taylor.[35]

In 1948, Rockwell proved tough to unseat, as the incumbent held key natural resource committee seats important to the Fourth Congressional District. President Truman and the Democratic Party's troubles in 1948 complicated matters, making Aspinall's chances "look very dark at this time." Aspinall ran an Edward Taylor–style campaign—short, intense, yet highly personal—and he visited all twenty-four counties of the massive rural congressional district. Endorsing Aspinall's candidacy, Walter Walker of the *Daily Sentinel* remarked that the people of western Colorado had been searching for a "worthy successor" to Edward Taylor since 1941. Facing an uphill battle against an incumbent blessed with unlimited personal financial resources, Aspinall nevertheless discovered several issues that resonated with the voters of the Fourth Congressional District. In 1947–48 the Republican-controlled Congress had moved in the direction of privatizing and loosening federal regulations over the West's natural resources.

In a series of well-publicized hearings, Rockwell and Congressman Frank Barrett (R-WY) pummeled US National Forest Service bureaucrats for attempting to restrain private interests on public lands. The influential *Daily Sentinel* took a dim view of Rockwell's antics, arguing that the region's long-term interests would be better served by well-managed federal watersheds. Both Aspinall and Truman benefited from the 80th Congress's parsimonious reputation. In several campaign stops Aspinall excoriated Rockwell and the Republicans for their budget cuts. Of course, by 1948 the Bureau of Reclamation and the Upper Colorado River Basin states were busy generating plans for the future of the river. Water development was "perhaps the most important" campaign issue for western politicians seeking national office in 1948.[36]

In an editorial that appeared two weeks before the election, *Daily Sentinel* editor Walter Walker remarked that the Bureau of Reclamation had indeed been spending some money in Colorado as Rockwell had argued, but it was spent unevenly across the state. The bureau, Walker contended, had spent vast amounts of money to study how to divert more water across the Continental Divide to the Front Range. By the same token, it had spent "much smaller amounts" on how to put water to use within the Colorado River Basin. Walker and Aspinall echoed national condemnation of the Republicans' parsimony. The *New Republic* had editorialized that the "development of the West depends on government capital. Private capital has not been and will not be able to finance such colossal projects" as those planned by the Bureau of Reclamation. With so many water projects being discussed and the Upper Colorado River Basin Compact nearing completion, Aspinall, Truman, and the Democrats emerged as champions of an enlarged federal presence in developing the American West during the 1948 campaign.[37]

Steaming through the state aboard his campaign train, Truman visited Grand Junction and many other towns, denouncing Republican efforts to stymie federal resource management. In Grand Junction, Truman exclaimed that "Republicans had no interest in the West—not in water, not in public power." As proof, Truman pointed out that the Republican Congress had slashed appropriations for western power and reclamation projects. "These are the life blood of the West," the president proclaimed. Wayne Aspinall credited Truman's support for his victory over the incumbent Rockwell. Aspinall moved to Washington, DC, and enjoyed a renowned career as a water politician. His fingerprints covered most legislation dealing with water in Colorado in the decades ahead. Perhaps more important, the Western Slope once again had a strong and able defender of its interests, well-positioned to balance the population and political advantages of Colorado's Eastern Slope.[38]

Aspinall's election eventually replaced some of the prestige and power Edward T. Taylor had once commanded. Since 1941, western Colorado had suffered from a "lack of genuinely aggressive work on the river problem" and needed a man of "Edward T. Taylor's type, determination, and influence." The congressional representation question loomed ever larger for the Western Slope in the late 1940s because of the threat of several more diversion plans to bring western Colorado water to the Front Range. The fact that people voted for the candidate with the strongest record on water protection helped Aspinall stay in Congress from 1948 to 1972.[39]

Wayne Aspinall's congressional career paralleled the passage and implementation of the Colorado River Storage Project. However, because of the size and gravity of the legislation and the interstate and intrastate controversies it would generate, drafting the CRSP took more than half of the 1950s until it became law. Because of its volatile intrastate water conflict environment, Colorado argued long and hard before reaching a small degree of unity to support a final version of the CRSP in 1956.

Colorado's rapid population growth also contributed to the renewal of the state's water wars after World War II. Many urban areas were unprepared for this development. Richard White points out that most cities "found their public services," including their domestic water supplies, stretched to the limit after the war. While California's increase was the largest, Colorado's population surge outstripped that of most other intermountain states. Much of the growth occurred along Colorado's Eastern Slope in war-related industries such as defense contracting and military bases. Government science, research, and defense work remained a cornerstone of Colorado's and the Front Range's growth well past World War II. On the Western Slope, the search for uranium to feed Cold War defense needs inspired a smaller yet significant population boom from Grand Junction to Durango. Western Slope water officials, especially Grand Junction's leaders, worried openly about the impact of the postwar population boom on water supplies. Denver shared this concern, and fears over a finite water supply drove the capital city's frantic quest for additional water.[40]

The 1940s saw few actual reclamation projects completed in the American West. However, to label this an era when nothing happened for Colorado's water program is misleading. It was a decade of careful, often intricate planning for the future. World War II allowed Colorado water officials, ranging from the CWCB to the Denver Water Board to the Western Slope's new water protection agency, the Colorado River Water Conservation District, to bide their time and begin serious planning. At the same time, federal water agencies, notably the Bureau of Reclamation, also entered a vigorous planning phase that resulted in the early plans for the Colorado River Storage Project. Individually, the states of Colorado, Wyoming, Utah, and New Mexico lacked the population and political clout to build massive and numerous water projects. California's prodigious growth provided an additional stimulus for Upper Basin water planning. As Marc Reisner eloquently phrased it, "If the upper basin didn't hurry and begin using its own entitlement [of the Colorado River], California seemed certain to try and 'borrow' it; if it succeeded, and millions of people then depended on that water, how would the upper basin ever get it back?"[41]

The Bureau of Reclamation responded to the Upper Basin's urgency with drafts of what became the massive CRSP. This gargantuan endeavor did something the individually powerless states of the Upper Colorado River Basin could not do—provide a basin-wide approach to the region's water problems. The CRSP's route to passage would not be smooth, and Colorado's political divisions would threaten to undermine the Centennial State's participation in the Upper Basin's water legislation. Heading into the 1950s, plans for the Colorado River Storage Project loomed large in Colorado, but questions over the Gunnison-Arkansas Project and Denver's bid for a Blue River diversion would also occupy Colorado water officials for much of the next decade.

NOTES

1. Colorado River Water Conservation District (hereafter CRWCD), "Report on CWCB's Position on Colorado's East-West Water Issues," May 20, 1938, folder "East-West Position, Colorado Water Conservation Board [hereafter CWCB]–CWCB-Trans-Mountain Diversion [hereafter TMD]," CRWCD, Glenwood Springs, CO.

2. Carl Ubbelohde, Maxine Benson, and Duane A. Smith, *A Colorado History*, 9th ed. (Boulder: Pruett, 2006), 310; Douglas Kupel, *Fuel for Growth: Water and Arizona's Urban Environment* (Tucson: University of Arizona Press, 2003), 133; Gerald D. Nash, *The American West Transformed: The Impact of the Second World War* (Lincoln: University of Nebraska Press, 1985). Nash discusses the idea that World War II was the major transforming event of the twentieth century.

3. Quotation in Peter Wiley and Robert Gottlieb, *Empires in the Sun: The Rise of the New American West* (New York: G. P. Putnam's Sons, 1982), 28; Steven C. Schulte, *Wayne Aspinall and the Shaping of the American West* (Boulder: University Press of Colorado, 2002), 49–52.

4. Mark W.T. Harvey, *A Symbol of Wilderness: Echo Park and the American Conservation Movement* (Albuquerque: University of New Mexico Press, 1994), 25–27.

5. CWCB Minutes, November 18, 1937, folder "East-West Position, CWCB-TMD," CRWCD, Glenwood Springs, CO.

6. Statement of Judge Clifford H. Stone, Counsel for the Colorado Water Conservation Board, January 15, 1938, Box 11, folder 3, Silmon Smith Papers, Colorado State Historical Society (hereafter CSHS), Denver.

7. CRWCD, "Report on CWCB's Position on Colorado's East-West Water Issues."

8. Ibid.

9. Taylor letter reprinted in the *Gunnison (CO) News-Champion*, March 17, 1938.

10. Duane Vandenbusche and Duane A. Smith, *A Land Alone: Colorado's Western Slope* (Boulder: Pruett, 1981), 265–67; History and Description of the Fryingpan-Arkansas Project, accessed August 20, 2009, www.secwcd.org/content/fryingpan -arkansas-project-history; CRWCD Minutes, January 21, 1947, folder "CRWCD Minutes, 1946–47," CRWCD, Glenwood Springs, CO.

11. CRWCD Minutes, n.p.

12. *Denver Post*, May 19, 1935; *Daily Sentinel* (Grand Junction, CO), November 22, 1934; *Denver Post*, Taylor obituary fragment, undated, ca. September 1941, Edward T. Taylor Papers, CSHS; Schulte, *Wayne Aspinall*, 22–23; Nancy Whistler, interview with Wayne N. Aspinall, February 15, 1979, Association of Former Members of Congress Project, Manuscript Division, Library of Congress, Washington, DC.

13. *Rocky Mountain News* (Denver), September 4, 1941. The article on Taylor's perpetual hold on the Fourth Congressional seat is in Box 1, folder 53, Edward T. Taylor Papers, CSHS; Silmon Smith to E. L. Dutcher, August 9, 1941, Box 3, folder 7, Silmon Smith Papers, CSHS.

14. Silmon Smith to Walter Walker, February 24, 1948, Box 4, folder 3, Silmon Smith Papers, CSHS; *Rocky Mountain News* September 4, 1941.

15. CRWCD Minutes, July 16, 1940, folder "CRWCD Minutes, 1940–41"; CRWCD Minutes, January 18, 1944, folder "CRWCD Minutes, 1943–44"; both CRWCD, Glenwood Springs, CO. As far back as 1938, Edward Taylor was working against federal appropriations for a Blue River survey, something he referred to as "the Bannister Scheme" after L. Ward Bannister, the notable Denver water attorney who had long advocated for the project. See Edward T. Taylor to Frank Delaney, Silmon Smith, and Dan Hughes, December 27, 1937, Box 168, folder 2, Frank Delaney Papers, University of Colorado at Boulder Archives (hereafter UCBA); Patricia Nelson Limerick with Jason L. Hanson, *A Ditch in Time: The City, the West, and Water* (Golden, CO: Fulcrum, 2012), 142–46.

16. Frank Delaney to Edward T. Taylor, March 3, 1938, Box 168, folder 2, Frank Delaney Papers, UCBA.

17. CRWCD Minutes, October 15, 1940, folder "CRWCD Minutes, 1940–41," CRWCD, Glenwood Springs, CO.

18. Frank Delaney to Frank C. Merriell, October 23, 1940, folder "River District WCPA, Basin States Water Law, Reserved Right, W. Colorado, etc."; CRWCD Minutes, October 15, 1940, folder "CRWCD Minutes, 1940–41"; both CRWCD, Glenwood Springs, CO.

19. CRWCD Minutes, July 20, 1943, folder "CRWCD Minutes, 1942–43," CRWCD, Glenwood Springs, CO.

20. CRWCD Minutes, January 19, 1943; CRWCD Minutes, July 20, 1943; CRWCD Minutes, October 11, 1943, all in folder "CRWCD Minutes, 1942–43," CRWCD, Glenwood Springs, CO.

21. CRWCD Minutes, January 19, 1943.

22. Ibid.

23. Clifford Stone, Statement to Committee of 14, Memo of Information in RE: Colorado River Basin, Made at the Request of Governor L. C. Hunt [Wyoming], by L. C. Bishop, Wyoming State Water Engineer, June 1, 1944, folder "Source Material, CWCB Minutes, RE: TMDCRD," CRWCD, Glenwood Springs, CO.

24. Colorado River Conservation Board Minutes, March 26–28, 1945, Box 4, folder 5, Silmon Smith Papers, CSHS.

25. Harvey, *Symbol of Wilderness*, 42–43; US Bureau of Reclamation, *The Colorado River, "A Natural Menace Becomes a Natural Resource": A Comprehensive Report on the Development of the Water Resources of the Colorado River Basin for Irrigation, Power Production, and Other Beneficial Uses in Arizona, California, Colorado, Nevada, New Mexico, Utah, and Wyoming* (Washington, DC: Department of the Interior, 1946), 15–17, 107.

26. US Bureau of Reclamation, *Colorado River*.

27. Upper Colorado River Basin Compact, Hearings before a Subcommittee on Irrigation and Reclamation, Committee on Public Lands, House of Representatives,

81st Congress, 1st Session, on HR 2325–2334, March 14–18, 1949, 24. See the Colorado River Compact, Article 3, section F, which indicates that "the amount which would be borne by each basin may be made in the manner provided in paragraph (g) [which allowed any two signatory states to give notice through their governors to appoint representatives] whose duty it shall be to divide and apportion equitably between the Upper Basin and Lower Basin the beneficial use of the unapportioned water of the Colorado River System, subject to the legislative ratification of the signatory States and the Congress of the United States of America." See the compact in Norris Hundley Jr., *Water and the West: The Colorado River Compact and the Politics of Water in the American West*, 2nd ed. (Berkeley: University of California Press, 2009), 355–56.

28. Most of this information is taken from the comments of CRWCD secretary Frank Merriell to the board of directors, July 16, 1946, CRWCD, Glenwood Springs, CO. See CRWCD Minutes, July 16, 1946, folder "CRWCD Minutes, 1946–47," CRWCD, Glenwood Springs, CO. See also *Kansas v. Colorado*, 185 U.S. 125 (1902); *Wyoming v. Colorado*, 259 U.S. 419 (1922).

29. US Bureau of Reclamation, *Colorado River*, 61–65; Harvey, *Symbol of Wilderness*, 44; Upper Colorado River Basin Compact, Hearings, 24.

30. CRWCD Minutes, July 16, October 15, 1946, folder "CRD Minutes, 1946–47," CRWCD, Glenwood Springs, CO.

31. Ivan C. Crawford, *Water Resources Planning in Colorado* (Denver: Colorado Water Conservation Board, 1957), 43; Jean Brietenstein, "The Upper Colorado River Basin Compact," *State Government* 22 (1949): 214–15; Colorado Water Conservation Board Minutes, September 27–28, 1946, Box 45, folder 12, George A. and James M. Pughe Papers, UCBA.

32. Harvey, *Symbol of Wilderness*, 45.

33. Ibid., 45–46; Justice Gregory Hobbs, "History of Colorado River Law, Development and Use: A Primer and Look Forward"(paper presented at the conference Hard Times on the Colorado River: Drought, Growth, and the Future of the Compact, Natural Resources Law Center, University of Colorado School of Law, Boulder, June 8–10, 2005), 8–9.

34. Upper Colorado River Basin Compact, Hearings, 67–68; Schulte, *Wayne Aspinall*, 49; Harvey, *Symbol of Wilderness*, 45–46.

35. For background on Aspinall's upbringing and early career, see Schulte, *Wayne Aspinall*, 1–36.

36. Wayne N. Aspinall Autobiographical Mss., 55–56, Box 1, Vivian Passer Papers, Colorado Mesa University Archives and Special Collections, Grand Junction; Bernard DeVoto, "Sacred Cows and Public Lands," *Harper's Magazine* (July 1948): 45, 44–45; Schulte, *Wayne Aspinall*, 41–42; Jon M. Cosco, *Echo Park: Struggle for Preservation* (Boulder: Johnson Books, 1995), 25.

37. Schulte, *Wayne Aspinall*, 43; *Daily Sentinel*, October 22 (editorial) and 28, 1948; Robert Rockwell to Silmon Smith, August 6, 1948, Box 4, folder 3, Silmon Smith Papers, CSHS.

38. Wayne Aspinall, Interview with Helen Hansen, Mesa County Oral History Project (OH-473), Part One, Museum of the West, Grand Junction, CO, August 10, 1981; *Daily Sentinel*, September 20 (Truman quotations), November 3, 1948.

39. Quotations in Silmon Smith to Walter Walker, February 24, 1948; Walter Walker to Silmon Smith, March 4, 1948, both in Box 4, folder 3, Silmon Smith Papers, CSHS. On March 8, 1948, Walker expounded upon the late Congressman Taylor's significance to Colorado River matters: "I have no hesitancy in saying that the late Edward T. Taylor had a keener grasp, a greater appreciation of the existing and potential phases of the Colorado River problems than any other man whether he has passed from earthly scenes or is now living. The fact of the matter is that I feel deeply and sincerely that had it not been for Edward T. Taylor, the Colorado River situation today would be far more critical and with a far greater potentiality of danger to our section of the state than exists at this time." See Walter Walker to Silmon Smith, March 8, 1948, Box 4, folder 3, Silmon Smith Papers, CSHS. Also see Silmon Smith to Clifford Stone, April 8, 1948, Box 45, folder 6, George A. and James M. Pughe Papers, UCBA.

40. Richard White, *It's Your Misfortune and None of My Own: A New History of the American West* (Norman: University of Oklahoma Press, 1991), 507, 514–16; CRWCD Minutes, January 16, 1946, folder "Colorado River District Minutes, 1946–47," CRWCD, Glenwood Springs, CO.

41. Marc Reisner, *Cadillac Desert: The American West and Its Disappearing Water*, rev. ed. (New York: Penguin Books, 1993), 145.

4
The Struggle for the CRSP

In a word, there is no water which can be diverted to Eastern Colorado
without interfering with the future development of Western Colorado.

Silmon Smith to Clair Hotchkiss, June 3, 1949[1]

PRELUDE TO A CONFLICT: COLORADO WATER PLANNING IN THE LATE 1940S

By the time the regionally transforming Colorado River Storage Project
(CRSP) was enacted in 1956, Colorado had struggled for more than ten years
to sort through its water difficulties. It took state politicians until 1955–56
to be able to present a semi-united front to the US Congress to ensure that
Colorado could claim its fair share of federal reclamation project monies, as well as monies associated with the CRSP. The greatest casualty of
Colorado's early- to mid-twentieth-century water wars was intrastate trust
and cooperation. It took Colorado until the 1960s to build better working
relationships between the Eastern and Western Slopes. However, even
after that point, distrust rather than open cooperation has been more the

DOI: 10.5876/9781607325000.c004

norm. In Colorado's mid-century water wars, the skirmish lines formed on two fronts: Denver's push for a Blue River diversion project and southeastern Colorado's ongoing plans for what was still known as the Gunnison-Arkansas Project. The Western Slope tried to accomplish three main tasks: to hold the line against further diversions, retain a large share of its own water supply, and put more water to work in western Colorado. Significantly, the Western Slope not only tried to resist these demands for new diversions, but it also started to question the operation and fairness of the Colorado Water Conservation Board (CWCB).

From 1946 to 1950, Colorado's two slopes attempted to solidify their strategic positions. Both halves of the state anticipated a vigorous political fight over the Front Range's impending diversion plans. In 1945, CWCB director Clifford H. Stone advised Western Slope officials that the two diversions, Blue River and Gunnison-Arkansas, were several years away from authorization. The delay was caused by the need to consider the massive planning documents generated by the US Bureau of Reclamation and the need to divide the Upper Colorado River Basin's waters among the states. In the meantime, the two slopes staked out their positions, anticipating that the ratification of an Upper Colorado River Basin Compact would reward Colorado with the majority of the Upper Basin's waters.[2]

Meanwhile, planning for the Gunnison-Arkansas Project also moved forward. The initial Bureau of Reclamation study of the project occurred in 1936. After authorization of the Colorado–Big Thompson Project in 1937, hopes soared along the Arkansas River that it was now southern Colorado's turn to turn on the water taps. After "withering on the vine" during World War II, optimism about the Gunnison-Arkansas Project's fate returned after 1945 as Colorado officials again tried to interest the Bureau of Reclamation in building the project. Initially, however, federal officials showed hesitancy about moving forward with Gunnison-Arkansas because of the extensive national financial commitment to build and complete Colorado–Big Thompson.[3]

In the meantime, political jousting over the next round of water diversions had started across the state. Western Slope water officials had observed that the Denver Water Board had continued what it considered token construction efforts on the proposed tunnel from the town of Dillon to Grants. To complicate matters, a lawsuit over the diversion was expected to be filed. The litigation had the potential to delay the project indefinitely as well as

cloud any attempt to graft the project onto any comprehensive western reclamation bill like the proposed CRSP. At the August 15, 1948, meeting of the
Colorado Water Conservation Board, Grand Junction water attorney Silmon
Smith reiterated what had become a standard Western Slope defense strategy against further diversions. The Delaney Resolution of 1935 and Senate
Document 80 had called for the protection of "present and prospective uses
of water within the [Colorado River] Basin." Western Slope leaders, however,
had long maintained that planning for future diversions could not be done
without first carrying out comprehensive studies of future basin-of-origin
economic needs. The need for such studies had long been a staple in the arsenal of Western Slope water leaders to slow the pace of diversion planning.[4]

Western Colorado's fears over impending water diversions became evident
in other forums as well. Both Silmon Smith and Frank Delaney maintained that
the Bureau of Reclamation had done little to investigate putting more Western
Slope water to use in western Colorado. In April 1948 Smith quoted bureau
representatives who had "stoutly maintained" that "there is no more land in
Western Colorado fit or properly situated for irrigation." Several months later,
Smith returned to this theme by arguing that Bureau of Reclamation funds
"were being lavishly spent to discover ways of diverting water [to the Eastern
Slope] with almost nothing being spent to discover future uses of water in
Western Colorado." At a meeting of the Policy and Review Committee of the
Gunnison-Arkansas Project, Frank Delaney echoed Smith's criticisms of the
Bureau of Reclamation. How could he adequately defend the Western Slope's
water future with so little official study data available to him?[5]

For Silmon Smith, a recent discussion with US Bureau of Mines personnel had awakened him to a new line of argument to help preserve Western
Slope waters. Bureau of Mines officials had informed Smith that in the "reasonably near future" a population of 500,000 would be crowding into western Colorado to assist with the extraction of oil shale. Smith stated, "I have
been shocked at the apparent fact that they [Bureau of Mines officials] have
reached their conclusion with practically no effort or forethought" about the
water needed to sustain such a large operation. Smith's realization foreshadowed a fundamental argument that would be used not only in the late 1940s
but over the next six decades: the necessity of reserving a large supply of
water in western Colorado to meet the needs of an imminent oil shale industry. Eastern Colorado water users would grow weary of the Western Slope's

FIGURE 4.1. Grand Junction attorney Silmon Smith helped shape water rights strategies for the Western Slope from the 1930s to the 1960s. Smith, blessed with dogged determination and an acerbic wit, served on the Western Colorado Protective Association, which helped negotiate a compromise over the Colorado–Big Thompson Project. Later, he served for more than ten years on the Colorado Water Conservation Board. *Courtesy*, Priscilla Mangnall.

steady refrain that a possible oil shale boom dictated the need to store or leave more water in western Colorado. Nevertheless, the oil shale "card" would prove to be one of the most effective arguments in Western Slope officials' water protection toolbox. To prepare for the oil shale boom, Smith had been quantifying the amount of water a full-blown industry would need. A massive oil shale industry had been predicted and anticipated by many Western Slope citizens since the first flourish of the industry in the 1920s. Smith and others believed that reserving water for oil shale–related development was not only prudent but necessary to protect the region's economic future.[6]

Silmon Smith began crusading to "discover definite future uses for this water which we all feel will be necessary for the final development of Western Colorado." In Smith's opinion, the CWCB's chief engineer, R. J. Tipton, had been more responsive to the needs of eastern Colorado than to those of western Colorado. In attempting to quantify the amount of future water the Western Slope would require for anticipated industrial and municipal growth, Tipton was on record saying that a mere 40,000 acre-feet would fill the need. Smith declared, "I have never been convinced that his [Tipton's] familiarity with or interest in Western Colorado and its future was sufficient to base our future upon his advice." Smith envisioned a synthetic fuel industry looming in western Colorado's immediate future. However, the two impending diversions (Blue River and Gunnison-Arkansas] could incapacitate an oil shale industry, causing it to be essentially stillborn.[7]

For decades, Silmon Smith had been accumulating a vast amount of data on Colorado's past, present, and projected water uses. His mistrust of what little data he could extract from Bureau of Reclamation sources drove the Grand Junction attorney harder to develop his own database and complete a study of the water issue. In the spring of 1949 Smith completed his *Analysis of Colorado's Share of the Colorado River and Its Consumptive Use, Present and Potential*. Smith's table started with the theoretical allotment of 7.5 million acre-feet for the Upper Basin. He then subtracted each state's allotment based on the Upper Colorado River Basin Compact, which was being ratified in 1949. Colorado's share was estimated at 51.75 percent of the Upper Basin's share, or 3,855,900 acre-feet. Smith proceeded to estimate current uses for both slopes, including the amount of Western Slope water already diverted to the Front Range (544,000 acre-feet). With that figure, Smith came to the crux of existing and future water wars: with an estimated 1.6 million acre-feet left for Colorado, which areas of the state would receive how much, and what would those regions use the water for?[8]

At this point, Smith arrived at the real point of his exercise: to prove that western Colorado and the Colorado River Basin had no more water to export. Smith proceeded to total the amount of "potential irrigation" needs by major watershed regions, including the Colorado, Gunnison, San Juan, Dolores, Yampa-White, and Little Snake Basins. Smith also attempted to extend his crystal ball by predicting future municipal and industrial needs, including the oil shale / synthetic fuel industries that had started planning for a commercially viable product in the late 1940s. Smith estimated that a well-developed oil shale industry would need 300,000 acre-feet per annum. Finally, if the proposed diversion amounts were added in to future water requirements (Smith listed the Gunnison-Arkansas, Blue River–South Platte, and a proposed Gunnison–Rio Grande diversion in this category), the Grand Junction attorney believed Colorado's share of the river would have a water deficit of more than 685,000 acre-feet. Engineer Frank Merriell had told the river district's board that every figure on Smith's list could likely be debated; however, the engineer regarded the oil shale figures that originated with Boyd Guthrie of the Rifle Oil Shale Experimental Plant "as the firmest thing in the list." Merriell believed that, if anything, Smith's oil shale figure of 300,000 acre-feet per year might be too low.[9]

The timing of Smith's *Analysis* coincided with former Bureau of Reclamation commissioner John Page's visit to Grand Junction. Page, a Nebraska native, had spent a long career in water management beginning with the US Reclamation Service (later renamed Bureau of Reclamation) surveying canal sites in Colorado. Starting in 1911, he worked as an assistant to the Grand Junction city engineer specializing in water issues. Later, he worked for the Boulder Canyon Project, and by 1935 he was heading the Bureau of Reclamation's Engineering Division. In 1936, following the death of Commissioner of Reclamation Elwood Mead, Page became the bureau's acting commissioner, assuming the post of commissioner from 1937 until 1943. In the post–World War II era, Page, living in Denver, worked from time to time as a consulting engineer for the Colorado Water Conservation Board. His appearance in Grand Junction came at the behest of the Grand Junction Chamber of Commerce. Page made it clear that he appeared as an ordinary citizen talking about water and was not speaking the "party line" for any one agency.[10]

Before Page's evening address, the Colorado River Water Conservation District directors held an afternoon meeting in Grand Junction and invited Page to address the group. Page began his remarks by indicating that he was "disturbed" over the Western Slope's reflexive resistance to Front Range diversion plans. As a Coloradan, Page hoped the water would be used somewhere in Colorado, or else it would flow across state lines to be used in California and the Lower Basin. In the evening the former commissioner addressed a chamber of commerce gathering attended by an estimated 570 people. Page astonished his Grand Junction audience with some of his remarks. He told the crowd that western Colorado had little or no need for further water supplies. No additional lands would require irrigation water, and the much ballyhooed oil shale and synthetic fuel industries would need "practically no water." Page flew against local conventional wisdom by doubting that a synthetic fuel industry would ever take wing.[11]

America first became an oil-importing nation in the late 1940s. This development, combined with Cold War defense needs, helped refocus national efforts toward developing an oil shale industry. A related development in the spring of 1949 was a report from W. C. Schroeder, chief of the synthetic fuels branch of the US Bureau of Mines, stating that at the Rifle Oil Shale Experimental Plant, scientists had taken Colorado shale to produce "everything you want, from motor gasoline to any kind of oil you want." Schroeder claimed that the existing processes were "sufficiently good so that they can produce oil from that shale as cheaply as you can get it in many places from the ground." With oil shale seemingly poised to become a commercial entity, the Western Slope wanted to make sure the industry had the water it would need to process the material and support the related growth of domestic infrastructure.[12]

Several years later Tell Ertl, a nationally renowned expert on oil shale, envisioned a "powerhouse" industry employing 80,000, stimulating a direct population growth on the Western Slope of 500,000 people. Ertl predicted that industrialization from oil shale would result in an eventual population of 1 million people along the 100-mile corridor between Glenwood Springs and Grand Junction. However, this impressive growth, which many people on the Western Slope had long predicted, would only occur "if the State of Colorado reserves water in the Colorado River." Ertl's statement, carrying the authority of hard science (he was a professor at Ohio State University), represented the type of information Western Slope water advocates had long desired. More than a year earlier, Frank Delaney had solicited this sort of information from Ertl. At that time Delaney had asked what had become the bottom-line question when it came to oil shale: "How much closer are we to actual [oil shale] development and what is new in the way of processes and additional data as to the use of the water?"[13]

Not only was the problem of reserving water for the synthetic fuel industry a major issue heading into the debate over what form a Colorado River Storage Project would take, but its immense but unrealized potential became a perennial card played often by Western Slope water officials to argue against further trans-mountain diversions. When expansion of the oil shale industry was discussed seriously again in the 1970s, the amount of water the industry needed once again became a contentious statewide issue. In recent years, as discussion of a commercial oil shale industry has predictably returned, the feasibility of a synthetic fuel industry continues to turn on the same two issues: the available technology and the need for an adequate water supply. Oil shale's significance in Colorado's twentieth-century water wars was its ability to shape discussions over statewide water allocations. As a result, the ghost of the hoped-for oil shale industry hovered over Colorado's deliberations concerning what projects to include in the state's requests for the enormous Colorado River Storage Project taking shape in the early 1950s.

Colorado's Battle over the CRSP: The Early Years

The Colorado River Storage Project began to take shape during the late 1940s. In the planning stages since World War II, the origins of the project were embedded in the great growth the Upper Basin states experienced during and after the war. Many states recognized that to accommodate future population and economic growth, it was necessary to collectively use their political influence to work with the Bureau of Reclamation to begin developing their shares of the Colorado River. The bureau had devised a massive plan that contained dams, reservoirs, and power facilities. After several years of tentative planning, by 1950 the Bureau of Reclamation's final blueprints were ready. The legislation would commission at least six high dams and more than fifteen "participating projects." It would also fund studies to determine the feasibility of future water projects. While most residents of the Upper

Colorado River Basin states supported the CRSP in some form, the project was threatened between 1950 and 1956 by several potential roadblocks, including taxpayer outrage at its enormous costs, the rise of a formidable alliance of national conservation groups, and internal discord within the state of Colorado over which projects should be included.[14]

Each half of Colorado had its water dreams invested in some form of a CRSP. Denver and the Front Range hoped to knit a Blue River diversion into the project. The Gunnison-Arkansas Project had always been considered a stand-alone enterprise, but some of its advocates believed the surest path toward authorization might be to fold it into the CRSP. The Western Slope's blueprint for the CRSP was more in line with its traditional needs: to build more storage in the region but with an eye to putting more of this water to use locally. More storage and local uses, the old saying went, offered the best protection against further diversions.

In July 1949 a spokesman for the Bureau of Reclamation, C. B. Jacobson, appeared before the Colorado River Water Conservation District (CRWCD) board and representatives from seven Western Slope counties to address what was already termed the Colorado River Storage Project. Jacobson indicated that Upper Basin states were being asked to select projects to include in the superstructure of the CRSP. The authorization of the huge Echo Park Project in northwestern Colorado and eastern Utah on the Green and Yampa Rivers alone could generate enough income through electricity sales to finance several key participating projects. Jacobson indicated that the bureau hoped to build dams at Echo Park, Split Mountain downstream from Echo Park, Flaming Gorge, Glen Canyon, a dam and reservoir tentatively named Curecanti on the upper reaches of the Gunnison, and Crystal Dam, also on the Gunnison. A dam at Bridgeport on the Gunnison River near Grand Junction was also included in the early plans.[15]

Echo Park, located within Dinosaur National Monument, was generally considered the linchpin of most early drafts of the Colorado River Storage Project. Echo Park was a large, narrow canyon high on the Yampa River near its confluence with the Green, and Bureau of Reclamation engineers deemed it a superb place to generate power while minimizing reservoir evaporation. As early as 1947, Bureau of Reclamation engineers were touting the Echo Park location because it could produce enough revenue from electricity sales to drive other water projects in the Upper Colorado Basin.[16]

The Colorado River Water Conservation Board had been devoting serious study to early Bureau of Reclamation reports outlining the shape of the Colorado River Storage Project. The CRSP would allow the Upper Basin to store vast amounts of water in what were termed Holdover Projects that would enable the four Upper Basin states to better meet their commitment of 75 million acre-feet (on a ten-year average) to the Lower Basin states. The larger Holdover Projects would also generate electricity to supply needed revenues to finance the repayment of both those projects and the smaller Participating Projects. The electricity revenues would be placed in a development account and be used to build the smaller projects (Participating Projects), which in general would not have favorable cost-benefit ratios by themselves. It was each state's responsibility to submit Participating Projects for possible inclusion in the CRSP. The Participating Projects would put water to use in the state and basin for both irrigation and municipal-industrial purposes. "Wherever feasible," the projects would include provisions for hydroelectric power development.[17]

The CWCB held hearings throughout Colorado in early October 1949 to obtain local views on how to shape the CRSP. At the Grand Junction meeting, attendees endorsed both the Echo Park and Gunnison River Reservoirs as project cornerstones. At the Pueblo meeting, longtime Fryingpan-Arkansas advocate Charles J. Biese applauded the entire project but felt certain that "investigations will show that there will be surplus Colorado River Waters within the share allotted Colorado" under the Upper Colorado River Basin Compact. Those surplus waters could be "made available for out of basin diversions to the Eastern Slope." While the Fryingpan-Arkansas Project had always been considered separate from the larger Upper Basin multi-state project, "Fry-Ark" (as it was generally known) advocates believed its turn would come either alongside the passage of CRSP or immediately thereafter. The Eastern Slope appeared ready to pounce on any water deemed "surplus."[18]

In December 1949 Colorado, through the CWCB, offered its comments on the Bureau of Reclamation's CRSP plan, prepared in March. Colorado registered general approval for the plan but had specific requests for inclusion as well as suggestions for changes in the bureau's blueprints. Colorado recommended the construction of two Holdover Project storage units: Echo Park and a large project called at the time the "Gunnison River Development." The exact shape and size of a Gunnison Project remained undetermined in

1949 because many local Gunnison-area citizens wanted either a small project or none at all. Complex negotiations on these points lay ahead. Colorado also asked to have several Participating Projects authorized: Paonia, Smith Fork, Silt, Pine River Extension, Florida, the Little Snake Project, and two units of the La Plata Project.[19]

In 1949, Colorado did not favor construction of the Glen Canyon Dam as one of the Holdover Projects. To Upper Basin states like Colorado, Glen Canyon appeared to offer benefits mainly to the Lower Basin. This was also consistent with Colorado's hopes to see two large reservoirs built that would clearly help Colorado: Echo Park and some to-be-determined structures on the Gunnison River. Colorado's official position as of December 1949 in regard to the Glen Canyon Dam was to support its construction but only after Holdover Projects like Echo Park were first built "higher up in the Basin."[20]

The question would soon be: after all the statewide debate, what projects did Colorado want to include in the CRSP? While the answers should have been relatively simple, no water question in this era could avoid becoming embroiled in the internecine strife that plagued the state over water. Not even the Western Slope could agree on the size and shape and ultimately the location of potential projects. Complicating matters, a large group of Gunnison citizens had started to mobilize against the idea of a large reservoir on the Gunnison River. CRWCD secretary-engineer Frank Merriell believed that without a large Curecanti Project, western Colorado would receive few benefits from the CRSP. Throughout 1951, the struggle with the Gunnison region over the shape and scope of a CRSP reservoir continued. The CRWCD Board of Directors met in Gunnison on April 5, 1951, to try to convince Gunnison citizens to support a large Curecanti Reservoir. Merriell worked to persuade local citizens of the need to sacrifice some free-flowing stream waters rather than see those waters diverted to the Front Range.[21]

The Upper Basin needed to build large storage reservoirs somewhere to meet its Colorado River Compact obligations to the Lower Basin. Echo Park would help, but a large reservoir on the Gunnison River would not only assist in achieving this compact requirement, it would also put more water to work on the Western Slope. The water released from the dam would also ensure ample irrigation water for the downstream Uncompahgre Project, especially later in the season. While some Gunnison River Valley lands would be inundated and thirty or more miles of stream fishing would be lost, new lands would be put into production because of the availability of irrigation waters.[22]

The CRWCD met with the Gunnison Watershed Committee two weeks later. Chaired by local attorney Ed Dutcher, a prominent figure in Gunnison River water matters, the committee indicated that 90–95 percent of Gunnison-area citizens were against any water project. Inundation would destroy twenty-three resorts, flood fine ranchlands near the stream, and bury two small towns (Iola and Sapinero). After Dutcher's appearance, Frank Delaney spoke and warned Gunnison-area residents that without the Curecanti Project, eastern Colorado would soon be trying to divert the Gunnison River to Pueblo and Colorado Springs. As Delaney phrased it, "Pueblo was in on the general scheme to get water away from Western Colorado."[23]

In the midst of this Western Slope squabble over what types of benefits the region should gain under a CRSP, several issues clarified themselves. Western Slope water officials continued to maintain that a large Curecanti Reservoir would not only help the state meet its downriver compact obligations but would also keep the Front Range out of the Gunnison River area. Gunnison citizens could agree with those two goals, but many also embraced a "not in my backyard" mentality. As a result, some momentum was gained for constructing a large reservoir near DeBeque or Bridgeport (also known to some as the Whitewater Project), both near Grand Junction, essentially to take the place of an Upper Gunnison River reservoir. Most western Colorado water advocates did not favor the Bridgeport option, however. It would be too costly, its desert location would have a high evaporation rate, and early studies seemed to indicate that the stored water would be of lower quality. In addition, a costly removal and relocation of a long stretch of Denver and Rio Grande Railroad track would be involved.[24]

Western Slope water officials outside the Gunnison Valley continued to hold out hope that a large reservoir could be built high on the Gunnison River. In a discussion with Henry F. Lake at a board meeting, editor of the *Gunnison News-Champion*, CRWCD secretary Frank Merriell challenged the editor to accompany him to inspect the horrifying impacts of trans-mountain diversion along the headwaters region of the Colorado River. Merriell specifically mentioned the diversions from the Fraser River, Vasquez Creek, and the Colorado–Big Thompson Project. Merriell remarked, "If the Gunnison people saw these diversions working and the hardships they cause they would have a much better idea of what they could afford to put up with to avoid diversion from their country." While many local groups were upset about the impact of a large reservoir on sport fishing, a major diversion such as the Gunnison-Arkansas would essentially destroy all stream fishing, "as it had been and now was, on every mile of stream in the country from which any water was diverted."[25]

While Colorado's CRSP planning process moved haltingly forward, the two major state diversion projects were also being discussed and debated. Both became increasingly tangled in the emerging CRSP debates, and each (the Blue River and Fryingpan-Arkansas Projects)[26] had the potential to undermine statewide unanimity toward the CRSP. By 1951, Denver's plans for the Blue River were being adjudicated in the court system. Western Slope water officials feared that if Denver received the early decrees date it hoped for, western Colorado would be unable to use the waters of Green Mountain Reservoir as originally intended—as replacement water for diversions to the Colorado–Big Thompson Project.[27]

In February 1951 the CRWCD passed a resolution concurring with the report of the statewide Fryingpan-Arkansas Policy and Review Commission, with only slight modifications. Because the Fryingpan-Arkansas report was endorsed by the CRWCD before a comprehensive survey of the Western Slope had taken place, the directors of the CRWCD felt the need to back-track and state that all future diversions would be held to what they believed was a state policy established during the struggle over the Colorado–Big Thompson Project. The policy of compensating water-exporting regions of the state and the need to conduct comprehensive water-use surveys of regions impacted by diversion dated back to the meeting of the State Planning Commission in Denver on June 15, 1935.[28]

THE CRSP, ECHO PARK, AND THE BLUE RIVER DIVERSION

The battle for the CRSP had spawned division not only between Colorado's two slopes but also within the Western Slope. Yet most Western Slope residents agreed with Grand Junction *Daily Sentinel* reporter George Sanford Holmes, who called the CRSP "vital." The CRSP would enable western Colorado to finally achieve industrial and agricultural expansion, "despite efforts by California and eastern Colorado to snatch our water." Without the CRSP, Holmes speculated, the sparsely populated Upper Basin would remain "largely an exploited colonial wilderness." Denver, however, tried to climb onboard the CRSP bandwagon in the early 1950s to receive federal support for its Blue River diversion. This action destroyed any semblance of state unity over participation in the CRSP. Before this issue came to light and could be fully aired, another problem threatened to undermine the entire Colorado River Storage Project: the construction of a large holdover storage unit within Dinosaur National Monument at a place known as Echo Park.[29]

Named by John Wesley Powell during his legendary 1869 exploration of the Green and Colorado Rivers, the Bureau of Reclamation had long regarded Echo Park a superior site for a large holdover reservoir. Secretary of the Interior Oscar Chapman had approved dams at Echo Park and downstream at Split Mountain within Dinosaur National Monument in April 1950. The Colorado River Water Conservation District endorsed the Echo Park unit as part of the CRSP in May 1951. The endorsement was given "in spite of the objections of many 'wildlife' organizations that this reservoir will ruin the monument." The CRWCD mentioned that the monument had been created with the "express understanding" that future water facilities were not to be precluded.[30]

Before an actual CRSP bill could be drafted, however, critics of the Dinosaur dams began to mobilize. Prominent conservationists like Horace Albright, Bernard DeVoto, and Arthur Carhart condemned Chapman's decision. Soon, new voices in the emerging post–World War II conservation movement began to chime in. Howard Zahniser of the Wilderness Society and David Brower, the new executive director of the Sierra Club, proved to be two of the most effective advocates in the struggle against the Dinosaur dams.[31]

The Echo Park controversy also marked the emergence of Fourth Congressional District congressman Wayne N. Aspinall as a national spokesman on water and natural resources issues. The Palisade, Colorado, politician took center stage as the controversy escalated. Initially, Aspinall strongly advocated construction of the two dams. As the conflict progressed and Aspinall's influence on the House Interior Committee grew, he became a voice for compromise, though he still preferred CRSP legislation that provided for at least one or, he hoped, two dams inside the national monument.[32]

Early in the Echo Park struggle, dam foes discovered their most persuasive argument: constructing a dam in a national monument or park would repeat the mistake of the twentieth-century Hetch Hetchy controversy in which John Muir, founder of the Sierra Club, failed to prevent construction of a dam in the lovely Hetch Hetchy Valley in Yosemite National Park. The Hetch Hetchy controversy had influenced the idea that national parklands were, in a sense, sacred spaces. In challenging the Bureau of Reclamation's long-awaited CRSP, the Sierra Club and other conservation groups "hearkened back" to the Hetch Hetchy case for inspiration. One Hetch Hetchy per century was more than enough for the new conservationists of the 1950s. The sanctity of National Park Service lands remained a key argument of dam opponents throughout the Echo Park struggle.[33]

Prior to 1953, Oscar Chapman had vacillated between supporting the Dinosaur National Monument dams versus placing them on hold because of pressure from the environmental community. John Geoffrey Will, secretary of the Upper Colorado River Commission,[34] noted that on two occasions Chapman had assured him that he had not changed his mind about Echo Park. Will's goal in 1952 was to convince the Department of the Interior to release the CRSP project report to the Bureau of the Budget. In a speech to the Paonia (Colorado) Chamber of Commerce in 1952, Will sounded a theme that would damage Colorado's relationship to the developing CRSP legislation over the next four years—the need for state harmony on water matters. In a statement that must have haunted Western Slope audiences, Will argued that instead of tearing each other apart, the state's politicians needed to act "as a unit" to work toward authorization of a large project for the Arkansas River Valley, authorization of "additional water for Denver," and the overall enactment of the CRSP.[35]

Will acknowledged that western Colorado's traditional complaint about being overlooked in the expenditure of reclamation investigation and planning funding remained valid. However, Denver had a legitimate need for more water, and it could expect to receive more from the Western Slope. To this point, Will argued, Denver had not supported the CRSP enthusiastically because there was nothing in the massive bill for the capital city. Denver's substantial political weight could be important to the bill if Denver received some "assurance that its needs for the future will not be overlooked." Will's remarks earned him few friends on the Western Slope, but they correctly anticipated the struggle over Denver's role in the CRSP that would unfold over the next several years.[36]

The Denver Water Board had been considering the Blue River diversion in some form for many decades. In early formulations of the Colorado River

Storage Project, the diversion was often discussed as a possible project but was not included in most potential configurations. One study asserted that the Reclamation Bureau had explicitly advised the Denver Water Board not to push for including Denver-Blue in the CRSP. Water Board attorney Glenn Saunders "had decided to disregard the Bureau's advice and push for its inclusion after 1952." This decision would not only inflame the simmering east-west diversion struggle, but it also threatened to jettison or severely curtail Colorado's overall share of the Colorado River Storage Project.[37]

Water officials in western Colorado continued to take a hard line against trans-basin diversion in the early 1950s. At a November 1951 meeting of the Colorado River Water Conservation District, Silmon Smith, Judge Dan Hughes (a member of the CRWCD Board of Directors), and Frank Delaney spoke about the long-promised Bureau of Reclamation report detailing "present and potential uses of water in western Colorado." Smith believed the bureau had no intention of completing this study and, if it were done, "such a report would show that there was not water enough to serve all the prospective uses." Smith did not believe that water existed for both the proposed Fryingpan-Arkansas diversion and compliance with the 1944 US-Mexico Water Treaty.[38]

Near the end of 1951, Silmon Smith resigned from the CWCB after serving for more than a decade. He left because he believed both the board and the Bureau of Reclamation felt immense "pressure" to respond favorably to the Front Range's requests for more diversions. The constant political pressure "was simply too great" for dissenting members of the CWCB.[39]

Both in the press and in the political arena, Western Slope officials felt increased pressure to answer charges that they were deliberately stalling from committing to further diversions. The traditional argument that western Colorado could not seriously consider any further diversion until the Bureau of Reclamation finished its long-awaited study seemed a transparent stalling attempt to many eastern Coloradans. A more serious charge could have been leveled against western Colorado for endangering the state's participation in the CRSP. Either way, it was time to move ahead with Colorado's water program. Bureau of Reclamation officials met with the CRWCD Board of Directors in January 1952 and reported that the board had found increasing amounts of western Colorado acreage that could be classified as irrigable. Bureau officials noted that they had also located additional reservoir sites and canal locations and examined some of the water needs of the synthetic fuel and oil shale industries.[40]

By mid-1952, the Curecanti Project near Gunnison looked as though it was going to be downsized from a projected 2.5 million acre-feet to slightly less than 1 million acre-feet. This plan was intended to placate local resistance to the large reservoir, yet it would still allow the Western Slope to put more water to work in the Upper Basin. It would also protect some Western Slope water from diversion to the Front Range. The nearby Crystal Dam on the Gunnison would allow the "little Curecanti" configuration to still be worthwhile to Western Slope interests, even if downsized to less than half the "big Curecanti" size. The Curecanti issue had become a major point of contention among western Colorado water planners. It seemed ironic to many that, for once, the Western Slope seemed to have the blessing of the CWCB and the Bureau of Reclamation for a large reservoir, only to face objections from local citizens who would be impacted by the waters. As CRWCD secretary Frank Merriell noted with obvious bitterness, "It's a hell of a note if the rest of us [on the Western Slope] cannot discuss what is best for Western Colorado without having to stop because it would offend the Gunnison people."[41]

THE DEATH OF CLIFFORD H. STONE

Colorado still had decisions to make in regard to project requests for the Colorado River Storage Project. However, some issues were becoming clear. Denver wanted to be included in the project's benefits and was preparing to go against the advice of the Bureau of Reclamation and ask that its Blue River diversion be included among Colorado's CRSP requests. The Western Slope also wanted numerous Participating Projects. The CWCB had worked hard to harmonize the interests of all sections of the state, largely through the untiring labors of the only director the CWCB had ever had: Gunnison's Clifford H. Stone. Stone had the respect of his Western Slope colleagues, and his national reputation as a reclamation expert afforded him some insulation from Front Range political criticism. Stone had the ability to do what he had been asked to do when he took the difficult job of leading the CWCB—keep Colorado's statewide interests paramount while trying to placate sectional interests.

In the fall of 1952, all the goodwill and trust Stone had engendered in fifteen years of work was suddenly threatened when word reached Colorado that Stone, age sixty-four, had suffered a fatal heart attack while attending a conference in New Orleans on October 22, 1952. The *Rocky Mountain News* referred to Stone as the West's "top-ranking water expert," adding that the law of the river that governed the Colorado River "was developed largely under his guidance." Colorado governor Dan Thornton noted that Stone had authored his own epitaph, which is "written in the history of our water conservation program since 1937." On the day of Stone's death, Colorado water officials immediately began assessing his legacy and, perhaps more important, the implications of his passing. Frank Merriell remarked that "it is damn sad news for us [the Western Slope] that Clifford Stone is no more with us. I do not know anybody who can fill the job and am only afraid it will be someone from Eastern Colorado, which would about complete our ruin."[42]

Most Western Slope water officials believed Stone had been the one person at the state level who always gave western Colorado a fair hearing. He was sometimes seen as the one huge obstacle against the untiring efforts of eastern Colorado to dispossess the Colorado River Basin of its remaining waters. Two days after Stone's death, Montrose attorney Charles J. Moynihan began lobbying for the appointment of Frank Delaney as Stone's successor. The Western Slope simply could not afford to leave Stone's successor "to chance or to the Eastern Slope." Moynihan believed eastern Colorado was already maneuvering to take control of the water board entirely away from the Western Slope. As Moynihan recalled in a letter to Delaney, "I was present with you in Denver when we had our first conference [in the mid-1930s] in connection with any possible plan to divert Western Slope water to the Eastern Slope" as part of what became the Colorado–Big Thompson Project. "Ed Taylor," Moynihan remembered, "led the way and saved our skins." Silmon Smith, who had served alongside Stone for eleven years on the CWCB, joined Moynihan in trying to induce Delaney to step forward and fill Stone's job. Delaney denied any interest in the position, undoubtedly recognizing both the amount of energy the thankless job would entail as well as his standing as a longtime Western Slope partisan. Both factors would have made the job difficult for Delaney.[43]

In the months following Stone's death, the Western Slope realized the precarious political position in which it found itself. Almost immediately, Merriell predicted that Stone's demise would result in "a more active and insistent demand for trans-basin diversion, which it will be harder for

Western Colorado to resist than when he was in command." Smith, Delaney, and Merriell made rapid connections between Stone's death and Eastern Slope moves to gain additional water. A "rational approach" to Colorado water questions would be "harder now" with Stone gone, Delaney remarked in June 1953. Delaney admitted that despite being on its guard, the Western Slope had not foreseen all of the Eastern Slope's political maneuvering that followed in the wake of Stone's death. As for the CWCB, without Stone "we shall get no help . . . where we can be constantly outvoted." While the Western Slope still hoped for a definitive study of its water availability and future water needs, without a leader at the helm of the CWCB who was sympathetic to its needs, little could realistically be expected.[44]

In 1953, Denver's sudden move to include the Blue River diversion as part of the Colorado River Storage Project sparked the next phase of Colorado's mid-century water wars. As one scholar assessed this development, "Denver shocked Colorado and the rest of the upper basin with its proposal" to build a "Blue River Unit" at a meeting of the Upper Colorado River Commission in Cheyenne, Wyoming, in early 1953 as part of the CRSP. The "Denver scheme," as Grand Junction *Daily Sentinel* newspaper reporter William Nelson quickly dubbed it, was met with a fast negative response from western Colorado.[45]

The *Denver Post* heralded the Denver Water Board's action in Cheyenne as a "dramatic and historic move." The move seemed justified to many on the Front Range because recent studies had revealed that at its current growth rate, Denver would exhaust its water supplies by 1962. The DWB press release noted that the only water available to the city was "diversion . . . from the tributaries of the Colorado." Denver also emphasized that by asking to join with the CRSP, it would throw its full political support behind the measure, which to this point only included Western Slope features for the state of Colorado. The strongest journalistic reaction from western Colorado came from Grand Junction's *Daily Sentinel*. "Show us, Denver," the *Sentinel* demanded, that the "transmountain diversion game will injure no [western Colorado] interest," as DWB attorney Glenn Saunders had asserted in Cheyenne on January 30, 1953. Potential damage to the Green Mountain Reservoir loomed large in the *Sentinel*'s criticism of Denver's actions. The newspaper also criticized Denver's choice to announce the move to the Upper Colorado River Commission rather than first gaining the approval of the Colorado Water Conservation Board.[46]

Denver's proposal to the Upper Colorado River Commission was made by Nicholas R. Petry, president of the Denver Water Board. It did not follow what by 1953 was standard Colorado water-planning protocol—to first have potential project proposals studied and approved by the Colorado Water Conservation Board. To most Western Slope water officials, Denver's actions demonstrated an unusually cavalier attitude toward the rest of the state. Less than two years before this time, the CWCB had passed the Frying Pan–Arkansas settlement (Operating Principles) that forbade further trans-mountain diversions until the long-promised studies of western Colorado water availability and economic planning were completed. In early February 1953 it still remained to be seen if the CWCB would endorse Denver's water proposal.[47]

Upper Colorado River Commission executive secretary John Geoffrey Will had lobbied to include the Blue River diversion in Colorado's CRSP requests. Will revealed his logic in a confidential letter to Frank Delaney on February 5, 1953, six days after Denver officially announced its intent to include the diversion in the CRSP legislation. Denver's political support was crucial to gain passage of a strong CRSP bill for Colorado and the other Upper Basin states. Denver had been "extremely cool" toward the CRSP until it began discussing the possibility of adding the Blue River diversion to the CRSP as a Participating Project. Will believed he had successfully convinced Denver to go after a modest-sized diversion for municipal water-supply enhancement only. Overall, Will believed that while the Western Slope would be losing some water, what it would gain would more than make up for any loss: political support for the entire CRSP program and more political pressure available to press the Bureau of Reclamation for both surveys and funding.[48]

The Colorado Water Conservation Board met on February 16, 1953, to consider Denver's request for including the Blue River diversion among Colorado's recommended CRSP projects. Western Slope water officials resolved to make a strong showing in an attempt to stifle the capital city's request. Water correspondent William Nelson listed a long series of arguments western Colorado officials could use against Denver at the CWCB meeting. Nelson believed Denver's proposed project was slated for municipal water purposes only, which might violate long-standing Bureau of Reclamation policy; that the Blue River diversion was already being fought over in the state and federal courts; and that the 1951 CWCB agreement to hold off on further diversions (after Frying Pan–Arkansas) would be violated. Nelson also underscored the diversion's threat to Green Mountain Reservoir, "built with taxpayers' money." If Green Mountain Reservoir was compromised, the workings of the Colorado–Big Thompson Project might be endangered. Nelson also saw both threats and injustice to planned and authorized Western Slope projects if this large, potentially expensive diversion was included in the CRSP. What would happen to the smaller Paonia, Smith Fork, Silt, and Collbran Projects? Finally, Nelson could not help adding, tongue-in-cheek: "Is this a case of Eastern Colorado trying to stage a Munich? Remember Hitler in 1938 declared, 'I want no more territory.' While he spoke, his generals planned World War II to grab the world."[49]

Matters between Colorado's two slopes came to a head in mid-February 1953. By then, Delaney had met in person with the DWB's counsel, Glenn Saunders, about Denver's plans; the two men engaged in a momentous showdown featuring verbal fireworks during a February 16, 1953, meeting of the Colorado Water Conservation Board. On the eve of the meeting at which Denver's proposal would be discussed and acted upon, Colorado governor Dan Thornton had framed the gathering as a vital "crossroads" in Colorado's water history. "Our future is at stake," Thornton warned. "I have great fear as to our success in securing any one of the three projects [CRSP, Denver-Blue, and Fryingpan-Arkansas] in the event there is substantial opposition from within Colorado."[50]

THE CONFERENCE COMMITTEE AND THE HILL REPORT

During the February 16, 1953, CWCB meeting, Frank Delaney had argued against the inclusion of Denver's diversion in the CRSP on several grounds, including the 1951 CWCB resolution forbidding further trans-basin diversions until a thorough study of the Western Slope's water needs had been completed. Glenn Saunders responded, noting that the CWCB had been created to promote all of Colorado's water interests and, furthermore, Denver would only need federal support as a loan—the city would ultimately repay the money for the diversion's costs. The meeting had reached an impasse. Western Colorado remained unalterably opposed to allowing Denver to proceed with the Blue River diversion as part of the CRSP, especially since litigation over the matter was still before the Colorado Supreme Court. Denver believed its future was tied to the diversion. Sensing no immediate resolution of the dispute, the next day the CWCB voted to authorize a five-member Conference Committee to oversee a detailed survey of future water needs for the state of Colorado. Until the survey was finished and its results had been considered, Colorado would continue to withhold its approval of projects considered for inclusion in the Colorado River Storage Project. Colorado's intramural water war was literally delaying the CRSP in its entirety. The Conference Committee was composed of two members from each slope and a chair, George Bailey of Walden in North Park. Eastern Slope representatives were Nicholas R. Petry of the Denver Water Board and H. H. Christy of Pueblo. The Western Slope representatives were Robert Delaney (Frank Delaney's nephew and law partner) and George Cory of Montrose.[51]

Trying to chart a strategy, Western Slope water officials had gathered in Grand Junction in early February and vowed to oppose Denver's Blue River diversion in the CRSP legislation. At the January 30 CWCB Board of Directors meeting, Western Slope members decided not to let the inclusion of Denver's project be submitted to a vote. Instead, after extensive caucusing, the CWCB agreed to appoint the Conference Committee. In a letter to Congressman Wayne Aspinall, the CRWCD's Frank Merriell called the water board "a discredited agency . . . [we] evidently cannot put any dependence in their word" since the board had repudiated its 1951 "no-more-diversion" pledge.[52]

In the midst of the state's water turmoil, following the January 30 meeting Governor Thornton acted to appoint a successor to Clifford Stone as director of the water board. It was clear to many Coloradans that much of the early 1953 escalation in the state's water wars could be traced to Stone's death and the ensuing water leadership vacuum. Thornton decided to appoint Boulder's Ivan C. Crawford to the post. A Leadville native, Crawford had recently retired as dean of the University of Michigan's engineering school. Crawford proved to be a weak leader when compared with Stone, and he would be unable or unwilling to stand up to the overwhelming political pressure applied by the Front Range to pursue more diversions.[53]

While the CWCB could recommend a study, it remained for the Colorado General Assembly to pass legislation and an appropriation to make the Conference Committee and its study a reality. Toward that end, the 39th Colorado General Assembly passed HB 457 in March 1953 to try to attempt what the Western Slope had been demanding from the Bureau of Reclamation for several decades: to make a "study of the water resources available from surface water supplies in that part of Colorado which rise[s] west of the Continental Divide, and a study of the present and potential uses thereof to the full extent necessary to a unified and harmonious development of those waters for beneficial use in Colorado to the fullest extent under the law." The CWCB Conference Committee would select and supervise the engineers charged with making the study. The state appropriation ($100,000) also provided for an industrial survey of western Colorado to be conducted by experts from the University of Colorado at Boulder. It was hoped that the studies would silence Western Slope critics who continued to allege that their water needs had never been adequately assessed.[54]

Prior to the formation of the Conference Committee, western Colorado water officials had begun to see the handwriting on the wall: continuing to follow a policy of absolute opposition to further Front Range diversions would be difficult. In early 1953, Frank Delaney concluded that the CWCB would not protect Western Slope interests with Crawford in charge. Perhaps even more problematical, Jean S. Breitenstein, the state water board's attorney, now dominated its policy directions. Breitenstein's advice was closely followed by the new CWCB director, Ivan Crawford. "It is my judgment that [Breitenstein] and the little group that are now dominating the policies of the Water Board want Denver and the Eastern Slope to get everything regardless of the effect it has on the future of Western Colorado," Delaney asserted in a letter to Colorado senator Ed Johnson in May 1953. At the time the Conference Committee was receiving its charge from the Colorado General Assembly, Governor Dan Thornton issued a statement that many in western Colorado construed as constituting open support for the Blue River diversion. Western Colorado had started to feel powerless in the face of the combined power of the Front Range, the reconfigured CWCB, and the governor.[55]

The CWCB and its Conference Committee considered many engineering firms to conduct the water survey, striking some applicants from the list because of close ties to one side of the state or the other. After careful deliberation the committee chose Raymond A. Hill of Los Angeles to conduct the study, from the firm Leeds, Hill, and Jewitt. The engineers targeted November 1, 1953, for its study completion date. Frank Delaney immediately expressed doubts about the short, six-month time frame for Hill to conduct the study. This would necessarily be a "hasty report" and may or may not do justice to the present and future needs of the Western Slope. Clearly, Delaney believed the Western Slope was taking a big chance by following the path of the Hill Report. Delaney had other concerns as well. If the report really did appear as scheduled in late October 1953, would the Western Slope have enough time to digest its implications and formulate an adequate response to its conclusions?[56]

Many Western Slope officials believed the Hill Report process had been controlled from the start by the Front Range, particularly the Denver Water Board. The same conspiracy-minded western Coloradans saw the study as an exercise to build political momentum for the Blue River diversion and its possible inclusion as one of Colorado's CRSP projects. Frank Delaney anticipated that the Hill Report's conclusions would be amenable to Front Range water planning. With Breitenstein, Crawford, and Will dominating the CWCB, little attention seemed to be paid to the "wishes or desires of the [sic] Western Colorado." In a letter to Frank Merriell, Delaney stated this even more strongly: Breitenstein, Will, Saunders, and "the other boys who are supposed to be influential in water matters . . . commenced to plot immediately after the death of Cliff Stone just how they would seek to rob us of our water."[57]

While western Colorado prepared for the worst, the *Denver Post* reflected the surging optimism emanating from Denver following the authorization of the Conference Committee and the Hill Report. The Western Slope, according to the *Post*, should be pleased that its water was finally receiving the careful study and analysis western Colorado has long asked for: "If the study shows the Western Slope has more water than she needs, Denver and the eastern slope will expect to be allowed to go ahead with plans for the diversion." However, "If the study shows the western slope needs all of Colorado's still unused Colorado River water, talk of further diversions to the eastern slope would be futile." The *Post* concluded that for the Western Slope, the "hour of decision" for its water future was at hand. A great deal indeed seemed to be riding on the outcome of the Hill Report.[58]

THE WESTERN SLOPE'S "HOUR OF DECISION" HAS ARRIVED

The 1952 election spelled the end of twenty years of Democratic presidential rule and also signified, as the *Denver Post* indicated, a crossroads in Colorado's twentieth-century water wars. The next four years would witness the struggle to enact the CRSP and also mark the emergence of the conservation community as a shaping force in national reclamation policy. The struggle for a dam within Dinosaur National Monument would be a "conservation crucible." Yet a new element would be added to the mix that would threaten Colorado's hopes for favorable consideration in the battle for the CRSP: Denver's plan to add the Blue River diversion to the state's package of CRSP projects. Following Bureau of Reclamation official O. E. Larson's presentation on the status of the CRSP at the October 20, 1953, meeting of the CRWCD, Frank Delaney took the floor and offered his reaction to recent events based on "thirty-seven years of experience in water matters." Throughout that long duration, Delaney had observed many things "proposed ostensibly for the benefit of Western Colorado that had turned out to be primarily for the use of Eastern Colorado in the diversion of more water." Citing examples of this trend, Delaney mentioned that immediately after the signing of the Upper Colorado River Basin Compact, the Bureau of Reclamation stood ready with reports endorsing two massive trans-basin diversions: Blue–South Platte and Gunnison-Arkansas. These issues had inflamed the state's water wars for almost a decade.[59]

The convening of the CWCB Conference Committee and the commissioning of the Hill Report had propelled the conflict between the two slopes to a higher level of contention. Raymond Hill was a distinguished hydrologist with a sterling record. Yet the Western Slope distrusted any study of Colorado's water supply that bore the fingerprints of the Denver Water Board and Front Range water interests. The loss of Clifford Stone and the impending Fryingpan-Arkansas diversion also contributed to the conspiratorial mind-set of western Colorado's water politicians. The Western Slope felt itself being "boxed into a corner" by the political power of eastern Colorado.

From the perspective of the early 1950s, the Front Range had strong advantages in Colorado's water wars. Not only did it appear to have the ear of the Bureau of Reclamation (at least from the perspective of the Western Slope), but its population had grown tremendously during World War II and in its aftermath. Denver was nicknamed the "second national capital" because of the number of federal agencies located there. Southern Colorado was also growing fast, and the Colorado Springs region had become a favorite place for the US military to build bases and command centers such as Fort Carson, the North

American Air Defense Command, and the Air Force Academy. The Rocky Flats Nuclear Weapons Plant opened in 1951 between Golden and Boulder. A host of private-sector defense contractors also had a huge presence on the Front Range, including Martin Marietta, Honeywell, IBM, Hewlett-Packard, and others. The Front Range's burgeoning growth and its place in the nation's Cold War defense needs gave it strong advantages in the bid for more water.[60]

The Western Slope, too, had demonstrated some impressive growth after World War II, emerging as an important region in the nation's Cold War American West. Western Colorado continued to articulate some of the same arguments it had been making for decades to hold on to its water—it had been promised thorough studies of its future water needs, it was just beginning to mature economically, and its oil shale potential made the region vital to the nation's short- and long-term energy future. Yet the Western Slope continued to face the same dilemma it had always experienced in its struggles with the Front Range: the western half of Colorado had the lion's share of the state's water supply but a shrinking share of the political power. While it was growing, eastern Colorado was growing faster. As a result, the pressure to submit to demands to relinquish more water through the CRSP, the Denver-Blue Project, and the Fryingpan-Arkansas Project would only increase in the years ahead.

NOTES

1. Silmon Smith to Clair Hotchkiss, June 3, 1949, Box 4, folder 4, Silmon Smith Papers, Colorado State Historical Society (hereafter CSHS), Denver.

2. CRWCD Minutes, April 16, 1945, folder "Colorado River District Minutes, 1945–46," Colorado River Water Conservation District (hereafter CRWCD), Glenwood Springs, CO.

3. Carol Jean Drake Mehls, "Into the Frying Pan: J. Edgar Chenoweth and the Fryingpan-Arkansas Reclamation Project" (PhD dissertation, University of Colorado–Boulder, 1986), 116–20.

4. Colorado Water Conservation Board (CWCB) Minutes, August 15, 1948, folder "East-West Position, CWCB-TMD," CRWCD, Glenwood Springs, CO.

5. Storage water to replace water transported over and through the mountains to the Front Range. See Silmon Smith to Clifford Stone, April 8, 1948, Box 45, folder 6; Silmon Smith to Hume S. White, November 19, 1948, Box 45, folder 10; Minutes of Meeting, Policy and Review Committee, Gunnison-Arkansas Project, November

24, 1948, all in George A. and James M. Pughe Papers, University of Colorado–Boulder Archives (hereafter UCBA).

6. Silmon Smith to Walter Walker, February 24, 1948, Box 4, folder 3, Silmon Smith Papers, CSHS.

7. Silmon Smith, *Analysis of Colorado's Share of the Colorado River and Its Consumptive Use, Present and Potential,* Box 2, folder 3; Silmon Smith to George Pughe, May 2, 1949, Box 4, folder 4, both in Silmon Smith Papers, CSHS.

8. Smith, *Analysis of Colorado's Share of the Colorado River.*

9. Ibid.; Frank C. Merriell to Clifford Stone, April 19, 1949, Box 170, folder 11, Frank Delaney Papers, UCBA.

10. See Page's biography in http://www.usbr.gov/history/CommissBios/page.html; also see Mark Reisner, *Cadillac Desert: The American West and Its Disappearing Water,* rev. ed. (New York: Penguin Books, 1993), 143, for comments on Page's leadership of the Bureau of Reclamation; "John Chatfield Page, 1887–1955," Vertical File, Loyd Files Research Library, Museum of the West, Grand Junction, CO.

11. CRWCD Minutes, April 19, 1949, folder "CRWCD Minutes, 1948–49," CRWCD, Glenwood Springs, CO; Silmon Smith to Clifford Stone, April 20, 1949, Box 4, folder 4, Silmon Smith Papers, CSHS.

12. Frank C. Merriell to Hume S. White, October 11, 1953; Robert Delaney to Frank C. Merriell, October 1953; Silmon Smith to Robert Delaney, October 14, 1953, Box 5, folder 6, all in Silmon Smith Papers, CSHS; Schroeder cited in *Daily Sentinel,* April 6, 1949.

13. Tell Ertl, "Water Requirements of Western Colorado because of the Establishment of an Oil Shale Industry," July 17, 1953; Frank Delaney to Tell Ertl, February 2, 1952, both in Box 168, folder 19, Frank Delaney Papers, UCBA.

14. Steven C. Schulte, *Wayne Aspinall and the Shaping of the American West* (Boulder: University Press of Colorado, 2002), 57; Mark W.T. Harvey, *A Symbol of Wilderness: Echo Park and the American Conservation Movement* (Seattle: University of Washington Press, 1994), 22.

15. CRWCD Minutes, July 28, 1949, folder "CRWCD Minutes, 1948–49," CRWCD, Glenwood Springs, CO; Proceedings of the Meeting of the Colorado River Basin States Committee, December 3, 1947, Box 9, no folder, Silmon Smith Papers, CSHS; Harvey, *Symbol of Wilderness,* 17, 29–30.

16. Harvey, *Symbol of Wilderness,* 17.

17. Comments of the State of Colorado Concerning "Interim Report," Colorado River Storage Project and Participating Projects Dated March 1949, Prepared by the Regional Director of Region IV, Bureau of Reclamation, Department of the Interior, Box 3, folder 41, William Nelson Papers, Colorado Mesa University Archives and Special Collections (hereafter CMUASC), Grand Junction; Colorado River

Storage Project, Hearings before the Subcommittee on Irrigation and Reclamation, House Committee on Interior and Insular Affairs, House of Representatives, 83rd Congress, 2nd sess., on HR 4449, 4443, and 4463 to Authorize the Secretary of the Interior to Construct, Operate, and Maintain the Colorado River Storage Project and Participating Projects and for Other Purposes, January 18–28, 1954.

18. Minutes of Hearings of Colorado Water Conservation Board held in Craig, October 3, 1949, Grand Junction, October 4, 1949, Durango, October 6, 1949, Pueblo, October 8, 1949, and Denver, October 10, 1949, Box 10, folder 1, Silmon Smith Papers, CSHS.

19. Comments of the State of Colorado Concerning "Interim Report."

20. Ibid. Two dams were actually proposed for Dinosaur National Monument: the large Echo Park Dam and a smaller dam downstream on the Green River at Split Mountain. See Harvey, *Symbol of Wilderness*, 89–91.

21. CRWCD Minutes, January 18, 1951; Meeting of the Board of Directors, CRWCD, April 5, 1951, both in folder "CRWCD Minutes 1950–51," CRWCD, Glenwood Springs, CO.

22. CRWCD Minutes, January 18, 1951; Meeting of the Board of Directors, CRWCD, April 5, 1951.

23. Meeting of the Board of Directors, CRWCD, with the Gunnison Watershed Committee, April 16, 1951, folder "CRWCD Minutes, 1950–51," CRWCD, Glenwood Springs, CO.

24. CRWCD Minutes, May 29, 1951, folder "CRWCD Minutes, 1950–51," CRWCD, Glenwood Springs, CO.

25. Ibid.

26. In 1950 the Gunnison-Arkansas Project was renamed the Fryingpan-Arkansas Project after it had undergone some significant reconfigurations. See CRWCD Minutes, January 17, 1950, folder "CRWCD Minutes, 1950–51," CRWCD, Glenwood Springs, CO.

27. CRWCD Minutes, February 19, 1951, folder "CRWCD Minutes, 1950–51," CRWCD, Glenwood Springs, CO.

28. Ibid.

29. This originated in a draft of a news story written by George Sanford Holmes, the *Daily Sentinel*'s Washington correspondent. See n.d., 1952, Box 3, folder 41, William Nelson Papers, CMUASC, Grand Junction.

30. Meeting of the Board of Directors of the CRWCD, May 29, 1951, folder "CRWCD Minutes, 1950–51," CRWCD, Glenwood Springs, CO; Harvey, *Symbol of Wilderness*, 89–91. Other studies give solid background to the Echo Park controversy. See John M. Cosco, *Echo Park: Struggle for Preservation* (Boulder: Johnson Books,

1995); Elmo R. Richardson, *Dams, Parks, and Politics: Resource Development in the Truman-Eisenhower Era* (Lexington: University of Kentucky Press, 1973).

31. Harvey, *Symbol of Wilderness*, discusses the criticism of Echo Park from the emerging conservation movement in many places throughout his study.

32. Schulte, *Wayne Aspinall*, 58; *Daily Sentinel* (Grand Junction, CO), August 17, 1951. The proposed dam lay within Aspinall's vast congressional district.

33. Robert W. Righter, *The Battle over Hetch Hetchy: America's Most Controversial Dam and the Birth of Modern Environmentalism* (New York: Oxford University Press, 2005), 191–93. The Hetch Hetchy controversy, Righter argued, influenced the enactment of the 1916 National Park Service's Organic Law, "the touchstone for managing the parks." According to the 1916 act, the agency's lands were to be managed "to conserve the scenery and natural and historic objects and the wildlife therein to provide for the enjoyment of the same in such manner and by such means as will leave them unimpaired for the enjoyment of future generations." Harold Bradley, a stalwart member of the Sierra Club who helped alert the organization to the impending disaster at Echo Park, thought the Echo Park struggle was similar to Hetch Hetchy, that "indeed, the two situations are so much alike that the campaign literature on both sides might be interchanged, with the appropriate names added." See Harvey, *Symbol of Wilderness*, 57; Schulte, *Wayne Aspinall*, 58.

34. Formed in the aftermath of the passage and ratification of the Upper Colorado River Basin Compact of 1948, the Upper Colorado River Commission was an interstate administrative agency composed of one commissioner representing each of the states of the Upper Colorado River Basin: Colorado, New Mexico, Utah, and Wyoming. One commissioner, appointed by the president of the United States, represented the interests of the federal government.

35. John Geoffrey Will, Report of the Secretary of the Upper Colorado River Commission, March 17, 1952; John Geoffrey Will, "Remarks of John Geoffrey Will to Paonia, Colorado Chamber of Commerce," ca. April 1952, both in Box 3, folder 44, William Nelson Papers, CMUASC, Grand Junction.

36. Will, "Remarks of John Geoffrey Will."

37. Saunders quoted in ibid.; Matthew Hildner, "Fight for the Faucet: The Denver Water Board, the Blue River, and the Metropolitan Water Supply" (MA thesis, Colorado State University, Fort Collins, 1999), 42; Patricia Nelson Limerick with Jason L. Hanson, *A Ditch in Time: The City, the West, and Water* (Golden: Fulcrum, 2012), 143.

38. CRWCD Minutes, November 10, 1951, folder "CRWCD Minutes, 1950–51," CRWCD, Glenwood Springs, CO.

39. Ibid.

40. CRWCD Minutes, January 22, 1952, folder "CRWCD Minutes, 1952–55," CRWCD, Glenwood Springs, CO.

41. CRWCD Minutes, April 15, 1952, July 12, 1952, folder "CRWCD Minutes, 1952–55," CRWCD, Glenwood Springs, CO; Frank C. Merriell to Frank Delaney, November 22, 1951, Box 169, folder 17, Frank Delaney Papers, UCBA.

42. *Rocky Mountain News* (Denver), October 23, 1952; Frank C. Merriell to Frank Delaney, October 22, 1952, Box 169, folder 18, Frank Delaney Papers, UCBA.

43. Charles J. Moynihan to Frank Delaney, October 24, 1952, Box 169, folder 4, Frank Delaney Papers, UCBA. Also see the correspondence surrounding Delaney's possible appointment to the CWCB director's position in Box 5, folder 6, Silmon Smith Papers, CSHS.

44. Frank C. Merriell to Hume S. White, October 29, 1952, Box 169, folder 18, Frank Delaney Papers, UCBA; CRWCD Minutes, April 28, 1953, folder "CRWCD Minutes, 1952–55," CRWCD, Glenwood Springs, CO; Frank Delaney to Frank C. Merriell, June 17, 1953, Box 170, folder "Water Correspondence Delaney-Merriell," Frank Delaney Papers, UCBA.

45. Hildner, "Fight for the Faucet," 43; William Nelson to W. M. Wood, February 2, 1953, Box 10, folder 20, William Nelson Papers, CMUASC, Grand Junction.

46. *Denver Post*, January 30, 1953; "Show Us Denver," ms. of *Daily Sentinel* article, Box 3, folder 41, William Nelson Papers, CMUASC, Grand Junction; press release mentioned in an article in the *Denver Post*, January 30, 1953.

47. William Nelson to W. M. Wood, February 2, 1953. In a letter to Frank C. Merriell written the same day (February 2, 1953), Nelson, who had been present in Cheyenne at the meeting of the Upper Colorado River Commission, submitted a detailed list of arguments the Western Slope could use against Denver's proposal. Included on this list were such ideas as the following: Denver's proposal was so huge that it was likely that all CRSP plans to date would need to be revised to take the Blue River diversion into account; "this is not the time to reopen the water war. Proposing a Denver diversion can do no less"; the Blue River–South Platte case remained in open litigation at the state and federal levels. "How can we justify a diversion until those cases are settled"; finally, the major argument the Western Slope had been putting forth for several years in opposition to the Blue River diversion—that the diversion (if it gets an early date) could undermine the purpose of the Green Mountain Reservoir, built for Western Slope compensatory storage as part of the Colorado–Big Thompson Project "with taxpayers' money." See William Nelson to Frank C. Merriell, February 2, 1953, Box 10, folder 20, William Nelson Papers, CMUASC.

48. John Geoffrey Will to Frank Delaney, February 5, 1953, Box 75, folder 15, Frank Delaney Papers, UCBA. After making his case to gain Delaney's support for

including Denver in the CRSP, Will concluded by saying that "the foregoing ought to be enough to satisfy you that there is ample water for an additional modest exportation to Denver, without the slightest risk to the Western Slope." Will believed Denver's entrance into the CRSP legislative crafting provided not a threat but an opportunity for the Western Slope. This view was not shared by the Western Slope and only provided further evidence of Will's defection to Denver's side of the water war. Also see John Geoffrey Will to George Cory, January 31, 1953, Box 2, folder 4, Silmon Smith Papers, CSHS.

49. William Nelson to Frank C. Merriell, February 2, 1953, Box 169, folder 5, Frank Delaney Papers, UCBA.

50. Quoted in Hildner, "Fight for the Faucet," 44.

51. *Rocky Mountain News*, February 18, 1953.

52. Frank C. Merriell to Wayne N. Aspinall, February 21, 1953; Frank C. Merriell to Ivan C. Crawford, March 7, 1953, both in Box 170, folder 1, Frank Delaney Papers, UCBA; *Rocky Mountain News*, February 18, 1953.

53. Frank C. Merriell to Wayne N. Aspinall, February 21, 1953.

54. CRWCD Minutes, April 28, 1953, folder "CRWCD Minutes, 1952–55," CRWCD, Glenwood Springs, CO; quotation in Ivan C. Crawford, *Water Resource Planning in Colorado* (Denver: Colorado Water Conservation Board, 1957), 57–58.

55. Frank Delaney to Senator Ed C. Johnson, May 6, 1953, Box 169, folder 1, Frank Delaney Papers, CSHS; Silmon Smith to Dan Thornton, Box 5, folder 6, Silmon Smith Papers, CSHS.

56. CRWCD Minutes, October 20, 1953, folder "CRWCD Minutes, 1952–55," CRWCD, Glenwood Springs, CO.

57. Frank Delaney to Silmon Smith, August 7, 1953, Box 5, folder 6; Frank Delaney to Frank C. Merriell, October 20, 1953, both in Silmon Smith Papers, CSHS; CRWCD Minutes, July 21, 1953, October 20, 1953, folder "Minutes of the CRWCD, 1952–55," CRWCD, Glenwood Springs, CO.

58. *Denver Post*, March 23, 1953.

59. Delaney to Smith, August 7, 1953; CRWCD Minutes, July 21, October 20, 1953; Delaney to Merriell, October 20, 1953.

60. Carl Ubbelohde, Maxine Benson, and Duane A. Smith, *A Colorado History*, 9th ed. (Boulder: Pruett, 2006), 333–34; Carl Abbott, *Colorado: A History of the Centennial State* (Boulder: Colorado Associated University Press, 1976), 236.

5

Water Wars at a Zenith, 1953-1956

This controversy has raged a long time. Our Colorado East-West water
war is not unlike the international East-West Cold War and it may take
time to persuade some to discard feelings engendered over a long period.

—*Barney Whatley to Governor Ed Johnson, May 8, 1955*[1]

The mid-1950s witnessed some of the most severe clashes in Colorado's
twentieth-century water wars. Continued conflicts over the shape of the
Upper Colorado River program, Denver's renewed efforts to secure additional Western Slope water, and the actions of Colorado Springs and Pueblo
in passing the Fryingpan-Arkansas Project led to a state of perpetual tension
between Colorado's eastern and western halves. By the 1960s, Colorado's
water planners were forced to take a more conciliatory intramural posture
because of renewed threats to the state's water allotment from the Lower
Colorado River Basin.

Several separate yet delicately intertwined events defined Colorado's
ongoing water wars during the mid-1950s. By 1953 the Colorado Water

DOI: 10.5876/9781607325000.c005

Conservation Board's (CWCB) Conference Committee had commissioned two studies that would help determine Colorado's immediate hydrological future, including a determination of which projects the state would attempt to include in the Colorado River Storage Project (CRSP). In addition, would Denver be allowed to include its long-hoped-for Blue River diversion within the structure of the massive Upper Basin Project? A final development influenced the renewal of Colorado's water conflicts: southeastern Colorado had been advocating a Gunnison-Arkansas (or Fryingpan-Arkansas) Project in one form or another since before passage of the Colorado–Big Thompson Project in 1937. Both the Blue River diversion and the Gunnison-Arkansas Project had been reported on favorably by the Bureau of Reclamation in the aftermath of ratification of the Upper Colorado River Basin Compact in 1949. It remained to be seen how both projects would fare as the nation returned to normal after another major war in Korea and the Upper Basin states sought to realize their share of the Colorado River system's waters.

THE HILL REPORT AND ESCALATING TENSIONS

As the deadline approached for the release of the Hill Report, the political atmosphere on the Western Slope grew increasingly pessimistic about the pending study's prospective content. Colorado River Water Conservation District (CRWCD) counsel Frank Delaney confirmed this after a conversation with engineer Raymond A. Hill in September 1953. Based on this discussion, Delaney believed Hill's "report was not the sort of thing Western Colorado could agree with." Western Slope water advocate William Nelson of the Grand Junction *Daily Sentinel* saw the Hill Report, Denver's diversion plans, and the Fryingpan-Arkansas Project as only the beginning of a much more ambitious attempt to destroy western Colorado's remaining water reserves. Denver was asking for 177,000 acre-feet for its Blue River diversion. However, the Blue River–South Platte Project, of which Denver's diversion of the Blue was but one part, threatened to take 600,000 acre-feet from the headwaters of the Colorado River. Similarly, Fryingpan-Arkansas was a small portion of the much larger Gunnison-Arkansas Project. Nelson believed that if the smaller projects were constructed, "proponents of both Blue–South Platte and Gunnison-Arkansas will commence yelling for further planning and consideration of their projects." Nelson believed there was "more than meets the eye in Denver's scheme." The study by Hill was only the first phase. Much larger project demands would flow from these beginnings.[2]

Hill's study, according to CRWCD board member F. M. Peterson, had been essentially forced on the Western Slope by the CWCB. Peterson agreed with Nelson that the water board was dominated by enemies of the Western Slope's interests.[3] Western Colorado operated under additional political handicaps. Governor Dan Thornton had been a strong advocate for Denver's diversion plans. Delaney speculated that Thornton's further political aspirations dictated his alliance with powerful Eastern Slope forces. Even after the authorization of Hill's study, Delaney continued to argue the need for the Bureau of Reclamation to do a complete Western Slope water-needs survey, believing it would be "more thorough" than the hastily cobbled Hill Report. In May 1953, well after the Colorado General Assembly had authorized the Hill study, Delaney was still imploring Senator Ed Johnson to light a fire under the Bureau of Reclamation to continue with its western Colorado water survey.[4]

Congressman Wayne Aspinall had been involved with Colorado's state water program since its inception in the 1930s as a state representative, state senator, and a charter member of the Colorado Water Conservation Board. Aspinall offered little comfort to his Western Slope constituents by reminding them that the Front Range likely had more political power in 1953 than it had at the time of passage of the Colorado–Big Thompson Act (1937). Aspinall indicated that "the immediate picture does not look too propitious for Western Slope development." In 1953 the Palisade, Colorado, legislator was a third-term congressman and a junior member of the House Subcommittee on Interior and Insular Affairs (Interior Committee). While Aspinall had replaced Republican representative Robert Rockwell in part because of Rockwell's perceived ineffectiveness on reclamation and public land questions, in 1953 Aspinall remained far from approaching the influence over reclamation policy exhibited by Edward T. Taylor.[5]

In anticipation of the Hill Report's appearance, Denver water officials skillfully prepared public opinion to support the expansion of the city's water system. Denver Water Board (DWB) engineer Harold Roberts indicated that Denver had made attempts to develop the Blue River as a water source since as early as 1914—something the Colorado River Water Conservation District consistently disputed. DWB attorney Glenn Saunders noted that "Denver

FIGURE 5.1. Wayne N. Aspinall, from the Western Slope town Palisade, succeeded Edward T. Taylor as western Colorado's most notable advocate of water development. His lengthy congressional career (1948–72) saw the authorization of most of Colorado's major water projects. *Courtesy*, Colorado Mesa University Archives and Special Collections, Grand Junction.

depends on the waters of the Colorado River and its tributaries for continued existence and growth. There is no more water in the Platte." Numerous studies indicated that without the Blue River diversion, Denver only had enough water to fuel its growth until 1962. By framing its demands as an impending crisis, Denver reached out to a general public that normally took its water somewhat for granted.[6]

Meanwhile, the Bureau of Reclamation issued a Supplemental Report on the Colorado River Storage Project, a necessary precursor to facilitate the legislative process toward congressional enactment. The report superseded earlier studies of the project while summarizing the state of thinking on the shape of the CRSP at the end of 1953, about the time Colorado received the Hill Report. The new study noted that not all units in the project would be constructed after enactment of the CRSP. As of late 1953, the major reservoir units recommended included Glen Canyon, Echo Park, Flaming Gorge, Navajo, and Whitewater. On the Western Slope, an internal debate continued over whether to substitute a Curecanti Reservoir on the Upper Gunnison River for the Whitewater unit on the lower portion of the river. Twelve Participating Projects were also still included. Yet Colorado's overall participation in the CRSP seemed somewhat limited as of 1953. No mention was made at this time of including Denver-Blue as a Participating Project as that topic continued to be debated within Colorado. Other Colorado Participating Projects that remained in the bureau's plans included Florida, Pine River Extension, Silt, Smith Fork, and Paonia.[7]

Heartening to many on the Western Slope was the continued inclusion of Echo Park as one of the major holdover storage units. Echo Park continued to suffer attacks from a growing coalition of conservation organizations, but at least through 1953 it remained central to the Bureau of Reclamation's plans for the CRSP. To the bureau, Echo Park and Glen Canyon were keys to the hydraulic future of the Upper Basin states. Centrally located in the Upper Basin, Echo Park would help control the Upper Green and Yampa Rivers and also provide water to be held by the larger Glen Canyon Reservoir, enabling the Upper Basin to meet its water delivery obligations to the Lower Colorado River Basin. By the end of the year, President Dwight Eisenhower's secretary of the interior, Douglas McKay, announced his approval of the Echo Park Dam, a decision that added fuel to the growing Echo Park–Dinosaur National Monument controversy. Heading into 1954, Echo Park remained alive and, if not well, at least firmly in the future water plans of Coloradans and the Bureau of Reclamation.[8]

Throughout Colorado, the Colorado River Storage Project and its Echo Park controversy temporarily took a distant second place to the arrival of the Hill Report, whose conclusions many believed would likely give one section of the state a clear political advantage over the other in setting Colorado's water agenda. The Conference Committee had commissioned Hill's firm to make the study so it could realize its original goals as expressed in HB 457: to study the "water resources available from surface water" in Colorado, west of the Continental Divide, and to study "the present and potential uses" so the state could use those waters "to the fullest extent possible under the law." The committee was also charged with assessing Denver's request to the CWCB to divert 177,000 acre-feet a year from the Blue River. The Hill Report, it was hoped, would give the Conference Committee the necessary information to act on the Colorado General Assembly's charge.[9]

THE HILL REPORT AND AFTERMATH

After months of speculation, advance condemnation, praise, and much guessing as to its ultimate contents, the Hill Report appeared on November 1, 1953. The study concluded that "uncommitted surplus" water that could be relied upon in Colorado amounted to 1.45 million acre-feet per annum. Hill broke down some of the possible variables confronting future water use in Colorado—in other words, potential claims on the "uncommitted surplus." Western Slope agricultural growth would likely occur, but that could only happen with massive federal subsidies. Hill did not envision that subsidies as high as $600 per acre would be likely. Hill also addressed possible Western Slope industrial growth, including an oil shale industry.[10]

Hill prefaced his analysis and water data by saying that the Colorado River states did not have enough water to satisfy their Colorado River Compact requirements. While Hill's study represented the first analysis to revise the river's annual capacity downward, the report vexed the Western Slope with its insistence that enough water capacity still existed to sustain some of the larger planned trans-basin diversions. Hill tallied 388,000 acre-feet already diverted annually, with firm plans for other diversions bringing the total to 503,000 acre-fee. Yet if there were no "legal nor economic barriers" to further diversions, a "very large quantity of water could be taken." These words loomed like green lights to Front Range water officials. The results were exactly what the Denver Water Board and other water agencies from eastern Colorado had hoped to accomplish by commissioning Hill's study.[11]

Hill also discussed the availability of water for both the Bureau of Reclamation's massive Blue River–South Platte Project and Denver's proposal for a Blue River diversion. It is easy for someone examining the documents from this era to confuse the two projects or to believe that they were one and the same. They were not. The proposal for the diversion had been discussed and planned for many years. Denver, in contrast, had contemplated some sort of Blue River diversion since the 1920s. The Blue River–South Platte Project, depending on which version is being discussed, contemplated diverting at least 430,000 acre-feet annually from western Colorado. Denver's Blue River diversion proposed bringing 177,000 acre-feet each year to the Denver water system. While Hill believed the Fryingpan-Arkansas Project's relatively meager diversion of 72,000 acre-feet per year remained feasible, the Blue River–South Platte Project and Denver's diversion of the Blue River would be impossible to build in tandem. Colorado would have to build one or the other. Hill did not see a large version of what had once been called the Gunnison-Arkansas Project as likely, especially at the level of 500,000 acre-feet annually envisioned by some of its early designs.[12]

Oil shale's "unlimited future" had always played a role in the Western Slope's defense of its water reserves. Western Colorado water officials made sure that Hill and his associates toured the Naval Oil Shale Reserve facilities near Rifle, Colorado, and had ample time to talk with some of the local people involved with oil shale promotion. Hill concluded that oil shale development "should be anticipated" and that the consumption of water for industrial, municipal, and other purposes "may reach . . . 300,000 acre-feet per year." This was approximately the same amount of water anticipated by Silmon Smith's estimates in 1950.[13]

The Hill Report is notable in several respects. Many on the Front Range read it as a confirmation of what they had long suspected—that western Colorado's irrigated agriculture would need huge federal subsidies to be cost-effective. Some sections of the report could also be construed as opening doors to additional trans-basin diversions. On the Western Slope, water officials pounced quickly on the report's implication that ample waters remained available for diversion. Silmon Smith, not surprisingly, believed Hill had overestimated the amount of water available.[14]

A final way to view Raymond Hill's study is to assess where it stands within the history of Colorado River water estimates. It was the first hydrological study to raise serious doubts about the 17.5 million acre-feet annually figure articulated in the Colorado River Compact of 1922. From 1930 to 1952, the river's annual flow had averaged only 11.7 million acre-feet—about 6 million acre-feet per year less than the accepted annual figure needed to meet its legal allocations. Unfortunately, the Bureau of Reclamation had formulated its manifold plans for the Colorado River based on the poorly done studies that informed the Colorado River Compact. As Marc Reisner told the story, even with Hill's study available, the Colorado River Storage Project of 1956 would be based on the bureau's own inflated figures rather than on any study that cast doubts about the 17.5 million acre-feet per year average. In the 1960s, when another ambitious basin-wide reclamation program was sought, the Colorado River's flow figures would be reconfigured once again.[15]

The Colorado General Assembly's Conference Committee, which had commissioned Hill's study as well as an analysis of the Western Slope's future economic growth by a team of University of Colorado scholars, still needed to make a report to the Colorado Water Conservation Board indicating how it wanted to implement or act upon Hill's findings. With strong words emanating from newspapers on both sides of the mountains prior to the meeting, Governor Dan Thornton called for "an immediate truce in the long battle for water between the eastern and western slope[s]." Unless the verbal sparring ceased, Thornton feared the future of the entire state, "particularly of Denver, may be jeopardized." The *Denver Post* indicated that the governor had called an "emergency meeting" to try to break the water deadlock on the eve of the Conference Committee's recommendations. The same article quoted Denver mayor Quigg Newton's standard refrain over the past few years: that without the Blue River, the capital city would run out of water before 1960. The *Post* also repeated the conventional wisdom in Denver about the Hill Report—that an "independent" water study had disclosed "plenty of water" was available for development by both halves of the state.[16]

On December 10, 1953, the Conference Committee reported its findings in a tension-filled meeting that demonstrated how far Denver had come in 1953 toward controlling the state's water decision-making. This would be underscored at the meeting of the Colorado Water Conservation Board scheduled for the next day. The Conference Committee voted 3 to 2 to release its "findings and recommendations." Western Slope representatives Robert Delaney and George Cory voted against the committee report. The Conference Committee endorsed the findings of the Hill Report and recommended constructing Denver's Blue River trans-mountain diversion within "the availability of water supply." The committee also favored the inclusion of both the DeBeque and Curecanti Reservoirs among Colorado's proposed CRSP projects.[17]

The CWCB met on December 11 to discuss and act upon the recommendations of the Conference Committee. After the CWCB began deliberating on the recommendations, Frank Delaney seized the floor to offer the Colorado River Water Conservation District's objections to including the Blue River Project in the CRSP. According to Delaney, the water board should not endorse the Blue River Project since its legality remained the subject of ongoing litigation. "At the very least," Delaney remarked, "the Water Board should remain neutral and impartial regarding matters in litigation between citizens or organizations in different sections of the state."[18]

John B. Barnard, a prominent Western Slope water attorney and a frequent spokesman for the Middle Park Water Conservancy District where the Blue River and its tributaries rise, charged Denver with misleading the public about the allegedly dire nature of its water situation.[19] After several more people from the Western Slope spoke, Harold D. Roberts took the floor. It was time to endorse the Hill Report and the actions of the Conference Committee. Roberts, a longtime attorney for the Denver Water Board, reminded the meeting that the US Congress was to hold hearings on the CRSP in one month's time in Washington, DC. Roberts spoke glowingly of Hill's study, calling it "the best that has been written" on the Colorado River. "My point," Roberts emphasized, "is that Denver can take that amount of water from the Western Slope [177,000 acre-feet annually] without harming anyone on the Western Slope." With that dramatic prelude, Roberts made a motion to adopt the findings of the Conference Committee as the policy of the CWCB and the basis of Colorado's instructions to its Upper Colorado River Commission representative. Western Slope representative George Pughe moved for a section-by-section vote on the original Conference Committee report. Pughe's attempt to delay or derail the final vote failed, and the CWCB voted 8 to 4 to adopt the Conference Committee's report as the policy of the water board.[20]

For two consecutive days, first at the meeting of the Conference Committee and then at the December 11, 1953, meeting of the CWCB, the Western Slope had felt the sting of the Front Range's raw political power by being outvoted both times. The Colorado River Water Conservation District retreated back to its Western Slope home for a December 19, 1953, strategy session in advance of another CWCB meeting scheduled for December 30 in Denver. After a thorough review of the events of the previous weekend, the CRWCD concluded that its "sole reliance" henceforth would need to be on the growing power of Congressman Wayne Aspinall, who had the ability to help shape pending CRSP legislation. Perhaps Aspinall could ensure that the Blue River diversion would not be included in the legislative package.[21]

The CRWCD Board also endorsed a CRSP without the Denver-Blue Project but one that included the Glen Canyon, Echo Park, Flaming Gorge, Navajo, and Curecanti Reservoirs, in addition to sixteen Participating Projects. In the midst of this discussion, Denver mayor Quigg Newton telephoned Frank Merriell to ask the CRWCD to work for the good of the state overall. Denver, the mayor remarked, had a "genuine stake" in western Colorado's prosperity, and the Western Slope should reciprocate this feeling toward the capital city.[22]

At the December 30, 1953, meeting of the Colorado Water Conservation Board, Denver hoped to gain the board's official endorsement of Colorado's share of the Colorado River Storage Project with the Blue River diversion included. Denver was mistaken in this assumption. The Western Slope still hoped to either delay or dislodge Denver's water plans. When the Western Slope's obstructionist plans became apparent, the CWCB appointed a Conciliation Committee with two members from each slope and a fifth member agreed to by each side. Representing the Western Slope were Frank Delaney and Silmon Smith, undeniably two of the most battle-scarred veterans (and least conciliatory survivors) of Colorado's water wars. Eastern Slope members were J. J. Sullivan and Robert Stearns. The fifth member chosen was Barney L. Whatley.[23]

The December 30, 1953, meeting turned into a raucous spectacle, with ample finger pointing and strong arguments on each side. Denver's water officials seemed particularly angry, apparently hoping the 8 to 4 vote on December 11 would have forced the Western Slope to willingly accede to Denver's demands. Nicholas Petry of the Denver Water Board accused western Colorado water officials of stalling and not giving the Hill Report the credibility it deserved. If the state did not unite on the water issue, it may "hinder progress . . . for one hundred years" in Colorado. Lecturing the CWCB, Petry reminded the board that it was time to get moving on Denver's water project: "You gentlemen voted 8–4 in favor of the Hill Report. The four dissenting votes were from the Western Slope. The State of Colorado, if united, could probably gain more from the Federal Government [through the CRSP] . . . now than ever before in history." Such partisan rhetoric did not set a very cooperative tone for the work of the Conciliation Committee.[24]

The Conciliation or Mediation Committee (as the press dubbed it) was equated to a "last-ditch effort" to negotiate a water truce before Congress came back into session to consider the CRSP on January 18, 1954. Though it met several times over the next two weeks, the Conciliation Committee failed to bring peace to the divided state. Delaney treated the committee to some of the usual, well-rehearsed Western Slope water defense arguments.

The Denver–Blue River Project, Delaney thundered, was opposed by "practically all of the 156,000 people residing in the Western one-third of the State of Colorado." The Western Slope also tried to reestablish the authority of the CWCB's action in regard to Fryingpan-Arkansas on February 22, 1951—which had ratified a CRWCD resolution supporting the Frying Pan Project but closed the door to any future diversions until a thorough watershed survey of the Western Slope had occurred. To Western Slope water officials, the hastily done Hill study did not meet this standard, while the Front Range, which was generally delighted with Hill's findings, believed the Western Slope had no more cause to complain about the absence of a complete water survey.[25]

Before the Conciliation Committee, Delaney recapitulated the argument he and other attorneys from the Western Slope had been making before the US District Court in the pending case over Denver's Blue River water claims. The court was being asked to determine the meaning and effect of Senate Document 80 and to adjudicate water rights from Green Mountain Reservoir. Delaney argued that the crux of the matter was that Denver had, "in effect[,] asked the Congress of the United States to undermine an investment that the United States has made in a reclamation project." Delaney also predicted that future, contemplated water uses for western Colorado would suffer— irrigation, oil shale, and other potential uses would lack an adequate water supply. Delaney's bleak portrait illustrated why it would be impossible for the Conciliation Committee to perform its task of finding middle ground.[26]

In notes prepared for the Conciliation Committee sessions, Frank Delaney indicated that the Colorado River Water Conservation District would "oppose any such [Blue River diversion plan] in Congress and wherever opposition seems appropriate." The Western Slope supported the overall concept of the Colorado River Storage Project but would continue to fight Denver's participation. The Western Slope believed it had one major card left to play in the controversy—the increasingly influential position on the House Interior Committee occupied by Fourth District of Colorado congressman Wayne N. Aspinall. Aspinall had moved quickly up the committee's seniority ladder, though his Democratic Party remained in the minority. It was clear that he was emerging as a key role player in congressional reclamation policy. Aspinall made it clear that during the upcoming hearings, he would not follow the wishes of the Denver Water Board and advocate for its Blue River diversion.[27]

With House hearings on the Colorado River Storage Project scheduled to begin on January 18, 1954, Colorado still had not officially heard from its Conciliation Committee. On January 14, Chairman Barney Whatley finally reported to the CWCB that his five-person committee had "worked very diligently" but was "unable to come up with anything." Turning the issue over to the water board, the CWCB voted 10 to 3 to approve Denver's project, though the ongoing litigation had the potential to disrupt the board's approval. The water board's resolution applauded the diligent efforts of the state, through the $100,000 Hill Report and the University of Colorado's survey of western Colorado's economic potential. In its resolution, the CWCB expressed support for the construction of Glen Canyon Dam and Echo Park. In addition, Colorado expressed no objections to the many "Participating Projects" recommended by the Department of the Interior. The water board also took the position that as much storage as possible was needed in Colorado at high elevations, though it went on record favoring facilities on the Upper Gunnison River and at DeBeque on the Colorado River.[28]

Turning finally to the controversial issue at hand, a carefully worded passage noted that Denver wanted to divert the Blue River, but Denver's right to the water was alleged to be in conflict with the rights of water stored in Green Mountain Reservoir and taken through the Green Mountain Dam as part of the Colorado–Big Thompson Project. Finally, a passage was inserted that Delaney had fought bitterly for: because of the impending lawsuits in the Colorado Supreme Court and the US District Court, "it would be improper for this Board to attempt to invade the process of the courts or to influence the pending legislation." Going to great lengths to justify its decision, the Colorado Water Conservation Board approved the inclusion of the Denver–Blue River Project as a CRSP Participating Project but noted that the impending litigation, the necessity of protecting the Colorado–Big Thompson Project, and the legal availability of enough water (either by litigation or "some other arrangement") could ultimately impact the project's feasibility. The CWCB also noted that every effort should continue by representatives of the Western Slope and Denver to arrive at a harmonious solution to what it termed the "unfortunate transmountain diversion controversy" that had caused such dissension in the state.[29] Denver had won a victory, to be sure, in its fight for the Blue River diversion. The victory, however, came at a great cost: the squandering of any hope of finding consensus within Colorado over the CRSP, which was finally taking shape before the US Congress. The next round of the struggle for Denver to be included in the CRSP would take place in front of Congress as part of Colorado's attempt to have an important part of its water program enacted at the federal level.

THE CRSP AND ECHO PARK

At the beginning of 1953 and the start of the Republican presidency of Dwight D. Eisenhower, the Colorado River Storage Project remained bottled up by financial exigencies related to the ongoing Korean War and the continuing question over the inclusion of Echo Park Dam in the project. Eisenhower and the Republican Party had long criticized the costs of Democratic programs, including public power and natural resource programs. The high price tag of the CRSP (over $1 billion) had the potential to influence the president and his advisers to reexamine the project's hefty cost. Maybe Echo Park could yet be preserved—if not by recognition of its sheer beauty, then because of its high cost. By late 1953, according to historian Mark Harvey, "much ground had been gained" in the conservationist campaign against dams in Dinosaur National Monument. Outgoing secretary of the interior Oscar Chapman had reversed course on the dams in the monument; President Eisenhower had indicated that he did not favor expensive river basin projects like the Tennessee Valley Authority and CRSP. Finally, in 1953 the Sierra Club and other conservation groups had started an energetic national campaign to crusade against the hated dams.[30]

Heading into the 1954 congressional hearings, Colorado's CRSP hopes were threatened on two fronts: by the emergence of the national environmental movement's opposition to the CRSP and by Colorado's lack of unity over its participation in the project. National and state controversies over the CRSP erupted as committees in both houses of Congress held hearings on several legislative versions.

Both supporters and opponents of the CRSP had opportunities to testify before the House Subcommittee on Irrigation and Reclamation in January 1954. Both proponents and foes of Denver's Blue River diversion also wanted their voices heard. While the Western Slope had complained of being out-voted by Denver in December and January CWCB meetings, Aspinall's strength on the Interior Committee became evident in the testimony allowed to be presented before the subcommittee. A veritable brigade of Western Slope witnesses appeared before the House of Representatives in support of western Colorado's water program. Western Slope residents Frank Delaney, Judge Dan Hughes, George Cory, Clifford Jex, L. R. Kuiper, George Pughe, and Frank Merriell all appeared. The Eastern Slope was limited to two witnesses: the Upper Colorado River Commission's Jean S. Breitenstein and the Denver Water Board's Glenn Saunders. A perusal of witnesses who appeared indicated that the Western Slope provided the most for this round of CRSP hearings, a clear demonstration of Congressman Aspinall's growing influence in national water politics.[31]

Two days before the Washington hearings began, the Upper Colorado River Commission held an unusual but much-needed meeting in Washington, DC, to act on the CWCB's recommendation to include Denver's diversion request in the CRSP bill. Congressman Aspinall served clear notice that he would not support the CWCB's endorsement of the diversion. According to a Grand Junction *Daily Sentinel* reporter present, after he spoke against the Blue River plan, "deep silence" greeted the congressman's remarks. With Aspinall's strong opposition, it appeared that "heroic efforts are necessary to unite Coloradans." The Upper Colorado River Commission's recommendations further angered Aspinall and most Western Slope water officials because not only did they include Denver–Blue River, but they deleted references to the Curecanti Project on the Gunnison River. Colorado's deeply divided water program endangered the state's overall participation in the CRSP.[32]

In the House hearings, Breitenstein and Saunders made strong pleas to include the Blue River diversion in the CRSP legislation. Breitenstein indicated that his role was to articulate the "official position of the State of Colorado." In his testimony, Breitenstein called the Denver–Blue River diversion "an important and desirable feature" of the CRSP, designed to augment a "well-managed" publicly owned water plant, one-sixth of whose customers were US government personnel. Breitenstein parroted the old Denver argument that the water system's present capacity was fast being surpassed by population growth and needed an infusion of a new supply. The only logical source of that supply was the Blue River.[33]

In the House committee's questioning of Breitenstein, Congressman Wesley D'Ewart (R-MT) jumped into the discussion, noting his close familiarity

FIGURE 5.2. Echo Park in Dinosaur National Monument. The controversy over whether to include dams in Dinosaur National Monument delayed consideration of the Colorado River Storage Project for several years. While no dams were built in Dinosaur, the 1956 Colorado River Storage Project began an era of frenzied water project construction in the Upper Colorado River Basin. *Courtesy,* David Lambert and FreeLargePhotos.com.

with the divided nature of Colorado water politics while indicating his hesitancy to commit large amounts of federal funds to a state that could not reach agreement within itself. "This committee," D'Ewart remarked, "is generally a little bit hesitant about building projects that would establish the prior use of the water within the state when the state itself does not agree where and how that water would be used." D'Ewart indicated that the committee had visited Colorado in 1953 and informed state water officials that they needed to reach stronger agreement on their water program before federal funding would be committed.[34]

Aspinall also locked horns with Glenn Saunders. In his testimony, Saunders observed that Denver's rapid growth dictated the need for additional water supplies. The city, Saunders asserted, "would be totally unable to continue to exist without transmountain water." In words that stung Aspinall and others from western Colorado, Saunders observed that "approximately half of our water just has to come from the Western Slope of Colorado . . . without it we could not live."[35]

Aspinall made it clear that he would not support any Denver or Front Range water bids unless his old political mentor Edward T. Taylor's formula was honored: acre-foot for acre-foot compensatory storage for the Western Slope. Aspinall maintained this stance during his questioning of Saunders. Saunders countered that the Colorado–Big Thompson Project's compensatory storage provision was not a binding, eternal contract between the two slopes. Aspinall responded that the 1937 agreement was meant to serve (through Senate Document 80) as the future "criterion for the determination of transmountain diversion in Colorado." In questioning by California representative Clair Engle, the committee's ranking Democrat, Saunders tried to minimize the rancor over Denver's bid to include the project with a provision that it would be constructed with a loan from the federal government. The CWCB, Saunders said, had made "tremendous efforts" to create as much state harmony as possible. However, "In a democracy we do not have unanimity." In this way, Saunders attempted to explain the escalation of Colorado's continuing water war to a congressional audience.[36]

Appearing on behalf of the CRWCD to oppose the Blue River diversion, Frank Delaney focused on the threat the diversion posed to the Colorado–Big Thompson Project. Denver was asking the courts for a 1921 priority date, which would make it superior to the date of the United States and the C-BT. If granted a 1921 date, the C-BT and any reclamation project with a later date could be shut down in years of water scarcity. Delaney's point, made frequently in public meetings in recent years, was that Denver was in effect asking Congress to "undermine an investment" the United States had made by building the Colorado–Big Thompson Project. To buttress his claim, Delaney pointed out that Denver had not accomplished any construction work on the Blue River diversion until the C-BT's Green Mountain Reservoir was "practically completed."[37]

Engineer Clifford Jex of Grand Junction took the stand specifically to oppose the Blue River diversion. "In recent years," Jex testified, "we have witnessed the uncommitted water supply of the [Colorado River] basin dwindle from millions of acre-feet to hundreds of thousands." Western

Colorado, he added, was relatively new to water development compared with neighboring Utah or eastern Colorado. By this logic the region needed to reserve a large amount of water for future economic growth. The Grand Junction *Daily Sentinel*'s Washington, DC, reporter George Sanford Holmes noted that Dan Hughes and Frank Merriell in particular had made strong impressions on the committee. Holmes predicted on January 22, 1954, that Curecanti at this point was a "toss-up" and that the Blue River diversion was "definitely disfavored" and would not likely be included in any bill passed during the present session.[38]

The question of whether to include the Echo Park Dam and Reservoir in the CRSP also occupied a large segment of the committee's time. David Brower, executive director of the Sierra Club, made national headlines by challenging the Bureau of Reclamation's estimates on evaporation rates at the Echo Park site. Western Slope water officials had gone into the hearings certain that the least of their looming problems would be gaining authorization for Echo Park. Western Colorado witnesses were far more motivated and prepared to attack Denver's diversion plans than they were to have to defend the Echo Park Dam site. The bulk of the defense of the Echo Park site fell to Aspinall, in whose Western Slope congressional district much of the project would be constructed. In a revealing question-and-answer period following Brower's testimony, Aspinall chided Brower and other environmentalists for their recent "discovery" of the majesty of Echo Park and Dinosaur National Monument. The congressman fired off a list of places in his congressional district that he believed were equal to Dinosaur National Monument in beauty. Had Brower and his environmentalist friends ever been to the Black Canyon of the Gunnison, Gore Canyon, Glenwood Canyon, Maroon Bells, Crystal Canyon, Hells Gate, or Hesperus Canyon? Why had the environmental community chosen Echo Park, above all, to make its stand? Aspinall argued that local citizens, familiar with the value of water and the region's economic potential, should have a strong voice in land-use decisions. Out-of-state visitors such as Brower or the occasional river runner did not know "the desires and longings of the people of the area" and merely wanted to use the area as a place to "go . . . play."[39]

Strong presentations during the 1954 hearings by Brower and other conservationists had created an avalanche of mail running as high as 80 to 1 against including the Echo Park Dam. However, Aspinall remained buoyed by his own district's strong support for Echo Park and a strong CRSP, without the Denver–Blue River diversion. In a statement to the press following the January 1954 hearings, Aspinall remarked that the people of his congressional district supported the CRSP, "but I wish to advise my colleagues that Western Colorado and its representative in Congress unanimously oppose" Denver's diversion plans in the project. In May the House Subcommittee on Interior and Insular Affairs approved a draft of a bill that did not include the Denver–Blue River diversion, an unsurprising result given Aspinall's ability to control the onslaught of testimony against Denver's proposal. Yet it did include the Echo Park Dam.[40]

In the House hearing aftermath, it became apparent that the conservationists had gained ground in the struggle against Echo Park Dam, and with off-year elections looming in November 1954, the CRSP remained stalemated before the House Committee on Rules. Denver's chances of including its diversion in the CRSP were severely diminished by the strong opposition of two of Colorado's most powerful national politicians: Western Slope natives Wayne Aspinall and Senator Ed Johnson. The struggle for a CRSP, with or without an Echo Park Dam and a Denver–Blue River diversion, would resume with the swearing in of a new Congress in 1955.[41]

In between the House and Senate hearings, in June 1954 President Dwight Eisenhower "delighted the upper basin" by endorsing the CRSP plans, after a $1.5 billion version of the project had met the approval of the US Bureau of the Budget. Eisenhower specifically cited the Echo Park and Glen Canyon Dams, calling them "strategically located to provide the necessary storage of water to make the plan work at its maximum efficiency." If the conservationists were going to delete Echo Park from the CRSP, they would have to do so against the president's will.[42]

Western Colorado's other abiding concern following the 1954 hearings was a growing onslaught of national public opinion against the Echo Park Dam. The *Rocky Mountain News* summarized one of the great fears of conservation organizations, other than the possible loss of a beautiful natural wilderness region: "Opponents see the Echo Park proposal as an encroachment upon the national park system, and wonder whether this would not set a precedent for more dams in other national parks." By the end of 1954, this once little-known arm of the national park system had become, according to Mark Harvey, a "symbol of endangered wilderness, the center of attention in the nation's environmental affairs." To Colorado's CRSP supporters, a real danger existed that the state might lose not only important federal resources because of incessant squabbling over which projects to include but also the Echo Park Dam, once viewed as the keystone of the entire CRSP by the Upper Basin states.[43]

With the 83rd Congress running out of time, the CRSP remained only a pipe dream for the Upper Colorado River Basin states. The House and Senate versions of the bill contained provisions for the controversial Echo Park Dam, but only the Senate version included Denver's request for the Blue River diversion. As 1954 wore on, in the aftermath of the so-called evaporation debate before the House subcommittee, more attention was given to a high dam at Glen Canyon as a substitute for Echo Park Dam, in the event that the latter continued to receive an onslaught of negative national publicity. Congress adjourned in the late summer of 1954 without taking further action on the Colorado River Storage Project.[44]

Heading into the off-year elections, Congress still had plenty of work to accomplish on the CRSP legislation. The political struggle to shape a CRSP would resume with the seating of the 84th Congress in January 1955. The Sierra Club and its conservation group allies saw the adjourning of Congress as a chance to get their message before the American people, especially the proposal "to invade Dinosaur National Monument to build Echo Park Dam." By the same token, Denver's struggle to gain its Blue River diversion by means of legislative authorization would also have to wait until the next Congress or be decided through other political maneuvers. The Western Slope, however, continued to hold two potentially strong cards in the state's contentious mid-century water poker game: the power wielded by Aspinall on the House Subcommittee on Irrigation and Reclamation and the hope of a favorable decision in the litigation still pending.[45]

William Nelson, the perceptive Western Slope editor of Grand Junction's *Daily Sentinel*, summarized the water wars heading into the 1954 election season. Nelson believed the Upper Colorado River Commission would ardently pursue another version of the CRSP in 1955, with both Glen Canyon and Echo Park as key components. Nelson, however, did not envision an easy path to passage. California's water interests were opposing the CRSP on several grounds, including the usual fear that any water put to beneficial use in the Upper Basin spelled less for use in the Lower Basin. Another fear hovered "like a cloud in the background" over all CRSP discussions—the question of

Native American water rights threatened to enter the proceedings. American Indian water claims had the potential to undermine water calculations for all seven Colorado River states. Nelson also believed the national conservation community had sufficient strength to stop the CRSP from enactment. The various conservation constituent groups had amassed a large mailing list of representatives and senators "who don't know the difference between the Colorado River and the Columbia River [and] are frightened by letters from their constituents." As for Colorado's ongoing water struggle, Nelson argued that the issue should never have found its way into the legislation; as long as the Denver–Blue River diversion remained in the bill, the CRSP's chance for passage remained problematic: "It never belonged there; it should never have been forced in there." Nelson did not envision Denver backing back down, and neither would western Colorado. At the close of his analysis, Nelson foreshadowed a potential solution to the Colorado controversy by indicating that the Colorado Supreme Court might settle the matter when it made its decision, expected sometime in the late fall of 1954.[46]

THE COLORADO SUPREME COURT MUDDIES THE WATERS

Political winds were shifting fast both nationally and within the state of Colorado. The Colorado Supreme Court delivered its opinion earlier than Nelson and many other interested parties expected. In fact, few predicted that the opinion would appear before the off-year elections scheduled for early November. On October 18, 1954, by a decision of 4 to 3, the Colorado Supreme Court decided the case of *City and County of Denver et al. v. the Colorado River Water Conservation District et al.* Essentially, the decision assured that the water stored in Green Mountain Reservoir would be available for the Western Slope's needs. Denver had sought to establish the right to divert that water with a priority date ahead of the priority right of Green Mountain Reservoir.[47]

Denver newspapers excoriated the decision. "Denver's hope for water is killed," cried the *Rocky Mountain News*. "Will the ruling halt growth of cities?" asked the *Denver Post*. Denver's era of expansion was essentially over, according to other *Post* articles. Entire subdivisions, already planned, would fail to materialize without promises of ample water. Plans for expansion of airline routes to Denver and the growth of the state's military and industrial sector were also believed to be endangered. The majority

FIGURE 5.3. William Nelson (1917–94), an unmitigated advocate of western Colorado's water rights, worked for the Grand Junction *Daily Sentinel* for forty-seven years, spending much of the time reporting Colorado water news. He became a widely recognized Colorado water expert, serving on various state and regional water boards, including the Colorado Water Conservation Board from 1956 to 1965. *Courtesy, Grand Junction Daily Sentinel.*

opinion, written by Chief Justice Mortimer Stone, upheld a two-year-old decision rendered in the district court by Judge William Luby of Summit County, who had initially ruled against the wishes of Denver and Colorado Springs. Colorado Springs was also seeking up to 18,000 acre-feet of divertible water annually. Stone, writing for the majority, found that Denver had not started work on a plan to divert water from the Blue River at the date the city had maintained. Denver's attorneys sought a much earlier priority date. Denver initially tried to convince the court that its plans extended back to 1914 and then, later, to the era of engineer George M. Bull's 1920s expeditions. The opinion declared that priority dates can be linked only to the date when the diversion plan is solidified and diligently carried out. Western Slope water officials had long argued that Denver had not implemented its early Blue River claims with the necessary due diligence. As the majority opinion stated: "It is undisputed that during a period of about 20 years, Denver had not even begun the actual construction of its project and had made no effort whatsoever . . . toward financing it, but only a laudable but fruitless attempt after nine years of inaction to induce the United States Reclamation Bureau to finance it."[48]

The dissenting opinion (labeled a "vigorous dissent") from three justices who hailed from the Denver area argued that Denver's water claims should date to 1927 instead of the 1946 date in the majority opinion. The logic of the dissent attempted to excuse Denver's inaction on the diversion as a product of the history of Colorado and the United States from the late 1920s until 1946. Colorado and the nation "lay prostrate" in the 1930s because of the Depression. Then World War II erupted, "diverting to the war effort materials and all productive effort of the nation and state." Finally, as soon as it was possible to resume normal activity, the Denver Water Board began construction of the diversion tunnel in 1946 and had been working on it ever since.[49]

By contrast, Grand Junction's *Daily Sentinel* attacked Denver's leading newspapers. An editorial concluded that "the puerile, hysterical approach taken by the Denver newspapers is disgusting. Both [Denver] papers moaned loudly that the decision of the Supreme Court setting Denver's priority date at June 24, 1946, wrecked Denver's chances of getting water from western Colorado. All of which is pure tommyrot. Its propaganda [is] designed somehow to scare the state into believing Denver."[50]

The political repercussions of the 4 to 3 Colorado Supreme Court decision still remained unclear. The decision was rendered two weeks before the important off-year elections. The decision reverberated through the state and impacted key voter decisions in November 1954. First and foremost, Chief Justice Mortimer Stone, author of the majority opinion, was a candidate for reelection to the Colorado Supreme Court bench for another ten-year term. After the decision became public, Stone's tenure in office was immediately threatened.[51]

In a letter to friends and supporters of Justice Stone, Frank Delaney urged "fair-minded Coloradans" to rally to counteract the "blaring and impassioned" headlines emanating from Denver's newspapers that attempted to "crucify" Justice Stone. In a personal letter to Walter Walker, the powerful editor of the *Daily Sentinel*, Delaney indicated that in recent years, Colorado Supreme Court justices from Denver had not been fair and impartial to sections of the state outside of Denver. Delaney speculated that the justices might fear the propaganda emanating from Denver newspapers on behalf of the Denver Water Board and others who shape state water policies and thus were "afraid to defy such influences." Particularly confounding to Delaney was the announcement of the decision approximately two weeks before the election. However, it seemed likely, he reasoned, that a member of the minority faction of the court leaked the decision to Denver's press. This unethical maneuver may have been done to intimidate the court and to try to influence Judge Stone "to change his mind at the last minute."[52]

In the minds of many Western Slope citizens, Justice Stone, a Republican, had rendered a courageous decision. As a result, Frank Delaney and other leading citizens of western Colorado tried to rally as many votes to Stone's side as they could in the last two weeks before the 1954 election. Delaney asked Walker to print supportive articles and editorials describing Judge Stone's judicial courage. Stone's defeat in 1954 could allow Denver-based judges to gain a majority on the Colorado Supreme Court. Delaney also sent Walker copies of proposed editorials, including one lauding the "sound decision" handed down by Stone and the majority and one praising Stone's judicial courage. Denver, according to Delaney, sought to gain an early water right date based on "nebulous plans and exploration," kept alive by flimsy construction efforts not at the site of the planned diversion.[53]

Colorado Supreme Court justice John R. Clark (who sided with the majority) offered encouragement to Delaney's campaign to support Chief Justice Mortimer Stone. Stone, Clark remarked, was subjected to a daily "malicious, one-sided" pummeling in the Denver press. Clark believed the Front Range press was attempting to increase political pressure to influence the court to reverse its decision. Clark called the Denver area's outrage a "pernicious, deliberate attempt" to pressure the court. Clark argued that "this case . . . furnishes a thorough demonstration that the people of Colorado outside of Denver must never permit a majority of this Court to be old-time residents of the city of Denver." Clark also believed it was unfair to Stone, a Fort Collins resident with Western Slope roots, to be pitted for reelection against Judge Henry S. Lindsley, a Denver resident. Clark indicated that Denver's domination of the Colorado Supreme Court had advanced to the place where "the tail expects to wag the dog." In the short time period up to the election, Western Slope Democrats found themselves in the strange position of supporting Republican Stone's candidacy for the bench over the Democrat Lindsley. An advertisement "paid for by a group of public-spirited laymen of both parties" declared that Justice Stone "took his political life in his hands when he wrote the recent water decision," adding that he made his decision on the merits of water law rather than "on the basis of Denver pressure."[54]

Despite the strong Western Slope effort on behalf of Stone, Lindsley easily prevailed in the election. The Denver Democrat ran far ahead of Stone in the Denver area, beating Stone by a wide 92,000 to 55,000 margin. The statewide tally was only slightly closer, 233,500 to 206,000. On the Western Slope, the intensive effort on Stone's behalf paid dividends, but as western Colorado was learning, the sheer power and concentrated political influence of the Front Range could control elections of all sizes, from statewide contests to a canvassing of the water board. Mesa County supported Stone over Lindsley by a vote of 9,527 to 5,476, and Garfield County gave the incumbent justice a margin of 3,526 to 929. Several other Western Slope counties gave Stone a solid edge as well. Colorado trended Democratic in 1954, and only in the supreme court race did the largest county in western Colorado, Mesa County, depart from state election trends.[55]

Less than a week after the Blue River decision, Denver decided to seek a reversal of the court's ruling. Under Colorado Supreme Court guidelines, re-hearings had to be requested within fifteen days of a decision. The Denver Water Board could also ask for an extension of time to draft the re-hearing plea. Sources for the city of Denver indicated that the Denver Water Board would likely follow the latter course. On October 27, 1954, Denver asked the court for more time, until December 14.[56]

BLUE RIVER: TOWARD A NEGOTIATED SETTLEMENT

The Blue River decision did little to heal the breach between the two sections of the state, but it had the effect of nudging Denver toward seeking a negotiated settlement on the Blue River diversion. This became the strategy Denver ultimately pursued. The Denver Water Board's initial reaction to the decision was to quickly appeal the case, but in December 1955 the court denied Denver's petition for a re-hearing. The DWB's legal counsel, Glenn Saunders, continued to emphasize Denver's need to access the Blue River. "It is hard to say what the total effect of the ruling is," Saunders said, "but one thing we know: Denver must have water from the Blue River."[57]

Heading into 1955, Denver had little choice but to pursue a policy of negotiation; the Western Slope and supporters of the Colorado–Big Thompson

Project could take comfort knowing that their water rights would be senior to Denver's Blue River rights. The Echo Park Project remained anchored in CRSP proponents' dreams for the Upper Colorado River Basin, though national conservation groups' insurgency reached new levels in 1955. Finally, in the US Congress the CRSP legislation would need to be reintroduced before a new Democratic-dominated Congress, which had overturned Republican control in the November 1954 elections. This development would have serious implications for the Western Slope and its bid to hold on to more of its water, as well as to develop additional water resources.[58]

Congressman Wayne N. Aspinall not only won reelection, but with Democratic control of the House of Representatives, Aspinall became the second-ranking (to California's Clair Engle) member of the House Interior Committee. Aspinall would chair the House Subcommittee on Irrigation and Reclamation and be in a strong position to shape the CRSP legislation.[59] For the first time since the long congressional tenure of Edward T. Taylor, western Colorado would have a congressman well positioned to not only protect the Western Slope's water but to help shape legislation in such a way that more water could actually be put to use on the Western Slope. Aspinall presided over the House Subcommittee on Irrigation and Reclamation for two key years as it shaped the final form of the Colorado River Storage Project. Until 1958, Aspinall was often the de facto chair of the House Interior Committee, with Engle frequently absent because of his campaign for a California Senate seat. After Engle won the election in 1958, Aspinall completed his climb to the top of the House Interior Committee and served as its chair for fourteen years.[60]

Colorado also elected a new governor in 1954. Former governor and senator Edwin ("Big Ed") Johnson, a Western Slope native from Craig in the northwestern part of the state, won the election over Republican state senator Donald Brotzman. Johnson had promised to help broker a settlement of the state's long-standing east-west controversy. Republican governor Dan Thornton, who had been serving since 1951 in an era where intrastate water relations had significantly deteriorated, had attended only four CWCB meetings. Johnson promised to be more "hands-on" in dealing with state water matters; he also promised to attend CWCB meetings. In remarks after the election, the governor-elect called for Coloradans to unite on water issues. If the Upper Basin was assured of its share of the river and if Upper Basin projects could be built before more work was done

FIGURE 5.4. Glenn Saunders, attorney for the Denver Board of Water Commissioners, was a fervent advocate of tapping the Western Slope of Colorado to ensure the Denver area's future water supply. *Courtesy*, Denver Water.

in the Lower Colorado River Basin, Johnson believed an era of harmony in state water relations could prevail. Johnson, who had been involved in state water issues since beginning a career in the state legislature in the 1920s, also understood a fundamental truth from which Colorado seemed to have strayed: to unite the state on hydraulic matters, it was often best to blame another region or state, usually California. Johnson noted that the Lower Basin states had used more than 60 percent of the Colorado River system's water over the past ten years and would continue this pattern of use because "they figure they'll get it all if they can prevent the beneficial use of the water" in the Upper Basin.[61]

At the end of 1954, the longtime counsel for the Colorado River Water Conservation District, Frank Delaney, submitted his resignation. He had held the position ever since the district was created (primarily through his actions) in 1937. Delaney indicated that he would continue in office until the appeals surrounding the Blue River litigation were resolved. The Colorado

River Water Conservation District board tabled Delaney's resignation pending action on several other matters, including, at Delaney's suggestion, creating an Executive Committee that would meet monthly, with the board of directors continuing to meet quarterly and by call for a special meeting.[62]

Delaney's resignation (accepted by the board at its November 6, 1954, meeting) and the reorganization of the CRWCD board with a new Executive Committee signaled a change in direction for the CRWCD. While the board had clearly shouldered the burden in litigation against the Eastern Slope, many believed it was time to broaden the scope of its activities. Frank Delaney believed the organization needed a stronger, central focus. The district's focus on the main-stem Colorado was often to the exclusion of smaller tributary streams. Broadening the focus of the district's action would induce more Western Slope areas to support the organization's activities. A Special Committee was appointed by the CRWCD Board of Directors to review the district's activities and make recommendations for changes in light of Delaney's resignation. The committee recommended replacing Delaney as soon as possible but allowing him to, in a sense, tutor his replacement. In addition, a new job description was developed for a director of the organization, with more emphasis on public relations and organizational activities. Less emphasis would be placed on engineering work, and, in the future, competent engineers would be hired on a case-by-case basis. This conclusion by the Special Committee sounded the death knell for the long career of Secretary-engineer Frank Merriell, whose tenure in recent years had been marked by concerns about his health, sprinkled with questioning about his overall organizational leadership. Finally, the Special Committee recommended expanding the district's size (to include additional Western Slope counties) to better raise funds to finance the attainment of the district's program—to promote and make available more water for western Colorado.[63]

In preparation for another round of CRSP battles in 1955, Upper Colorado River Commission secretary and general counsel John Geoffrey Will spoke to the Joint Legislative Subcommittee on Water Problems of the Colorado General Assembly on December 29, 1954. As an advocate of a CRSP with the Blue River diversion included, Will appeared to be trying to assuage doubters who had raised questions about the legislation from both out-of-basin diversion and conservationist perspectives. In November and December, Denver newspapers had characterized Western Slope efforts to block the Blue River diversion in the CRSP legislation in the worst possible light. Will's speech to the legislative committee was a ringing endorsement of the diversion without once mentioning the controversial project by name. In discussing the Upper Colorado River Basin Compact of 1949, Will pointed out that neither the 1922 Colorado River Compact nor the 1949 compact prohibited transferring water out of a river's natural basin, as some critics had alleged. Prohibitions on such diversions would be disastrous for the Upper Basin's major cities, such as Albuquerque, Denver, Colorado Springs, Pueblo, and Salt Lake City.[64]

1955–1956: Two Controversies Settled

In January 1955, to no one on the Western Slope's chagrin, John Geoffrey Will resigned as secretary and counsel of the Upper Colorado River Commission; he was replaced by Ival V. Goslin, a "skilled politician" who would have a much better working relationship with all segments of Colorado's water bureaucracy. In another key development, Frank Delaney agreed to be Colorado's representative to the Upper Colorado River Commission. These developments, along with Congressman Aspinall achieving more congressional power, would rebound to the benefit of the Western Slope in upcoming years.[65]

By February 1955, new CRSP bills had been introduced in both houses of Congress. In March and April, Aspinall's House Subcommittee on Irrigation and Reclamation held its hearings on the legislation, but with far less rancor than in 1954. Of the five CRSP bills under committee consideration, only Aspinall's versions did not contain provisions to authorize the Blue River diversion.[66] Prior to the start of the hearings, Aspinall indicated to Frank Delaney that he hoped to push hard for more western Colorado Participating Projects, but he also warned Delaney that what Colorado wanted and what it would get in the CRSP would likely be two different things. Aspinall indicated that he always tried to carry out the wishes of local (CRWCD) and state (CWCB) authorities where desired water projects were concerned, but in this case many of the planned Participating Projects had yet to be cleared by the requisite federal reports (surveys and studies by the Bureau of the Budget); if they were insisted upon, the entire CRSP could be held up. Aspinall seemed to be asking Delaney and other Western Slope water officials to trust him—he would get the desired projects listed as possible Participating Projects within the CRSP. Western Slope water officials were obviously pushing Aspinall to try to include many of their long-desired projects in the actual CRSP bill. Aspinall stated that he could not see the logic of holding up the entire CRSP edifice "to get consideration of all of the projects suggested."[67]

In a statement at the start of the subcommittee's hearings, Aspinall fore-shadowed a position he would take over the next fifteen years about the amount of water—or lack of water—available to Colorado River Compact signatory states. His position would not only impact his position toward the CRSP but would also color his stance toward the West's water battle-royal of the 1960s—the bid to pass Central Arizona Project legislation. According to Aspinall, most analyses of the Colorado River flow since the compact was signed in 1922 indicated that not enough water existed for the seven states to put their compact entitlements to use. Aspinall fell back on this argument time and again during his long forthcoming tenure as chair of the Interior Committee. However, in 1955 Aspinall made the point to gain political favor for more reclamation projects in his Western Slope congressional district. His region's mineral resources remained largely "untapped." With only slight exaggeration, he remarked that "only a few miles from my home lie mountains of oil shale" and other important minerals. These minerals only awaited what the CRSP could provide in ample amounts: "the availability of power at reasonable rates and the availability of domestic and industrial water."[68]

At the start of the subcommittee hearings, the Colorado congressman from the Denver area, Democrat Byron G. Rogers, closely questioned Assistant Secretary of the Interior Fred Aandahl about the conflicting versions of the House bill. Rogers received assurances from Aandahl that the Department of the Interior had no objections to Section 11, which authorized the Denver–Blue River diversion as part of the CRSP.[69] In questioning Aandahl, southeastern Colorado representative J. Edgar Chenoweth tried to tie the movement for a CRSP to his longtime effort to enact the Fryingpan-Arkansas Project. Chenoweth reminded the assistant secretary to confirm that President Eisenhower had visited sites in Colorado where both the CRSP and Fryingpan-Arkansas would be constructed. In his most recent message to the Bureau of the Budget, partly as a favor to the Republican Chenoweth (who feared that his tenure in office was linked to his ability to deliver the Fryingpan Project), Eisenhower recommended the construction of both the CRSP and the Fryingpan-Arkansas Project. Opposition to Chenoweth bringing the Fryingpan-Arkansas Project into the conversation was an issue Western Slope and Denver-area water officials could agree upon. Fryingpan-Arkansas, while a significant project, would remain in the background until some form of a CRSP had been passed. With Wayne Aspinall in control of the committee process, this was all but assured.[70]

The usual parade of Colorado witnesses came before Aspinall's committee during the 1955 House hearings, including Western Slope water brokers Judge Dan Hughes, John B. Barnard, Robert Delaney, Frank Merriell, and Silmon Smith. Colorado state officials who testified included Denver mayor Quigg Newton and Ivan C. Crawford of the state water board. A host of national conservation leaders also appeared to try to discredit the Echo Park Dam. Lower Basin witnesses appeared with the goal of either derailing or modifying the CRSP to their collective advantage. Hughes, a Montrose resident since 1904, stressed the need to secure water for the region's future industrial growth. Hughes was also critical of the Bureau of Reclamation program that favored large, downstream reservoirs over the construction of smaller units higher on the streams. He blamed part of this problem on the bureau's failure to complete the long-promised reclamation survey of western Colorado. As Hughes noted, the region had been promised detailed surveys since at least 1940, with only a segment of the region having been subject to comprehensive study.[71]

Silmon Smith delivered strong testimony in favor of more Western Slope water storage, arguing that "over 70 percent" of the Colorado River system's water originates in western Colorado—four times the amount of water contributed by any other Upper Basin state. Smith reiterated an argument that had been heard by Colorado's neighboring states since the era of *Kansas v. Colorado*: on the basis of the water it furnished annually, western Colorado should be considered "a 70-percent stockholder." In all versions of the CRSP to date, western Colorado stood to benefit very little, while "the plan" seems "designed primarily for development outside the [Colorado River] basin by the transmountain diversion of water." Middle Park Water Conservancy District attorney and future CRWCD counsel John Barnard both echoed and enlarged Smith's arguments while steering away from the controversial Section 11.[72]

Denver mayor Quigg Newton, who had lobbied hard for the Blue River diversion for several years, also appeared before the committee, confining his remarks to the importance of the diversion for his city's future. Newton noted that drought conditions in 1953 and 1954 coupled with rapid growth projections necessitated an urgent expansion of Denver's municipal water system. Using an effective Cold War–era argument, Newton pointed out that Denver felt a strong obligation to continue its water service to the many federal installations in the area. Newton also emphasized that the Blue River diversion would be no different than Los Angeles, "at a considerable distance from the Colorado River," receiving several million acre-feet from the river through diversion. Denver, Newton reminded the committee, was second to Los Angeles as a major city dependent on the Colorado River.[73]

Finally, Robert Delaney, the nephew of Frank Delaney and the latter's law partner, offered testimony. Delaney made no pretense about the purpose of his appearance: "I appear in opposition to Section 11 of HR 270 and 2386"— Denver's Blue River diversion. Delaney told the committee that Denver's "belated insertion" of the Blue River diversion into the CRSP was nothing more than a blatant exercise in "power politics"—with the more populated and politically powerful Eastern Slope running roughshod over the wishes of western Colorado. Delaney charged that Section 11, as written, was vague and ambiguous and that Denver had produced so many versions of this project that it was difficult to tell which one Section 11 referred to. Sounding increasingly like his famous water attorney uncle, Robert Delaney alleged that Denver's real purpose in securing the 180,000 acre-feet annually was so the city could "sell and speculate with its water supplies."[74]

Near the conclusion of the March 11, 1955, hearings, Congressman John Saylor (R-PA), a strong opponent of federally subsidized reclamation and an ardent friend of conservation interests, attacked the Blue River diversion. Saylor asked Quigg Newton how he could justify taking water from the Western Slope after witnesses such as Silmon Smith had testified that western Colorado could put all of the remaining waters to which Colorado was entitled to beneficial use, waters that arose on the Western Slope in the Colorado River Basin. Both Newton and Denver Water Board attorney Harold Roberts replied tersely to Saylor: "The Western Slope cannot use . . . all of the remaining water to which Colorado is entitled, without excessive federal subsidy." The Colorado River Compact allowed for river water to be

FIGURE 5.5. Two key Western Slope water strategists, Judge Dan Hughes of Montrose, Colorado (*left*), and Congressman Wayne Aspinall (*right*). *Courtesy*, University of Colorado–Boulder Archives.

used in the entire state, not just on the Western Slope. Attorney Roberts seconded Newton's remarks and pointed out to Saylor that Colorado water law did not require water that arises in a basin to stay in that basin.[75]

The proposed Echo Park Dam came back into the congressional hearings picture on March 17, 1954, when General Ulysses S. Grant III representing the US Planning and Civic Association, the Sierra Club's David Brower, Howard Zahniser of the Wilderness Society, and other conservationists appeared to give testimony. California also sent a series of witnesses who hoped to discredit the entire CRSP as a danger to California's growing need for a generous supply of Colorado River water. Most of the Lower Basin witnesses hailed from California and feared that Upper Basin reclamation development would impair delivery of water to the Lower Basin region, either in quality or quantity.[76]

From the perspective of western Colorado, the aftermath of the 1955 CRSP congressional hearings had produced several possible scenarios that could transpire over the next few months. One question that lurked in many minds was, how would Congress reconcile the various bills containing versions of the CRSP? The Senate bill continued to contain Section 11 providing for Denver's access to Blue River waters. In the House, several possible avenues remained for a CRSP to travel, including some favoring Denver's approach. However, because of his commanding position, Wayne Aspinall's version of the legislation would produce a CRSP without Denver's diversion included in the bill.[77]

Governor Ed Johnson had been elected in November 1954 in part because of his "can-do" reputation. One of the issues he seemed most assured about in the 1954 campaign had been his ability to get the two slopes to cooperate and put an end to their long-term water feuds. Johnson, however, found himself in the middle of the struggle between the two slopes over the Blue River diversion. Longtime Colorado Democratic politician and attorney Barney L. Whatley had been asked by the governor to present his views on the festering Blue River problem. In a memorable response, Whatley remarked that the "controversy has raged a long time. Our Colorado East-West water war is not unlike the International East-West cold war and it may take time to discard feelings engendered over a long period." Whatley succinctly summarized the issue as the Eastern Slope's immediate needs versus the Western Slope's fears over "its own future and not so much about present necessities." As for the state in general, Whatley advised Governor Johnson to nail down every gallon of water for Colorado and "decide how to divide it among ourselves when and if the time comes when we have to do so."[78]

The Echo Park Dam continued to present severe problems for Upper Basin water proponents. Though the Senate had passed the bill with the Echo Park Dam included in April 1955, the dam had always faced a tougher road in the House, which became the focus of an intense anti-dam barrage by conservation organizations. In early June 1955, anti-dam congressman John Saylor introduced an amendment to eliminate Echo Park Dam, which the House Subcommittee on Irrigation and Reclamation voted down. Meanwhile, Aspinall and other Upper Basin reclamation supporters finally admitted that the time had arrived to reassess their support of Echo Park Dam; salvaging most of the CRSP would be preferable to losing the entire project because of the controversial dam located in Dinosaur National Monument. Meeting just two days after Saylor's amendment had been rejected, the Subcommittee on Irrigation and Reclamation voted 15 to 9 to delete the controversial dam from the House bill.[79]

In September 1955, Aspinall addressed the board of directors of the Colorado River Water Conservation District to deliver both good news and bad
news. The positive message (from western Colorado's perspective) concerned the failure of the Fryingpan-Arkansas Project to gain a rule to come
before the House. The bill had passed the Senate but would fail again in the
House of Representatives. Aspinall's sour note concerned the prospects for a
strong Colorado River Storage Project that would fully reflect the hopes of
his Western Slope constituents. While a bill would likely pass in the next year,
it might not be the legislative package western Colorado had hoped for. The
prospects for Echo Park's inclusion looked increasingly dim. In fact, if the bill
was brought to the floor with Echo Park reinserted in late 1955, it would likely
fail, according to Aspinall.[80]

After hearing Aspinall's speech, the CRWCD board again expressed its disapproval of the Senate version of the CRSP (still containing Section 11) and
passed a resolution pleading with Congress to add more "proportional benefits" for western Colorado into the bill. The Western Slope believed it was on
the losing end of pending water developments in 1955, with Echo Park facing
possible extinction and Curecanti, after several years of wrangling, reduced
to a much smaller version. Furthermore, many of the Participating Projects
in western Colorado required further Bureau of Reclamation study. Looming
over it all was the strong possibility of losing more water to the Eastern Slope
through the Blue River diversion (either in or out of the CRSP). The Fryingpan-
Arkansas Project also seemed to be a distinct possibility in the near future.[81]

At a July 1, 1955, CRWCD Board of Directors meeting, Frank Delaney
explained why the district had desperately resorted to a policy of court
action against Denver's attempt to divert the Blue River. Denver, according
to Delaney, had repudiated a historical cornerstone of cooperation between
the two slopes—Senate Document 80.[82] Green Mountain Reservoir holds
152,000 acre-feet of water, of which 52,000 acre-feet were reserved for downstream or Western Slope users impacted by diversion to the Front Range.
Delaney argued that Senate Document 80 was a valid contract binding
all Colorado water users. However, in the Blue River controversy, Denver
had proceeded in the adjudication to try to obtain rights antedating Green
Mountain Reservoir's water rights. Court decisions over the course of several years had set Denver's water right to the Blue River junior to that of
Green Mountain Reservoir—June 25, 1946. In November 1954 the Colorado

Supreme Court confirmed this date and remanded the case to the Summit County District Court to award a decree to the United States for the waters of the Green Mountain Reservoir and power plant.[83]

Denver had consistently argued that the Senate Document 80 stipulations were not applicable to the Blue River case. In a brief filed with the court on August 2, 1955, Delaney had responded to the court's directives: does federal or state law apply in this case? What is the force and effect of Senate Document 80—is it a law or a contract? Finally, do Denver and co-litigant Colorado Springs have a preferential right to the Blue River for domestic purposes as opposed to the prior right of the United States at Green Mountain Reservoir for electrical generation? Delaney, naturally, argued that federal law is supreme in this case because Green Mountain Reservoir would protect the water rights of downstream, Western Slope water users. The cities based their claims for domestic water preference on Article 16 of the Colorado Constitution and the Colorado River Compact (Article 4[b]), which Delaney asserted was not meant to apply to intrastate water issues.[84]

In a March appearance before the Senate Committee on Interior and Insular Affairs, Denver Water Board attorney Allan Mitchem explored this argument of Denver's domestic need and its legal superiority by pointing out that while the Green Mountain Reservoir power plant had an earlier claim to the water, Denver's proposed municipal water use was "superior" to power generation. Denver's goal in Section 11 of the Senate's CRSP bill was twofold: to be able to buy at fair market value the government's power rights at Green Mountain and to bargain for rights-of-way to construct its water delivery system to Denver through federally owned lands.[85]

A SETTLEMENT AND CRSP's PASSAGE

Denver's water establishment had other strategies to unveil in 1955 to buttress its attempt to gain additional water. Appearing at the height of the controversy over Denver–Blue River was a report commissioned by the Denver Water Board by the Chicago consulting engineering firm Alvord, Burdick, and Howson that attempted to provide more arguments in a politically neutral disguise from out-of-state experts designed to supplement the case for Denver's need to augment its water supply. Denver's population had boomed by an estimated 43 percent since the end of World War II, severely straining the city's limited water resources. The engineering firm identified possible water sources to expand Denver's water system: maximum development of South Platte sources, more complete development of the Moffat Tunnel system, expansion of the Williams Fork Reservoir and its water collection system, and, inevitably, the significance of including the Blue River diversion in any plans for Denver.[86]

The report also mentioned a possible storage reservoir that seemed to be receiving increased discussion in Denver's water planning: Two Forks Reservoir. Alvord, Burdick, and Howson discussed Two Forks under the rubric "Remaining Storable Flow of the South Platte." The report indicated that Two Forks could not be a substitute for "additional trans-mountain projects" like the Blue River diversion. If Denver failed to construct the Blue River project, the city would be in a severe quandary—its current water supply could squeak by for ten more years by aggressively using every drop of South Platte water, but the city would face inevitable water-supply hardships by the 1960s. In predicting this dire scenario, the report parroted the arguments Denver's political and water establishment had been making for almost a decade.[87]

When Denver threatened to go back to the courts to gain a re-hearing on its Blue River claim, it opened a fresh avenue that would lead to a settlement of the decades-long water war. The addition of Harold Roberts to Denver's legal team led to a change in overall strategy in Denver's fight for a Blue River diversion. Rather than fight with western Colorado, Denver focused its energies on reaching a negotiated settlement. Denver stood ready to propose a settlement with the US government that included payment for power reserve losses at Green Mountain Dam and possible movement toward compromise on the amount of water to be diverted.[88]

In short, Denver embraced a strategy of negotiation rather than continuing down the path of hard litigation. Symbolic of this change of attitude was the replacement of ardent Western Slope foe Glenn Saunders by Roberts as the lead attorney on this matter. Roberts proved to be a "more effective negotiator than his colleagues, and his presence resulted in more productive discussions with Denver's opponents." Saunders, for all his tenacity, could be contentious and someone his Western Slope foes often regarded as a "devious schemer." His long-standing feuds with Western Slope officials are well-documented.[89]

In his book *The Last Water Hole*, historian Dan Tyler delivers a blow-by-blow account of the steps leading to settlement of the Blue River controversy, emphasizing the role of the Northern Colorado Water Conservancy District in reaching an accord with Denver's water interests.[90] Before switching to a strategy of negotiation, Denver had opened a new legal campaign in the Summit County District Court, asking again for a judgment on water rights at the Bureau of Reclamation's hydroelectric plant at Green Mountain Dam. The parties involved, including Denver and Colorado Springs on the one side and the Colorado River Water Conservation District, Northern Colorado Water Conservancy District, and the US government on the other side, wrangled with the question that from Denver's perspective came down to this: is water for power generation more vital than the domestic needs of a growing community? Denver tried to argue that Green Mountain water was needed for a drought-hampered city that was fast outgrowing its water supply. After the case was transferred to the US District Court, all sides began working toward an out-of-court settlement that was finally reached in early October 1955.[91]

On September 23, 1955, Silmon Smith, one of the Western Slope attorneys, received a letter from J. Lee Rankin, assistant US attorney general, indicating that a plan for an out-of-court settlement had been discussed at his Washington office among members of the federal government, its co-litigants from the Northern Colorado Water Conservation District and various Western Slope water agencies, and the cities of Denver, Colorado Springs, and Englewood. At the meeting, suggested forms of judgment were discussed for "concluding amicably" the long-festering controversy. The details of the possible settlement would soon become known, and after an almost decade-long struggle, the various parties involved would work toward a final settlement. Even Western Slope water attorney John B. Barnard agreed that Denver's attitude had changed for the better. The Denver Water Board now expressed a "reasonableness which we on our side had not detected before in the Denver attitude."[92]

Denver offered some clear concessions in the proposed compromise. Denver agreed to only take water for domestic uses—a longtime sticking point with Western Slope water officials. The city also had to pay the Bureau of Reclamation for power revenues lost at Green Mountain Dam. The Front Range cities would receive water that would normally flow into Green Mountain Reservoir—a key feature of the Colorado–Big Thompson Project. Thus the Northern Colorado Water Conservancy District had taken a stand against the project, along with the federal government and Western Slope water agencies. However, eastern Colorado cities could only divert after they had met their obligation to fill Green Mountain Reservoir with 154,645 acre-feet of water every year. In other words, Denver had to recognize that the power generation rights at Green Mountain Dam were senior to Denver's municipal needs. The formal agreement signed on October 12, 1955, also recognized Senate Document 80 as the controlling instrument in both the Colorado–Big Thompson and Blue River diversions. Storage rights for the 52,000 acre-foot Western Slope C-BT replacement water and the 100,000 acre-foot "power pool" of water for Western Slope beneficiaries were given a priority date of August 1, 1935, along with C-BT diversions through the Alva B. Adams Tunnel. Denver's Roberts Tunnel and Dillon Reservoir were awarded junior rights of June 24, 1946. The Western Slope's major concession was surrendering direct flow rights on the Blue River as junior to the Green Mountain Reservoir. As Frank Delaney remarked, "That water is gone forever as far as we are concerned."[93]

All sides greeted the "final shots" in this great mid-century water war with elation. The Denver Water Board estimated that the city could divert 177,000 acre-feet per year, though that high figure would depend on precipitation cycles.[94] Denver newspapers lauded the "brilliant" work of DWB counsel Harold Roberts, who had worked himself into what the newspapers called "exhaustion." However, it was later revealed that Roberts had suffered a heart attack that caused him to be absent from the final negotiations. The *Rocky Mountain News* hailed the accord as a "major step toward Colorado unity." The *Denver Post* termed it "momentous." US district judge Lee Knous termed the agreement a "milestone" in the state's attempt to solve its water problems "both inter-state and intra-state." An ecstatic Denver mayor Will F. Nicholson Jr. lauded the agreement as "a tremendous victory for Colorado—a high point in state history." Denver can now "keep our date with destiny." Of course, Denver was delighted that it would have enough water, once the dam and diversion tunnel were completed, to be able to serve a city of 1.5 million people. Front Range business leaders also believed the pact ensured the migration of more businesses to the region, since they now had the assurance of an ample water supply.[95]

Western Slope reaction to the agreement was slightly more circumspect, but a ready sense of relief could be detected. Grand Junction's *Daily Sentinel*, still in a fighting mood, indicated that the Western Slope "won more points than it lost in the negotiations," a perspective with which the Denver newspapers would have taken issue. Western Slope negotiator John B. Barnard admitted that he was disappointed with some of the provisions but termed the consent decree (as it was known) "pretty doggone good" overall for western Colorado. Grand Junction attorney Silmon Smith, who represented several western Colorado water associations during the last eleven days of negotiations, also expressed satisfaction with the agreement, noting that it was "beneficial to western Colorado . . . We made progress protecting interests of the Western Slope."[96]

The Blue River Accord augured well for Colorado's water future on several levels. After years of intrastate bickering that neighboring states had taken advantage of, Colorado, in Denver mayor Will Nicholson's words, had "served notice" to all states fighting for a share of the Colorado River "that the western slope and the eastern slope can get together." Even more immediately pertinent, the agreement signaled that Colorado was ready to move in a united fashion toward passage of the Colorado River Storage Project. Frank Delaney, who was usually much more restrained than optimistic, predicted that the agreement would greatly improve the CRSP's overall chances of passing in 1956. Colorado's intrastate disunity had compromised the state's ability to build tangible benefits in the overall bill. The Western Slope's primary objection to CRSP, Section 11 of the Senate version of the bill, would now be withdrawn.[97]

With Colorado's internal struggle settled and compromises in the works over Echo Park Dam, the long, twisted route to passage of the Colorado River Storage Project had suddenly became more direct. In the fall of 1955, with the support of dozens of national and regional conservation organizations, environmental leaders like Howard Zahniser and David Brower ratcheted up the pressure to make certain another Hetch Hetchy disaster would not befall Dinosaur National Monument. Zahniser, executive director of the Wilderness Society, attempted to guarantee against further Hetch Hetchys by attaching a proviso to the bill protecting the sanctity of the national park system against future reclamation projects. After another round of negotiations on Capitol Hill, Zahniser gained these assurances from Congressman Aspinall and other congressional leaders who, in turn, insisted on a cessation of conservation-group opposition to the overall CRSP. The route to passage now seemed open. Accordingly, the Council of Conservationists, a provisional alliance of conservation organizations that had opposed the CRSP with Echo Park, now advised members of Congress to support the project.

The organization's change of heart resulted in many House and Senate votes in favor of the CRSP's enactment.[98]

On March 2, 1956, the House voted 256 to 136 in favor of the Colorado River Storage Project. A week later, a House-Senate conference committee ironed out differences between the House and Senate versions of the bill, paving the way for its final passage on March 28. An ecstatic Wayne Aspinall called the committee's action a "glorious event." He particularly thanked the Upper Colorado River Commission and its "valiant, helpful, and effective" director, Ival V. Goslin, who had taken over the leadership of the commission in 1955. In Aspinall's estimation, Goslin had done more than anyone else to unite the Upper Basin states behind the project, states that had been "hopelessly divided" as recently as the summer of 1955.[99]

On April 11, 1956, President Dwight D. Eisenhower signed the Colorado River Storage Project into law, ending five years of both intrastate and interstate wrangling. Colorado and the Upper Basin states had finally managed to pass legislation that would positively change the lives of citizens of Wyoming, Colorado, Utah, and New Mexico. Four major reservoirs would be constructed: Glen Canyon, Flaming Gorge, Navajo Dam in New Mexico on the San Juan River, and the Curecanti Project on the Gunnison River in western Colorado. The CRSP also authorized the construction of eleven Participating Projects, including Western Slope projects Florida, Paonia, the Pine River Extension, Silt, and Smith Fork. In addition, the CRSP gave priority to project planning reports that could lead to the construction of several long-hoped-for Colorado projects, including Parshall, Troublesome Creek, Rabbit Ear, Eagle Divide, San Miguel, Bluestone, Ohio Creek, East River, West Divide, Battlement Mesa, Tomichi Creek, Bostwick Park, Grand Mesa, Dallas Creek, Savery–Pot Hook, Dolores, Fruit Growers Extension, Animas–La Plata, and Yellow Jacket. Colorado projects dominated the long list of planning reports to be ultimately acted upon by the secretary of the interior.[100]

With the passage of the Colorado River Storage Project, Colorado had achieved not only a temporary truce in its mid-century water war but a milestone in its efforts to plan for the state's water future. The CRSP provided a blueprint for future Upper Basin and Colorado water development efforts. Curecanti would need to undergo further investigation before construction could begin (morphing into Blue Mesa and, with other features,

FIGURE 5.6. The completed East Portal of the Roberts Tunnel. Named for the Denver Board of Water Commissioner's lead attorney, Harold D. Roberts, the 23.3-mile aqueduct conveyed Western Slope waters from Dillon Reservoir to the South Platte River near Grant, Colorado. *Courtesy*, Denver Water.

later renamed collectively the Wayne N. Aspinall Unit of the Colorado River Storage Project). Many of the Participating Projects would also be built over the next ten or more years. Often, however, projects slated for planning priority would become heavily contested as the Upper Basin states competed for increasingly scarce reclamation funds. In other words, though Colorado projects dominated this section of the CRSP bill, merely being listed as a Participating Project did not assure future construction. Some of the projects discussed in the planning section of the CRSP were eventually constructed, while others remain un-constructed to this day.

The Colorado River Storage Project was a galvanizing episode for both reclamation advocates in the Upper Colorado River Basin and the nation's conservation advocates. Congressman Wayne Aspinall emerged from this episode in a commanding position, prepared to dominate congressional

FIGURE 5.7. Formal opening ceremony of the Roberts Tunnel, East Portal Outlet Works, July 17, 1964. Western Slope waters that gather in Lake Dillon pour out of the tunnel toward the South Platte River to fill a series of reservoirs that constitute the major part of Denver's water storage. The water discharge is approximately fifty second-feet of water into the North Fork of the South Platte River, bringing water from the Western Slope into Denver by way of the N. S. Marston Filter Plant. *Left to right*: Nicholas R. Petry, E. L. Mosely, Mrs. Petry, Will F. Nicholson Jr., Denver mayor Thomas G. Currigan, Hudson Moore Jr., George R. Morrison, Bill Nicholson Sr., Carl Brauns, G. L. Stapp, R. B. McRae, and Ted Adams. *Courtesy,* Denver Water.

FIGURE 5.8. Several of Colorado and the Western Slope's most important water politicians gather to dedicate the Rife Gap Dam September 8, 1967, part of the Silt Participating Project of the Colorado River Storage Project. From left to right: "Big Ed" Johnson, two-term governor of Colorado and three-term senator; Congressman Wayne Aspinall; Frank Delaney of Glenwood Springs, for many decades the animating force behind many of the Western Slope's water protection initiatives. The fourth person is unidentified.

reclamation policy for the next fifteen years. Aspinall learned practical lessons in committee politics that he would soon apply as first the de facto chair and then, following the 1958 election, the chair of the House Committee on Interior and Insular Affairs. Aspinall's influence over the nation's water and natural resource policies remained strong in the years ahead. His political influence helped the Western Slope counterbalance the power of the growing Eastern Slope and the Lower Colorado River Basin.[101]

The controversies surrounding the CRSP and Echo Park also transformed the nation's conservation movement. Over the next decade, conservation was broadly reborn and redefined as the environmental movement. The Echo Park controversy signaled that an increasing number of Americans were willing to embrace an "activist brand of conservation which had begun to transform into environmentalism." Reclamation advocates who celebrated the passage of the CRSP as the birth of an era of hydraulic plenty would have to contend

FIGURE 5.9. Glen Canyon Dam under construction and bridge from the overlook. Authorized in 1956, the dam was completed in 1963 and soon Lake Powell began filling behind it. The site of the dam, fifteen miles north of Lees Ferry, Arizona, is in a narrow Colorado River gorge. The dam was dedicated in 1966. *Courtesy*, Colorado Mesa University Archives and Special Collections, Grand Junction.

in the near future with an energized and growing segment of the population who believed less development represented a desirable conservation value for the American people. The defeat of the Echo Park Dam imparted energy to

FIGURE 5.10. Glen Canyon Dam and Page, AZ. Glen Canyon Dam, with Lake Powell behind it, was one of the major projects authorized by the 1956 Colorado River Storage Project, along with Flaming Gorge Dam (Utah), Navajo Dam (New Mexico), and the Wayne N. Aspinall Unit. *Courtesy,* Colorado Mesa University Archives and Special Collections, Grand Junction.

those Americans who wanted not only to protect the national park system but to advocate a vision of protecting wilderness areas within the nation's public lands. Environmentalism, as it would evolve in the 1960s, would be defined implicitly as one of reclamation's staunchest obstacles.[102]

AFTERMATH

Even with the CRSP passed and the Blue River diversion settled, Colorado's water truce remained tenuous at best. The reality of a Colorado Water Conservation Board dominated by an Eastern Slope director, Ivan Crawford, continued to inspire a high level of wariness in the western portion of the state. Partly in response to the Western Slope's distrust of state water-planning

FIGURE 5.11. Morrow Point Dam waterfall. Constructed as part of
the Colorado River Storage Project, Morrow Point Dam, Blue Mesa
Dam, and Crystal Dam constitute the Wayne N. Aspinall Unit of the
Wayne Aspinall Storage Unit. The Wayne N. Aspinall Unit, formerly
the Curecanti Project, is one of four primary projects of the Colorado
River Storage Project. The others include Glen Canyon, Navajo, and
Flaming Gorge. *Courtesy*, Colorado Mesa University Archives and Special
Collections, Grand Junction.

efforts, the Colorado Water Conservation District began its reorganization in 1955–56 with Frank Merriell' s retirement. Merriell's replacement, Phillip Smith, took the helm in December 1955. The CRWCD also created an Executive Committee of six members, including the president of the board and representatives from the White and Yampa Basins, as well as the Upper Colorado, Lower Colorado (toward Grand Junction), and Gunnison River region. Essentially, the CRWCD would have almost one meeting a month, with the Executive Committee meeting between the quarterly meetings of the regular, larger board of directors. With the Blue River diversion controversy settled and the CRSP passed, Frank Delaney, who had essentially created the CRWCD, could officially retire as its attorney. He submitted his resignation on April 17, 1956, and the board accepted it with "great reluctance." Delaney was replaced by attorney John B. Barnard Sr. of Granby, who had taken an increased role in CRWCD affairs in recent years.[103]

There had also been serious discussion in 1955–56 about expanding the size of the CRWCD, in part to politically counterbalance western Colorado's misgivings regarding the water board. More counties would mean greater political clout and increased tax revenues to carry out the CRWCD's water protection mission. In 1955 the Colorado General Assembly approved the expansion of the river district's boundaries when the original eight counties of Summit, Eagle, Garfield, Mesa, Pitkin, Delta, Gunnison, and Montrose were joined by Grand, Moffat, Routt, Rio Blanco, and Ouray Counties. The CRWCD's president in 1955, F. M. Peterson of Delta County, made it clear that the purpose of an expanded district would be to protect "our water from the Eastern Slope and California."[104]

As the controversy over the CRSP and the Blue River diversion wound down, discussion increased among Western Slope water officials about trying to alter the composition of the Colorado Water Conservation Board to make it more geographically balanced and less likely to tip in favor of the Eastern Slope. Ever since Clifford Stone's death and Ivan Crawford's ascension, the Western Slope had distrusted the CWCB, with the low point the fiasco surrounding the commissioning and recommendations linked to the 1953 Hill Report. The legitimacy of the CWCB would continue to be questioned on the Western Slope until a new director of the organization could be found.

Despite the chronic misgivings of some Western Slope officials, in the aftermath of the Colorado River Storage Project, Colorado appeared to be in a stronger, more unified position on water matters than it had enjoyed in many years. Within two years, Congressman Aspinall would appear before the House Committee on Appropriations trying to override the Eisenhower administration's "no new starts" cost-saving reclamation policy. Aspinall, knowing that many of the CRSP's long-term benefits might accrue to the Western Slope, asked for an increased congressional financial commitment over an eight-year period to jump-start the program. The appropriations committee responded favorably to Aspinall's request, approving money for seven projects he chose plus two additional projects. Aspinall's commitment to timely construction of the CRSP-authorized projects would lead to accusations within Colorado that he was a less-than-fervent supporter of the long-hoped-for Fryingpan-Arkansas Project diversion. As soon as the CRSP passed the US Congress, supporters of Fryingpan-Arkansas "jumped to the front of the line" demanding action on their project. The Fryingpan-Arkansas Project was one of several issues that would undermine Colorado's water unity in the years ahead.[105]

Despite solid progress toward fostering a state water policy consensus, Colorado remained divided as it entered the post-CRSP era. The state's water unity in ensuing years often depended on the degree of the threat posed by forces originating outside the state's borders. In the next decade, not only would Fryingpan-Arkansas dash hopes of a unified approach to state water planning, but the Western Slope's desire to build some of its long-hoped-for projects listed in the CRSP as Planning Projects (including Animas–La Plata, Dolores, and West Divide) would be wrangled over during the 1960s. New threats also began to inhabit Colorado's water universe, including Arizona's bid to fashion its Central Arizona Project. In addition, the environmental movement would emerge from its grand victory at Echo Park energized and ready to reshape public perceptions of the federal reclamation program. The 1960s would often pit the new environmental community against western politicians, reclamation bureaucrats, and vested local interests who hoped to finally construct water projects planned for decades. New role players would take their place in the water debates, whether they originated in California and Arizona or with the emerging environmental movement. All of these forces had the potential to undermine Colorado's water plans and hopes for unity.

NOTES

1. Barney Whatley to Governor Ed Johnson, May 8, 1955, Box 2, folder 1, Silmon Smith Papers, Colorado State Historical Society (hereafter CSHS), Denver.

2. Delaney quoted in CRWCD Minutes, October 20, 1953; William Nelson to F. M. Peterson, both in Box 20, folder 10, William Nelson Papers, Colorado Mesa University Archives and Special Collections (hereafter CMUASC), Grand Junction. The Western Slope's skepticism toward the Hill Report is clear in the CRWCD Minutes, July 21, 1953, and Frank Delaney to Silmon Smith, August 7, 1953, both in Box 5, folder 6, Silmon Smith Papers, CSHS.

3. F. M. Peterson to William Nelson, May 5, 1953, Box 20, folder 10, William Nelson Papers, CMUASC, Grand Junction.

4. Frank Delaney to Ed C. Johnson, May 6, 1953, Box 169, folder 1, Frank Delaney Papers, University of Colorado at Boulder Archives (hereafter UCBA).

5. Wayne N. Aspinall to Frank Delaney, May 11, 1953, Box 168, folder 15, Frank Delaney Papers, UCBA.

6. *Rocky Mountain News* (Denver), September 15, 1953.

7. Supplemental Report on Colorado River Storage Project and Participating Projects Upper Colorado River Basin, October 1953, Box 4, folder 2, William Nelson Papers, CMUASC, Grand Junction.

8. Supplemental Report on Colorado River Storage Project; Mark W.T. Harvey, *A Symbol of Wilderness: Echo Park and the American Conservation Movement* (Seattle: University of Washington Press, 1994). Harvey discusses the evaporation rate controversy in chapter 6, 153–79.

9. Ivan C. Crawford, *Water Resources Planning in Colorado* (Denver: Colorado Water Conservation Board, 1957), 57–58.

10. Leeds, Hill, and Jewitt, Consulting Engineers, *Report on Depletion of Surface Water Supplies of Colorado West of the Continental Divide*, Prepared under Authority of HB 457, 39th Colorado General Assembly, 1st Regular Session, Bulletin no. 1, Surface Water Series, Colorado Water Conservation Board, William Nelson Papers, CMUASC, Grand Junction. Note: I found the Hill Report in the Nelson Papers on a shelf containing items yet to be accessioned.

11. Ibid., 1–8, 51; Marc Reisner, *Cadillac Desert: The American West and Its Disappearing Water*, rev. ed. (New York: Penguin Books, 1993), 261–64. Reisner asserts that Hill's figures were met with disbelief by the Bureau of Reclamation, which would not let any pessimistic assertion of the Colorado River's capacity get in the way of a large Colorado River Storage Project.

12. Leeds, Hill, and Jewitt, *Report on Depletion of Surface Water Supplies*, 52–58.

13. Ibid., 58–59.

14. Matthew Hildner, "Fight for the Faucet: The Denver Water Board, the Blue River, and Metropolitan Water Supply" (MA thesis, Colorado State University, Fort Collins, 1999), 46–47; Dan H. Hughes to Frank Delaney, December 5, 1954, Box 168, folder 21, Frank Delaney Papers, UCBA; Reisner, *Cadillac Desert*, 272.

15. Reisner, *Cadillac Desert*, 272.

16. *Denver Post*, December 7, 1953. In the fall the *Rocky Mountain News* had reported that Denver's growth "was doomed without the Blue River." The Blue, in a widely used phrase, was the "last water hole in the West." This argument was used with increasing frequency by the Denver Water Board and its friends in the media. The *News* article parroted Denver's legal argument that its claims to the Blue River extended back to 1914 and its first filings for the water occurred in the early 1920s. See *Rocky Mountain News*, September 15, 1953.

17. Crawford, *Water Resources Planning in Colorado*, 58–60; Hildner, "Fight for the Faucet," 47. The "Findings and Recommendations of the Colorado Conference Committee" contained ten recommendations for the CWCB to act upon at its December 11 meeting. It is clear that its most specific recommendation dealt with its endorsement of the Blue River diversion. The findings also recommended that Colorado insist on the two Western Slope reservoirs, DeBeque and Curecanti, which the state water board had favored. The other recommendations were glittering generalities, likely designed to show apparent state water unity. The Conference Committee's main purpose was to hide the controversial nature of its tenth recommendation to endorse the Blue River diversion.

18. Colorado Water Conservation Board Minutes, December 11, 1953, Box 75, folder 15, Frank Delaney Papers, UCBA.

19. Barnard succeeded Frank Delaney as counsel to the CRWCD in 1955.

20. Colorado Water Conservation Board Minutes, December 11, 1953.

21. Ibid.; CRWCD Minutes, December 19, 1953, folder "CRWCD Minutes, 1952–55," Colorado River Water Conservation District (hereafter CRWCD), Glenwood Springs.

22. CRWCD Minutes, December 19, 1953.

23. Colorado Water Conservation Board Minutes, December 30, 1953, Box 46, folder 6, George A. and James M. Pughe Papers, UCBA; Crawford, *Water Resource Planning in Colorado*, 60–61.

24. Colorado Water Conservation Board Minutes, December 30, 1953.

25. In the document "Suggestions of Points to Be Considered as Basis of Compromise," December 30, 1953, Box 80, folder 5, Frank Delaney Papers, UCBA. The Western Slope hoped to reaffirm the CWCB's February 22, 1951, policy to withdraw the Denver Blue diversion from any CRSP legislation, to bring the entire state together to support the CRSP legislation, to leave 300,000 acre-feet for oil shale development in western Colorado, and several other provisions relating to river

regulation. Not surprisingly, Western Slope negotiators also wanted to "complete as rapidly as possible the surveys now being conducted by the Bureau of Reclamation in Western Colorado to determine potential uses of water in Western Colorado." See "Suggestions of Points to Be Considered as Basis of Compromise," n.d., Box 80, folder 5, Frank Delaney Papers, UCBA.

26. "Suggestions of Points to Be Considered as Basis of Compromise"; Statement from Frank Delaney, Glenwood Springs, Colorado, n.d. [prepared for presentation to the Conciliation Committee], Box 80, folder 2, Frank Delaney Papers, UCBA.

27. Hildner, "Fight for the Faucet," 47–48; notes for the committee in Frank Merriell to Frank Delaney, Box 160, folder "Water Correspondence, Delaney-Merriell, July–December 1953," Frank Delaney Papers, UCBA; Steven C. Schulte, *Wayne Aspinall and the Shaping of the American West* (Boulder: University Press of Colorado, 2002), 59–60.

28. Crawford, *Water Resource Planning in Colorado*, 63–65.

29. Ibid., 64–65.

30. Harvey, *Symbol of Wilderness*, 147, 175.

31. Colorado River Storage Project, Hearings, Subcommittee on Irrigation and Reclamation, House Committee on Interior and Insular Affairs, 83rd Congress, 2nd Session, on HR 4449 et al., January 1954, iii–iv; Hildner, "Fight for the Faucet," 48–49.

32. *Daily Sentinel* (Grand Junction, CO) draft article, January 16, 1954; George Sanford Holmes to Burt Meyers, Western Union telegram, January 17, 1954, Box 4, folder 2, William Nelson Papers, CMUASC, Grand Junction. See the Resolution of the Upper Colorado River Commission, January 17, 1954, Box 4, folder 2, William Nelson Papers, CMUASC, Grand Junction.

33. Colorado River Storage Project, Hearings, 1954, 307–13.

34. Ibid., 316–17.

35. Ibid., 336–37; Schulte, *Wayne Aspinall*, 60.

36. Colorado River Storage Project, Hearings, 1954, 336–37; Schulte, *Wayne Aspinall*, 60; Hildner, "Fight for the Faucet," 49.

37. Colorado River Storage Project, Hearings, 1954, 620–21.

38. Ibid., 456–69, 486–94; George Sanford Holmes to William Nelson, Western Union telegram, January 22, 1954, Box 4, folder 12, William Nelson Papers, CMUASC, Grand Junction.

39. Schulte, *Wayne Aspinall*, 61; Colorado River Storage Project, Hearings, 1954, 235–37, 831–32.

40. Frank Delaney had written to Aspinall advising him to support the CRSP bill even without Echo Park included. Delaney's reasoning was that southwestern

Colorado wanted a bill that included Glen Canyon and a CRSP without the Echo Park Dam and would still allow for a dam on the Gunnison. See Frank Delaney to Wayne Aspinall, May 18, 1954, Box 168, folder 15, Frank Delaney Papers, UCBA. Aspinall quoted in George Stanford Holmes, "Aspinall Files Statement Endorsing Storage Project; Opposes Denver Diversion Plan at This Time," Box 4, folder 12, William Nelson Papers, CMUASC, Grand Junction.

41. Schulte, *Wayne Aspinall*, 60–61; Hildner, "Fight for the Faucet," 49–50; Elmo R. Richardson, *Dams, Parks, and Politics: Resource Development and Preservation in the Truman-Eisenhower Era* (Lexington: University Press of Kentucky, 1973), 142–44; Jon M. Cosco, *Echo Park: Struggle for Preservation* (Boulder: Johnson Books, 1995), 76–77; George Sanford Holmes, draft article, *Daily Sentinel*, February 4, 1954, Box 4, folder 12, William Nelson Papers, CMUASC, Grand Junction.

42. Harvey, *Symbol of Wilderness*, 211–12.

43. Ibid., 205; *Rocky Mountain News*, April 18, 1954; Colorado Water Conservation Board Minutes, June 21, 1954.

44. Harvey, *Symbol of Wilderness*, 223; Sierra Club News Release, "Sierra Club Commends Congress for Blocking Echo Park Dam," August 31, 1954, Box 4, folder 10, William Nelson Papers, CMUASC, Grand Junction.

45. Sierra Club News Release, "Sierra Club Commends Congress."

46. William Nelson to Edgar L. Dutcher, September 8, 1954, Box 4, folder 1, William Nelson Papers, CMUASC, Grand Junction.

47. Frank Delaney, Statement about Judge Mortimer Stone, October 21, 1954, Box 168, folder 18, Frank Delaney Papers, UCBA; *City and County of Denver et al. v. the Colorado River Water Conservation District et al.*, 276 P.2d 992 (1954).

48. Opinion quoted in *Rocky Mountain News*, October 19, 1954; *Denver Post*, October 19, 1954.

49. Patricia Limerick with Jason L. Hanson, *A Ditch in Time: The City, the West, and Water* (Golden, CO: Fulcrum, 2012), 143–49.

50. *Daily Sentinel*, October 20, 1954. William Nelson, the Western Slope's water reporter and a man active in western Colorado water politics (and a future member of the CWCB) termed Denver's reaction to the decision "phony and hysterical." Denver's "screaming" proved to Nelson that Denver knows and had known for some time that the amount of water in the Blue River is limited and that there is "much less water in western Colorado than many persons, even those in western Colorado, realize." Nelson, "The Westerner," *Daily Sentinel*, October 25, 1954.

51. Frank Delaney, Statement about Judge Mortimer Stone, October 21, 1954; Frank Delaney to Walter Walker, October 22, 1954, Box 169, folder 10, Frank Delaney Papers, UCBA.

52. Delaney, Statement about Judge Mortimer Stone, October 21, 1954.

53. Frank Delaney proposed editorials, "A Sound Decision" and "Judicial Courage"; Frank Delaney to Walter Walker, October 22, 1954, all in Box 169, folder 10, Frank Delaney Papers, UCBA; *Daily Sentinel*, October 24, 25, 26, 1954.

54. John R. Clark to Frank Delaney, October 25, 1954, Box 168, folder 17, Frank Delaney Papers, UCBA; *Daily Sentinel*, November 1, 1954.

55. *Daily Sentinel*, November 3, 1954.

56. Ibid., October 28, 1959; *Denver Post*, October 23, 1954.

57. Daniel Tyler, *The Last Water Hole in the West: The Colorado–Big Thompson Project and the Northern Colorado Water Conservancy District* (Niwot: University Press of Colorado, 1992), 208–9; Hildner, "Fight for the Faucet," 51–52; Saunders quoted in Limerick and Hanson, *Ditch in Time*, 148–50.

58. Tyler, *Last Water Hole*, 208–9.

59. Engle was acutely aware of the internecine squabbles within Colorado. In a 1953 congressional hearing on Fryingpan-Arkansas where he became acquainted firsthand with Colorado's east-west struggles, Engle rather famously told Colorado officials that if they had differences of opinion, they should go "back home" and settle them among themselves. As Engle phrased it, "I do not propose to sit up there and tell the people of Colorado how they ought to use the water. They can put it on their land or mix it with their whiskey." See *Daily Sentinel*, November 3, November 15, 1954.

60. Schulte, *Wayne Aspinall*, 62–64, details these developments. Grand Junction's *Daily Sentinel* observed that Aspinall would be in a "strong and favorable position to fight not only for the [Colorado River] Storage Project but for other reclamation projects without which the West would stagnate." See *Daily Sentinel*, November 7, 1954.

61. *Daily Sentinel*, November 6 and 7, 1954.

62. CRWCD Minutes, October 19, November 6, 1954, folder "CRWCD Minutes, 1952–55," CRWCD, Glenwood Springs; *Daily Sentinel*, October 20 and 22, 1954; George Sibley, *Water Wranglers: The 75-Year History of the Colorado River District—a Story about the Embattled Colorado River and the Growth of the West* (Glenwood Springs: Colorado River District, 2012), 171–72.

63. CRWCD Minutes, November 6, December 4, 1954, folder "CRWCD Minutes, 1952–55," CRWCD, Glenwood Springs. A movement to organize an All-Western Colorado Water District to maximize western Colorado's limited political and financial resources had seemed to sputter and fail in late 1954. This development was undoubtedly behind the CRWCD's discussion to possibly expand the district's borders. See also, Sibley, *Water Wranglers*, 171–78.

64. John Geoffrey Will, "Remarks Made at a Meeting of the Joint Legislative Subcommittee on Water Problems, Colorado Legislature, Denver, Colorado," December 29, 1954, Box 4, folder 3, William Nelson Papers, CMUASC, Grand Junction;

John B. Barnard to William Nelson, December 1, 1954, Box 2, folder "PWCD–Williams Fork Reservoir, Parshall Project Correspondence," John B. Barnard Papers, American Heritage Center, University of Wyoming (hereafter AHC), Laramie.

65. Tyler, *Last Water Hole*, 423.

66. The three bills containing provisions for the Blue River diversion were introduced by Representatives Manuel Fernandez (D-NM), William A. Dawson (R-UT), and Byron G. Rogers (D-CO). Rogers represented a congressional district framed by the City and County of Denver. For a brief overview of Rogers's career, see his *New York Times* obituary, January 2, 1984.

67. Wayne Aspinall to Frank Delaney, February 11, 1955, Box 168, folder 15, Frank Delaney Papers, UCBA.

68. Ibid.

69. Colorado River Storage Project, Hearings, Subcommittee on Irrigation and Reclamation, House Committee on Interior and Insular Affairs, 84th Congress, 1st Session, on HR 270 et al., 1955, Part 1, 45.

70. Ibid., 44–45.

71. Ibid., Part 2, 424–26.

72. Ibid., 426–37.

73. Ibid., 443–49.

74. Ibid., 450–53.

75. Ibid., 477–78; *Denver Post*, March 11, 1955.

76. Schulte, *Wayne Aspinall*, 62; Colorado River Storage Project Hearings, 1955, 1097–98.

77. CRWCD Minutes, April 19, 1955, folder "CRWCD Minutes, 1952–55," CRWCD, Glenwood Springs.

78. Ed Johnson Speech, December 20, 1954, Box 15, folder 7, Edwin C. Johnson Papers, University of Denver Archives, Denver, CO; Barney Whatley to Edwin Johnson, May 8, 1955, Box 1, folder 1, Silmon Smith Papers, CSHS.

79. Harvey, *Symbol of Wilderness*, 270–73; Schulte, *Wayne Aspinall*, 63–64.

80. CRWCD Minutes, September 17, 1955, folder "CRWCD Minutes, 1952–55," CRWCD, Glenwood Springs.

81. Ibid.

82. Senate Document 80 protected senior Colorado River water rights from the impact of diversion by the Colorado–Big Thompson Project through the operation of Green Mountain Reservoir.

83. CRWCD Minutes, July 1, 1955, folder "CRWCD Minutes, 1952–55," CRWCD, Glenwood Springs.

84. See "In the United States District Court for the State of Colorado, in the Matter of the Adjudication of Priorities of Water Rights in Water District no. 36

for Purposes of Irrigation, Civil no. 5016, and for Purposes Other than Irrigation, Civil no. 5017, Brief of Northern Colorado Water Conservancy District in Response to Questions of Law on Pretrial Hearing," August 2, 1955, Box 75, folder 8, Frank Delaney Papers, UCBA; *Rocky Mountain News*, March 2, 1955.

85. *Rocky Mountain News*, March 2, 1955.

86. Alvord, Burdick, and Howson, Engineers, *Report on Future Water Supply, Denver Municipal Water Works* (Chicago, March 1955), 2–3. This copy was accessed in Box 185, folder 9, Frank Delaney Papers, UCBA.

87. Ibid., 78–79.

88. Limerick and Nelson, *Ditch in Time*, 147–50.

89. Tyler, *Last Water Hole*, 210–11; Hildner, "Fight for the Faucet," 52–53; *Denver Post*, January 20, 1964.

90. See Tyler, *Last Water Hole*, 207–15.

91. Ibid., 210–17; *Denver Post*, January 20, 1964.

92. J. Lee Rankin to Silmon Smith, September 23, 1955, Box 2, folder 4, Silmon Smith Papers, CSHS; Hildner, "Fight for the Faucet," 55–57; Tyler, *Last Water Hole*, 212–15.

93. Tyler, *Last Water Hole*, 214–15; Hildner, "Fight for the Faucet," 57–59; Limerick and Hanson, *Ditch in Time*, 147–150; *Rocky Mountain News*, October 6, 1955.

94. Denver Water Board attorney Glenn Saunders estimated that the average amount of water Denver received would be 177,000 acre-feet per year. However, in wet years it could be as high as 200,000 acre-feet and in dry times as low as 100,000 acre-feet. See *Rocky Mountain News*, October 6, 1955.

95. Ibid., October 6 and 7, 1955; *Denver Post*, October 6, 1955. President Dwight D. Eisenhower, who frequently vacationed in Colorado and the Denver area, took a strong personal interest in the Blue River negotiations. In the final days of closed-door negotiations, the president was on record hoping the issues could be settled "in the best interests of all concerned." See *Daily Sentinel*, October 5, 1955.

96. *Daily Sentinel*, October 6, 7, 13, 1955.

97. *Denver Post*, October 6, 1955; *Rocky Mountain News*, October 6, 1955.

98. Schulte, *Wayne Aspinall*, 66; letter from Washington, New Mexico Newspapers Washington Bureau, December 16, 1955; William Nelson, "Upper Colorado Now Likely to Receive Some Support from Conservation Groups," undated, both in Box 4, folder 3, William Nelson Papers, CMUASC, Grand Junction; Harvey, *Symbol of Wilderness*, 279–85.

99. Wayne N. Aspinall to Upper Colorado River Commission, March 29, 1954; Wayne N. Aspinall to Frank Delaney, May 24, 1956, both in Box 82, folder 11, Frank Delaney Papers, UCBA. Goslin (1911–91) worked in water resources for more than fifty years. He cooperated closely with Aspinall on numerous projects over the

decades. From 1955 to 1979 he served as executive secretary of the Upper Colorado River Commission and later served as executive director of the Colorado Water Resources Development Authority. As secretary of the Upper Colorado River Commission, he was responsible for administering the Upper Colorado River Basin Compact. See Linda C. McGhee and John Newman, *Guide to the Ival V. Goslin Water Resources Collection* (Fort Collins: Colorado State University Water Resources Archive, 2007).

100. Schulte, *Wayne Aspinall*, 67; Harvey, *Symbol of Wilderness*, 284–85; "An Act to Authorize the Secretary of the Interior to Construct, Operate, and Maintain the Colorado River Storage Project and Participating Projects, and for Other Purposes," Public Law 485, 84th Congress, 2nd Session, Chapter 203, S. 500, April 11, 1956.

101. Schulte, *Wayne Aspinall*, 68; Tommy Neal, interview with Steven C. Schulte, Grand Junction, CO, January 4, 1997, transcript in author's possession.

102. Schulte, *Wayne Aspinall*, 67–68; Harvey, *Symbol of Wilderness*, 287–93; quotation in Hal K. Rothman, *The Greening of a Nation: Environmentalism in the United States since 1945* (Fort Worth: Harcourt Brace, 1998), 48; Mark W.T. Harvey, "Loving the Wild in Postwar America," in Michael Lewis, ed., *American Wilderness: A New History* (New York: Oxford University Press, 2007), 193–99.

103. CRWCD Minutes, December 17, 1955; January 17, February 22, April 17, 1956, folder "CRWCD Minutes, 1956," CRWCD, Glenwood Springs; John B. Barnard to Frank Delaney, March 16, 1955; F. M. Peterson to John B. Barnard, January 11, 1955; John B. Barnard to F. M. Peterson, January 13, 1955; John B. Barnard to William H. Nelson, June 1, 1955, all in Box 12, folder "CRWCD Correspondence 1956," John B. Barnard Papers, AHC. The CRWCD also moved its offices and gained more office space by relocating to the First National Bank building in Glenwood Springs. The CRWCD hired a secretary and retained the services of a bookkeeper. Sibley, *Water Wranglers*, 106–7, 171–77, also surveys the 1950s river district reorganization.

104. F. M. Peterson to John B. Barnard, January 11, 1955.

105. *Congressional Quarterly Fact Sheet*, January 23, 1959, 109; Schulte, *Wayne Aspinall*, 82.

6
Into the 1960s

A Tenuous Unity

There is no reason that western Colorado should have a representative in Congress. If we were so organized we could divide Colorado into east-west strips for congressional districts and all of Colorado's representatives in the Congress of the United States would be from eastern Colorado.

Glenn Saunders, February 1958, speaking at a water conference in Rocky Ford, Colorado[1]

From 1957 into the 1960s, Colorado's water wars waxed and waned, though the primary factors feeding the continued conflict remained the same. Denver continued its efforts to enlarge its municipal water system. The Western Slope devised arguments and policies to protect its disappearing water and reserve some for future economic growth. Oil shale's prospects were touted as a key to western Colorado's future. State water-planning efforts helped dampen sources of intrastate conflict. The appointment of Felix L. Sparks as director of the Colorado Water Conservation Board significantly helped paper over some of the state's regional differences. Perhaps most important for western Colorado, from 1958 to 1972 the Fourth District congressman

DOI: 10.5876/9781607325000.c006

for Colorado, Wayne N. Aspinall, presided over the House Committee on Interior and Insular Affairs. Aspinall was in a position to shape the most important pieces of legislation impacting the American West, including reclamation statues. These years also saw the Western Slope and the state of Colorado construct some of their most significant water infrastructures.

From the Fryingpan(-Arkansas) to the Political Fire

The late 1950s and 1960s also witnessed a concerted effort by Colorado water officials to help the state gain its share of the Colorado River Storage Project (CRSP). In the process, Colorado saw an opportunity to ensure its economic future. Many of the projects listed under the heading "CRSP Participating Projects" were located in western Colorado. The construction of these enterprises would help the Western Slope realize its most basic water maxim: that Colorado River water and that of its tributaries belong and should first be used in the area where it originates—western Colorado. The CRSP had two functions from Colorado's perspective. The four large storage reservoirs (Glen Canyon, Flaming Gorge, Navajo, and Curecanti) would hold runoff to be released to help the Upper Basin states meet their Colorado River Compact requirement of 75 million acre-feet in any ten consecutive years. The Western Slope's most immediate CRSP benefits would accrue from construction of some of its Participating Projects, including the Florida, Paonia, Pine River Extension, Silt, and Smith Fork Projects.

While the CRSP Participating Projects began to take shape, two major water controversies dominated Colorado in the 1950s and 1960s: the bid to build the long-debated Fryingpan-Arkansas Project and the struggle to pass legislation for a Central Arizona Project. Both sets of projects proved controversial, not only within the state but throughout all seven Colorado River Basin states.

Political leaders from Colorado Springs to Pueblo gazed with envy at northern Colorado's successful achievement of the Colorado–Big Thompson Project in 1937.[2] Early drafts of what would become the Fryingpan-Arkansas Project emphasized using Gunnison River Basin water and diverting it through trans-mountain tunnels to the Arkansas River Valley. Early Gunnison-Arkansas plans called for a system of canals to take the water to the base of Marshall Pass, where a twelve-mile tunnel under the Continental Divide would carry the water to the Arkansas River. From there, it would flow to Pueblo and other cities and be put to use by the people of southeastern Colorado. The 600,000–700,000 annual acre-foot diversion would lay waste to the Gunnison Valley's agricultural prospects and severely undermine Colorado's ability to help meet its Colorado River Compact obligations. For these reasons, from its conception, most Western Slope officials opposed the massive Gunnison-Arkansas Project.[3]

As World War II wound down, the Bureau of Reclamation and the western states began dusting off and reformulating old reclamation plans. When southeastern Colorado water interests tried to revive Gunnison-Arkansas diversion after the war, the sheer size of the plan crystallized strong opposition. While the project was being reconfigured and revised into the smaller Fryingpan-Arkansas, the Colorado Water Conservation Board and other Upper Basin interests were busy negotiating the Upper Colorado River Basin Compact and drawing up early plans for a Colorado River Storage Project. Fryingpan-Arkansas would not be recommended for inclusion in the massive CRSP. It would have to pass judgment as a stand-alone project.[4]

Yet given the hostility of the Western Slope toward further diversions, there was a good chance that it would fight even a scaled-down version of the original Gunnison-Arkansas diversion plan. In the late 1940s the Colorado Water Conservation Board formed two policy and review committees to begin formulating a statewide consensus for both the Gunnison-Arkansas and Denver–Blue River diversions. The Gunnison-Arkansas Policy and Review Committee actually gained the support of many people on the Western Slope when southeastern Colorado water advocates agreed to limit the project to what had originally been conceived as only the first phase of the entire project. The project was also renamed the Fryingpan-Arkansas Project. As one of the project's principal proponents, Charles J. Biese, remembered, the original plan for the Gunnison-Arkansas Project was "so big in size that it drew all kinds of opposition, and it became obvious that the only way you could ever get any federal funding would be to drop the major diversion" and limit it to the first phase, the Fryingpan-Arkansas Project. "This was agreed to reluctantly," Biese recalled, "but was necessary."[5]

Fryingpan-Arkansas thus emerged in a Colorado political universe preoccupied by the much larger and, from a statewide perspective, more significant task of shaping a CRSP that would enable Colorado and the Upper Basin to build multiple water projects and meet their obligations under the Colorado

River Compact. Yet in southeastern Colorado, "Fry-Ark," as it was lovingly known, was viewed to be as significant as life itself. However, the rest of Colorado seemed either indifferent to the project or, in the case of western Colorado, suspicious of or hostile to another raid on its fast-diminishing water supplies. One fact is certain: from the perspective of the early 1950s, Fryingpan-Arkansas faced a rough pathway to passage. While Fryingpan-Arkansas could gain the approval of the Colorado Water Conservation Board and could count on the support of the state's senators, obtaining cooperation from the Western Slope, the Colorado River Water Conservation District (CRWCD), and the increasingly powerful Fourth District congressman Wayne Aspinall proved extremely challenging for Fry-Ark proponents.

After two years of deliberation, in 1950 western and southeastern Colorado came to an agreement on a set of operating principles for a proposed Fryingpan-Arkansas Project. The Gunnison-Arkansas Policy and Review Committee had been formed on November 24, 1948, by the Colorado Water Conservation Board (CWCB). The committee included representatives from the CWCB, the Colorado Game and Fish Commission, western Colorado, the Arkansas Valley, and the city of Colorado Springs. The principles were clearly influenced by the Colorado–Big Thompson Senate Bill 80 guidelines. On February 22, 1951, the committee's findings were approved by the Colorado Water Conservation Board. The principles provided for the construction and maintenance of the Aspen Reservoir on the Roaring Fork River, above the town of Aspen. The reservoir would provide 28,000 acre-feet of replacement water for some of the water diverted to southeastern Colorado. The operating principles also assured Western Slope water users that water stored in Green Mountain Reservoir (as described in Senate Document 80, 75th Congress, 1st Session, June 15, 1937) "shall not be diminished by this project." Concurrently and not surprisingly, the CRWCD asked the state water board not to approve further trans-mountain diversions until a complete survey of future state water needs was completed. The board agreed not to support any more federally funded trans-mountain diversions until the long-awaited survey had been completed.[6]

From 1950 to 1956, western Colorado was entangled not only with the Fryingpan-Arkansas Project but also with shaping the Colorado River Storage Project, fighting Denver's attempt to include the Blue River diversion in the CRSP. On May 4, 1951, the Fryingpan-Arkansas Project received national momentum when Secretary of the Interior Oscar Chapman approved the project, calling it "vital" to the future of southeastern Colorado. The chief congressional advocate for the project, southeastern Colorado congressman J. Edgar Chenoweth, agreed to support Denver's inclusion of the Blue River diversion in the CRSP in return for additional eastern Colorado support for Fryingpan-Arkansas. The state of Colorado had clearly placed Fryingpan-Arkansas on the political "back burner" during these years, but southeastern Colorado's water interests still intended to try to get the bill passed alongside the larger and generally more significant CRSP legislation.[7]

In the 1954 election year, western Colorado congressman Wayne N. Aspinall became entangled with Fryingpan-Arkansas, almost to the detriment of his political career. The Fryingpan-Arkansas Bill, after being favorably reported from the House Committee on Interior and Insular Affairs during the 83rd Congress, failed on a House of Representatives floor vote, 188 to 195. Eastern Coloradans were both disappointed and angered by this turn of events. At the same time, the project's near-passage frightened many Western Slope residents who feared yet another raid on their water. During the fall of 1954, Aspinall got caught in the middle, blamed for the bill's last-minute failure in the House and castigated by many Western Slope residents who feared he was agreeing to the giveaway of western Colorado's water.[8]

According to the Grand Junction *Daily Sentinel*, the election stakes for western Colorado were high because if the Republicans retained control of the House of Representatives, Representative John P. Saylor (R-PA) would chair the Subcommittee on Irrigation and Reclamation. A predictable foe of large-scale reclamation, Saylor was also an ardent conservationist (and an advocate of legal recognition of wilderness lands) who envisioned his role on the committee as a brake on its disposition to rubber-stamp western water projects. While Saylor questioned the need for many components of the CRSP, including Echo Park Dam, he reserved a special dislike for Fryingpan-Arkansas. Because of this attitude, Saylor was considered, perversely, somewhat of a hero in Pitkin County. *Daily Sentinel* writer George Sanford Holmes considered that a Saylor chairmanship was "a contingency that should scare the daylights out of Colorado voters interested in developing their own water resources."[9]

With election day looming, Wayne Aspinall frequently found himself publicly equating his mission in the US Congress with that of his political mentor, Edward T. Taylor—to not give away a drop of western Colorado's water. Colorado River Basin water, Aspinall asserted, should be used in western Colorado "where the water falls and the snow melts." During the campaign, Aspinall experienced firsthand the volatile nature of Colorado's water politics. He never again made the mistake of putting himself in a position to appear less than 100 percent committed to retain Western Slope water. Despite the confusion over his position on Fryingpan-Arkansas, Aspinall managed to prevail by 4,500 votes, though he was trounced in Pitkin County by two opponents: his Republican foe and, in a raucous last-minute write-in campaign, Pennsylvania's John P. Saylor.[10]

Aspinall also believed he had won because of one fact repeated over and over during the 1954 campaign: that his reelection would make him second in seniority on the House Committee on Interior and Insular Affairs (Interior Committee). If the Democrats could win back control of Congress, Aspinall stood a good chance to chair the Subcommittee on Irrigation and Reclamation. He had started his odyssey up the ladder in 1949 as fourteenth in seniority. After 1954, the chair of the House Interior Committee, arguably the most powerful position from which to effect land and resource policy in the American West, was within his grasp.[11]

Southeastern Colorado water officials faced a dark situation after the 1954 elections. Aspinall's congressional victory, combined with Republican loss of control over the House of Representatives, vaulted the Palisade congressman to the chairmanship of the Subcommittee on Irrigation and Reclamation. Both the CRSP and Fryingpan-Arkansas would pass through his subcommittee on their respective routes to the Interior Committee and the House floor. A more realistic calculation of Fry-Ark's chances for passage seemed to be dawning on the bill's supporters such as Frank Hoag Jr., publisher of the Pueblo, Colorado, *Star-Chieftain*. Since Aspinall had announced his intention to seek passage of the Colorado River Storage Project ahead of Fry-Ark, "it is foolhardy for us to knock our heads against a stone wall." What Hoag really wanted was for Colorado's senators and Front Range congressmen (like Chenoweth) to work hard to support the CRSP and thus make Aspinall feel obligated to reciprocate with a strong stand for Fryingpan-Arkansas. Hoag and Chenoweth were likely reacting to resolutions such as the one passed by the Colorado River Water Conservation District in January 1955 affirming the water project strategy announced by Aspinall after the 1954 election: to first authorize the CRSP before considering the Fryingpan-Arkansas Project.[12]

Fryingpan-Arkansas legislation continued to flounder in 1955–56 and beyond, failing again to obtain a ruling in 1956 after the CRSP had become law. Its margin of defeat was even greater than two years before. Aspinall continued to confound his eastern Colorado counterparts by failing to speak in support of the measure from the House floor in 1956. As a respected voice in reclamation matters and chair of the Subcommittee on Irrigation and Reclamation, many non-western House members looked to Aspinall for clues as to how to vote on traditional western matters like federal reclamation. If he were ardently in favor of the bill, it stood a much better chance of passage.[13]

FRYINGPAN-ARKANSAS: AUTHORIZATION AT LAST

Fryingpan-Arkansas languished in Congress until the early 1960s. Southeastern Colorado water advocates scorned Aspinall for failing to move with more speed on this legislation. Several new developments caused the bill to be delayed, including Aspinall's goal of funding authorized CRSP projects and moving some of the so-called CRSP Participating Projects closer to enactment. Aspinall became chair of the House Committee on Interior and Insular Affairs in 1959; from that position he could dictate not only when many bills passed but the terms surrounding their enactment. Until Fry-Ark became law in 1962, southeastern Arkansas water advocates routinely blamed Aspinall for not "aggressively assisting us." The Fourth District Colorado congressman became a scapegoat for Fryingpan-Arkansas's failure to gain earlier passage.[14]

Responding to Western Slope criticisms of the Fryingpan-Arkansas Project, water officials worked to revise the project to better suit the interests of Aspen-area residents and the Western Slope in general. The replacement storage reservoir in early drafts of the bill had been the relatively small Aspen Reservoir, which only had a capacity of approximately 26,000 acre-feet. At a 1956 meeting of officials of the Bureau of Reclamation, the Pitkin County Water Association, the Colorado River Water Storage Association, and some members of the Colorado Water Conservation Board, the potential impact of Fryingpan-Arkansas on western Colorado was discussed. Phillip Smith, the new secretary-engineer of the CRWCD, reviewed the history of trans-basin diversions from a Western Slope perspective during the meeting, noting that in the early history of diversions, Western Slope citizens "raised little or no objections to them [diversions], feeling that the waters could be spared without serious harm." However, with increasing numbers of small diversions and more planned proposals for large diversions, the Western Slope was being asked to "satisfy the insatiable appetites of [the] Eastern Slope interest in Colorado River water."[15]

Smith was undoubtedly referring to the Colorado–Big Thompson Project and quite likely the early plans for the Gunnison-Arkansas Project. Smith made a simple but strong point that represented the thinking of many western Coloradans. If the Western Slope continued to trade away its water for lesser amounts in compensatory reservoirs, "the future growth of Western Colorado is foretold and dark indeed."[16]

A possible path toward meeting western Colorado concerns about Fry-Ark began to open in 1957. CRWCD meetings began to discuss constructing a larger reservoir in the Aspen area that would replace the smaller-capacity Aspen Reservoir. At a July 16, 1957, meeting, Phillip Smith spoke about possibly filing for 100,000 acre-feet of water at the Ruedi Reservoir site. Such a large Western Slope reservoir could even be used to diminish the amount of water earmarked for Fryingpan-Arkansas during low water years. In what was clearly a demonstration of wishful thinking, Smith hoped a 100,000 acre-feet Ruedi-site water right might also render Fry-Ark infeasible.[17]

At the same meeting, the Western Slope revealed yet another strategy it had been following to combat further trans-mountain diversions: Smith indicated that he had been filing for water rights on every possible stream "susceptible to transmountain diversion in the Upper Gunnison Basin" where the water supply would support possible CRSP Participating Projects. The CRWCD board supported the secretary-engineer's activities and passed a resolution urging him to continue to file for water near the Ruedi site and throughout the Upper Gunnison region.[18]

Because of the Western Slope's insistence on revising Fry-Ark and with Congressman Aspinall in a more influential position after the 1958 elections, the Fryingpan-Arkansas Project underwent a major reconfiguration in the late 1950s. The new Ruedi Reservoir would hold almost four times the capacity of the Aspen site. Ruedi would be used for replacement and regulatory purposes in both the Fryingpan and Roaring Fork Rivers. Retaining adequate stream flow had long been a concern of Pitkin County residents. Western Slope water rights impacted by the diversion of project water to southeastern Colorado would also benefit from Ruedi Reservoir's storage capacity. In the revised 1959–60 drafts of Fryingpan-Arkansas, 69,200 acre-feet of water would be diverted annually across the Continental Divide to the Arkansas Valley. Existing Western Slope water rights on the Fryingpan and Roaring Fork Rivers would be decreed as senior to project waters. The newly designed Fryingpan-Arkansas Project, which included the Ruedi Reservoir, began taking shape as soon as Felix L. Sparks was appointed director of the Colorado Water Conservation Board. To Sparks, the tension between the Eastern and Western Slopes over the Fry-Ark diversion had delayed the overall enactment of a more vigorous state water program. Sparks became a primary advocate of a reconfigured project with the larger Ruedi Reservoir.[19]

The new Fryingpan-Arkansas Project, the product of years of study, wrangling, and political turmoil, brought a degree of peace and cooperation between southeastern Colorado and the Western Slope. In 1958 the two regions had almost "broke[n] into a holocaust" when the Western Slope filed for conditional water decrees to the Basalt and West Divide Projects while Fryingpan-Arkansas failed to file for a decree. Later in 1958, with tensions rising, Governor Stephen McNichols and Felix Sparks intervened by forming a bi-slope committee to work on the new set of operating principles reflecting the replacement of Aspen Reservoir with Ruedi and to resolve decree priority dates. The new operating principles would guide the project and protect the interests of both parts of the state.[20] However, even if Fry-Ark was taking final shape by 1959, it was still not ready for action in the US Congress. That process would require a more propitious moment. House Committee on Interior and Insular Affairs chair Wayne Aspinall remained committed to advancing Fry-Ark, but only after Congress had budgeted for some of the CRSP's crucial components.[21]

Aspinall worked especially hard on the CRSP Curecanti Project, located on the Gunnison River in the heart of his congressional district. Curecanti had followed a difficult route to inclusion in the CRSP bill. Curecanti had been downsized considerably from earlier plans in response to Gunnison Valley citizen concerns. It also required more feasibility studies after the CRSP's passage. In the late 1950s, after President Dwight D. Eisenhower had announced a "no new starts" policy for federal reclamation projects, Aspinall remarked that the federal reclamation program appeared "in more difficulty" than at any time since he had entered Congress in 1949. Both Aspinall and reclamation commissioner Floyd Dominy believed the outlook for new reclamation project starts for 1960 "was very dark." After vetoing a large public works bill containing provisions for many water projects (including some CRSP projects), the Democratically dominated Congress overrode Eisenhower's veto, allowing monies to flow to authorized CRSP projects. Once Curecanti's construction had started, Aspinall allowed himself to devote more energy to move Fryingpan-Arkansas through Congress.[22]

In 1961, Aspinall pledged to "carry the fight" for Fry-Ark's passage before the new 87th Congress. Southeastern Colorado water officials expressed delight at Aspinall's declaration, which some characterized as the Western Slope legislator's strongest expression of support for the project to date. The *Denver Post* joyfully welcomed Aspinall's apparent change of heart toward Fry-Ark because he was "regarded as one of the most influential Western members of the House." Unfortunately for its supporters, Fryingpan-Arkansas remained saddled with too many feasibility and fiscal questions to assure a fast 1961 passage. The new secretary of the interior and former Arizona congressman Stewart Udall termed the project a "two-time loser" before Congress. Udall also expressed disdain for the bill's chief sponsor, J. Edgar Chenoweth, because of the legislator's conservative stand on many social issues. However, with Aspinall finally behind the bill, Udall and other members of the Kennedy administration needed to be somewhat circumspect for fear of endangering the administration's ambitious conservation agenda, as most land and water bills had to pass Aspinall's purview. On May 3, 1961, Udall and the Department of the Interior recommended the enactment of Fryingpan-Arkansas.[23]

Fryingpan-Arkansas received the approval of Wayne Aspinall's House Committee on Interior and Insular Affairs in the fall of 1961. Aspinall and other supporters of the bill decided to bide their time and clear up some other issues associated with the bill and then send a clean Fry-Ark and New Mexico's Navajo–San Juan–Chama bill to the House Committee on Rules and beyond in 1962. For the first time, the chances of passage of the controversial Colorado water diversion appeared strong. A May 26, 1961, *Aspen Times* editorial somewhat sheepishly admitted that the paper had been wrong in opposing the project for so many years. Two weeks later the *Times* attempted to calm any lingering Pitkin County and Aspen-area fears over Fryingpan-Arkansas by discussing the project's benefits to Aspen, the Western Slope, and Colorado at large. "We in Aspen," the newspaper proclaimed, "are not living in a vacuum."[24]

The Kennedy administration had failed to pass one single piece of significant reclamation legislation in 1961, its first year in office. Heading into 1962, Aspinall labeled Fryingpan-Arkansas the "top piece" of legislation for that year. After agreeing to move the New Mexico water bill first, Aspinall promised a "do or die" effort on Fry-Ark. Navajo–San Juan–Chama sailed through the House of Representatives on May 23, 1962, after a strong lobbying campaign highlighted by the appearance of a delegation of Navajo leaders. The two projects now went their separate ways because of the New Mexico project's one advantage: "Indians" as beneficiaries, as Aspinall succinctly phrased it. After a difficult struggle to obtain a rule for Fry-Ark, debate on the measure occurred. A floor vote on the legislation happened the following day. Aspinall spoke for the project, and the Kennedy administration made clear its full, if belated, support for the reclamation project. Aspinall informed his congressional colleagues that the rumored Colorado water war sparked by the proposal had been resolved by changes in the bill, and the legislation "has the unqualified support of the entire State."[25]

The decade-long struggle to pass the Fryingpan-Arkansas Project finally reached its conclusion in the summer of 1962. The bill cleared the House on June 13 while the Senate voted its approval on August 7. Fry-Ark became law with President Kennedy's signature on August 16. Still fearing a backlash from Western Slope voters for his support of the bill, Aspinall went to great lengths to identify the project's benefits for western Colorado. Aspinall touted the project's water storage for the Western Slope in the Ruedi Reservoir, noting that it would offer strong support for the nascent oil shale industry. Ruedi Dam and Reservoir would enable western Colorado's streams to be kept alive and flowing during the peak summer and fall diversion periods. Aspinall believed Fry-Ark, in its 1962 form, offered many tangible benefits for the Western Slope.[26]

The story of Fryingpan-Arkansas is another telling case study in Colorado's twentieth-century water wars. Fry-Ark illustrated the problems of balancing the legitimate water needs of the southeastern Arkansas Valley with the necessity to protect the future water requirements of the Western Slope. The timing of the Fry-Ark diversion with other major episodes in Colorado's water wars gave this project particular volatility in the context of state water politics. Back when the Gunnison-Arkansas Project was first introduced and discussed statewide, it appeared on the heels of the hard-fought and controversial Colorado–Big Thompson legislation. The Western Slope rightly believed it had lost a large share of the Colorado River Basin's water, about 310,000 acre-feet annually. Fryingpan-Arkansas suffered a planning delay because of World War II and the need after the war to negotiate the Upper Colorado River Basin Compact. By 1950, Fryingpan-Arkansas had become suffocated legislatively by the nationally and regionally significant Colorado River Storage Project legislation. Not only did the titanic battle for the CRSP obscure Fryingpan-Arkansas, the emotional struggle for Denver's Blue River diversion also forced Fry-Ark into the background.

Western Slope anger, largely directed against the Denver Board of Water Commissioners and its Blue River power play, created a backlash of determination to limit and prevent further diversions, including Fryingpan-Arkansas. The *Colorado Water Congress Newsletter* credited Colorado Water Conservation Board director Felix Sparks for his ability to mend long-standing Eastern versus Western Slope fractures to enact Fry-Ark. The project's authorization represented "a great personal victory" for Sparks, "who used every method from friendly persuasion to tough talk and head-cracking to iron out differences" between the two slopes. Wayne Aspinall's significant role must also be highlighted. The Western Slope congressman was referred to as Colorado's water "quarterback." Aspinall determined the timing of Fry-Ark's passage, and his strategy to bring it to the floor when he did ensured its success. The thirty-year odyssey of the Fryingpan-Arkansas Project had reached a conclusion.[27]

INTO THE 1960S AND AWAY FROM INTRASTATE STRUGGLES

The appointment of Felix "Larry" Sparks as director of the Colorado Water Conservation Board represented a milestone event in the middle of the wrangling over the Fryingpan-Arkansas Project. Sparks, who hailed from the small Western Slope town of Delta, worked to rebuild statewide confidence in the Colorado Water Conservation Board, as more than a group dominated by Front Range interests. A World War II hero, Sparks was the commanding officer of the 3rd Battalion of the 157th US Army Infantry Regiment that entered and liberated the Dachau Concentration Camp. Following World War II,

Sparks earned a law degree at the University of Colorado and served as Delta County, Colorado, district attorney and a member of the Colorado Supreme Court before being appointed to the CWCB by Governor Stephen McNichols in 1958. It is fair to say that ever since the death of Clifford Stone in 1952, the Western Slope had believed its interests were not being safeguarded by the Colorado Water Conservation Board. Sparks would emerge as a strong, mediating voice for state water matters in the years ahead.[28]

Sparks's energetic and unifying impact on the state's water program could be seen in the early months following his appointment. Addressing the Executive Committee of the Colorado River Water Conservation District in late 1958, he urged western Colorado water users to put aside their differences with the Eastern Slope and enact Fry-Ark. Fry-Ark, according to Sparks, had taken up a great deal of CWCB staff time and has "constantly slowed" Colorado's overall water program. Sparks's rallying cry for state unity focused on the dangers posed by other Colorado River Basin states: "We are constantly under attack from every state," not only adjoining states but those in the Lower Basin as well. In stressing the need for state unity, Sparks echoed and complimented the strategy for a unified statewide water program advocated by Congressman Wayne Aspinall. Sparks and Aspinall would help lead Colorado toward greater unity in the volatile 1960s.[29]

Despite occasional flareups and resumption of skirmishes between Colorado's two slopes, open intra-slope warfare seemed to diminish heading into the 1960s. Several major developments impacted a change in the state's water political culture as it related to water decision-making. In 1961 the legendary Colorado politician Big Ed Johnson effused over the CWCB's "progress and effectiveness" under the leadership of Sparks. "No man has done more for water conservation and utilization than he," Johnson remarked. Prior to Sparks's appointment, the Western Slope had explored ways to engineer the dismissal of Ivan C. Crawford, who had succeeded Clifford Stone as head of the CWCB in 1953. Crawford was essentially a caretaker head of the CWCB, who usually seemed most available to listen to the persuasive arguments emanating from the Eastern Slope. Crawford held a provisional appointment from 1953 to 1957, never a permanent position. Western Slope board members, including William Nelson of Grand Junction and F. M. Peterson of Delta, had explored ways to remove Crawford from his position. Peterson favored removing Crawford as long as his critics had the votes "to get the job done" and had a viable candidate in mind to take the position, especially someone "the Western Slope could trust" and a person who could "dominate the water efforts in the other states." Crawford's unsteady tenure had led to a crisis of trust in the state water board from western Colorado's perspective.[30]

Other developments helped lead to an alteration in the temper of Colorado's water politics environment. In July 1957, in an attempt to foster state water policy unity, Colorado governor Stephen McNichols initiated discussions to form a Colorado Water Congress (CWC). The idea stemmed from McNichols's frustration with intrastate fighting over the Fryingpan-Arkansas Project, which the governor believed had resulted in delaying the project's enactment. The CWC, McNichols hoped, would not replace the Colorado Water Conservation Board but instead would supplement that board's mission. It would include representatives of all water-user groups throughout Colorado and would devise a system to determine priority for future water projects. Above all, the new organization would attempt to mediate the water disputes between eastern and western Colorado.[31]

Throughout the second half of 1957, discussions of McNichols's CWC proposal percolated across western Colorado. Initially, the Western Slope appeared reluctant to actively pursue the governor's idea. The region's experience with the Colorado Water Conservation Board during the 1950s likely made it less than enthusiastic to organize another statewide water organization. During an informal discussion of state water issues at the November 1957 National Reclamation Association meeting, CRWCD secretary-engineer Phillip Smith commented that "there was virtually nothing in the field of water policy affecting the use of Colorado River water in Colorado on which the two areas [Eastern and Western Slopes] could agree." Such sentiments did not bode well for an immediate resolution of Colorado's ongoing water skirmishes or for building a new water organization.[32]

Despite misgivings over the possibility of a new water organization, in the late fall of 1957 discussions throughout the state intensified regarding the formation of such a group. At a meeting of the Colorado State Bar Association in late 1957, a steering committee was formed with traditional Western Slope foe, Denver Water Board attorney Glenn Saunders, at its head and four other members, including John B. Barnard Jr. of the CRWCD. The steering committee would frame the issues to be considered during the first general meeting of the CWC, which would be called at an undetermined date. The group contacted nineteen outstanding water authorities in Colorado. According to a memoir written by Barnard, the nineteen selected were water leaders who had been the most active and "bitterly engaged" in Colorado's historical water wars. It was apparent, according to Barnard, that each of these men had fought hard, long, and ably for his section of the state over the past decades. The question came to be: would they fight with the same ardor for their state? Early on, the steering committee and the group of nineteen agreed that the CWC would try to focus on issues on which there was substantial Colorado-wide agreement; by the same token, the group "would sweep under the carpet the matters on which there were substantial disagreements."[33]

At a statewide water conference held on December 30, 1957, a group of water engineers and attorneys gathered at the Denver Chamber of Commerce Building to discuss pressing state water-related issues and to further refine plans for the proposed water congress. The group of twenty-some men included only four from the Western Slope: John B. Barnard Sr., John B. Barnard Jr., Duane Barnard, and Phillip Smith. With Glenn Saunders acting as chair, the group met an additional three times. At the conclusion of these meetings, an expanded steering committee agreed to meet again to develop an agenda for the proposed Colorado Water Congress.[34]

John B. Barnard Sr. drafted a proposed platform to present to the CWC steering committee. Before submitting it, Barnard asked the dean of Grand Junction's water attorneys, Silmon Smith, to analyze the document. The acerbic Smith lamented that Colorado's water issues "will not be settled in my lifetime." Besides, "I have been an impotent observer of the giving away of considerable [amounts] of Colorado's water and I am not about to act as window dressing for any more such activities." As for Barnard's CWC platform recommendations, they were clearly the work of someone concerned with the perennial issue of future Western Slope water supplies. A "basic consideration" inserted by Barnard reminded delegates that Colorado had been divided by both physical and historical barriers. The settling of western Colorado in the early 1880s had rendered it at a disadvantage in regard to water development. Barnard then turned to a standard Western Slope water defense argument: "The yet unrealized potential for agricultural, mineral, economic, and industrial development in Western Colorado is of great importance to the state and the nation."[35]

Barnard also included ideas about the need for a statewide water organization. Calling the Continental Divide a "psychological barrier" as well as a physical divide, he admitted that the state's water wars had monopolized the time and energies of so much of Colorado that statewide water development had been neglected. Nearby states understood Colorado's divided history over water and had taken advantage of the Centennial State's inability to act in a unified manner. Colorado, he pointed out, remained the only state in the Rocky Mountain region without a statewide water association. To dampen the controversy, Barnard believed the CWC should only consider and discuss matters where "substantial agreement" existed among all sectors of the state. In other words, the proposed CWC should never foster further state sectional discord. Finally, Barnard included a section on Colorado's water conflicts and how to resolve them. His suggestion seemed to be a thinly veiled attack against the work of the CWCB since the death of Clifford Stone in 1952. "Colorado has failed to adequately assemble and disseminate the facts" when intrastate water conflicts have arisen, Barnard argued. As a result, he proposed dividing Colorado's water problems into those that needed to be solved immediately and those not susceptible to an immediate solution. To effect solutions to state water issues, Barnard (and apparently several more members of the CWC steering committee) recommended strengthening the Colorado Water Conservation Board on matters ranging from expanding its paid professional staff to creating a more immediate "continuous and intimate relationship" between the board and various regional water agencies throughout the state.[36]

After helping to draft a proposed platform for the new water congress, Barnard and Phillip Smith agreed to work with a group of about twenty officials to decide which of the state's water problems the new organization would eventually tackle. Barnard indicated that the Western Slope would cooperate only if hot-button issues like Colorado River trans-mountain diversions were off the table. Barnard told the group that western Colorado considered the Colorado River and its protection within Colorado "the first and most important water problem before the State of Colorado and its people."[37]

Revised at a January 1958 meeting, the proposed CWC platform was presented to the governor and attorney general. In his report to the CRWCD Board of Directors, Barnard revealed his true intent in taking such great interest in forming the CWC—to advance the idea of a definitive engineering, hydrological, and legal study of the Colorado River by the state of

Colorado, a study that, depending on who you talked to, had either failed to be done to this point or failed to yield credible results, as in the case of the Hill Report. With a certain sense of déjà vu, Barnard reiterated for the seemingly millionth time that western Colorado needed to ascertain the amount of water required for future development *"to form the basis of a limitation on transmountain diversions* [emphasis added]."[38]

While the Western Slope provided ideas to shape the CWC, western Colorado maintained a vigilant attitude through the early months of the organization's formation. Eastern Colorado's enthusiastic embrace of the proposed congress set off alarm bells in the minds of many Western Slopers. For example, western Colorado feared giving the CWC the leeway to settle intrastate issues by vote of the entire membership. CRWCD counsel Barnard observed in January 1958 that the Colorado River District should be "vigilant" in its participation in the statewide water group. If the CWC did not protect Colorado River water, "we must be prepared to oppose it in its activity." This point was dramatically driven home in late February 1958 when Barnard's fears became reality.[39]

Barnard and the Denver Water Board's Glenn Saunders were invited to address a large group of water users in the Arkansas River town Rocky Ford. Barnard stated to this eastern Colorado audience that if and when Fryingpan-Arkansas were authorized, there would no longer be additional water available to other parts of the state since western Colorado would need to tap the little water that remained to ensure its own economic future. Saunders responded to Barnard's address by referring to the Western Slope's attitude toward state water problems as "provincial." The Western Slope's historical answer to east-west Colorado water negotiations was usually an "emphatic 'No.'" Saunders told the audience that "he was not convinced that the need for the amount of water claimed by Western Colorado [for future uses] was justified." Plenty of water existed for both slopes, according to Saunders.[40]

In a statement dripping with sarcasm, Saunders all but mocked the often quoted Western Slope assertion that its coal and oil shale could make it an American version of the famed Ruhr Valley. If this was true, Saunders remarked, Denver would be willing to turn back its trans-mountain diversions to make that development possible. In other words, Saunders doubted that the oil shale revolution would ever occur. Most disturbing to Western Slope ears was Saunders's assertion that if western Colorado did not cooperate and share its water with eastern Colorado, the Front Range would use its population, wealth, and political strength to "accomplish the transmountain diversions it needs." Saunders continued: "There is no reason that western Colorado should have a representative in Congress. If we were so organized we could divide Colorado into east-west strips for congressional districts and all of Colorado's representatives in the Congress of the United States would be from eastern Colorado."[41]

The CRWCD's Phillip Smith, also in attendance at Rocky Ford, reported that the eastern Colorado audience appeared shocked by Saunders's tirade, which the CRWCD minutes characterized as "vitriolic and vengeful." It is thus little wonder that Barnard, after returning from Rocky Ford, confessed to William H. Nelson, longtime member of the Colorado Water Conservation Board and associate editor of the Grand Junction *Daily Sentinel*, that he had "never liked the idea of a Water Congress." Above all, Barnard believed a statewide water organization such as the CWC should not concern itself with intrastate controversies. The possibility of being outvoted by Front Range interests would always be a danger in such an organization. So, what should western Colorado do about the proposed CWC? Non-participation was not an option. Such an action would only foment unified opposition to Western Slope interests. The safest course, according to Barnard, was to participate and shape the group so it could not harm western Colorado.[42]

Informed of Saunders's inflammatory remarks at Rocky Ford, Congressman Wayne Aspinall asked Saunders to explain his comments. Western Colorado has always bickered and quarreled over water, to the detriment of both Colorado and the Western Slope, Saunders asserted. Yet western Colorado had a greater interest than eastern Colorado in statewide cooperation. In what could only be construed as a threat to Aspinall, Saunders indicated that some eastern Colorado factions favored an all-out fight to "destroy Western Colorado and its influence" by re-drawing congressional districts. Saunders urged Aspinall to curb those "provincial self-seekers" from the Western Slope who were attempting to foment discord over water issues. Such divisions would only play into the hands of other Colorado River Basin states and, perhaps even more alarming, fuel the continuing efforts of the federal government to undermine western states' water rights.[43]

In early May a cross-section of the state's water establishment, including Glenn Saunders, Felix Sparks of the CWCB, and several of the stronger voices for western Colorado water protection, met at the Grand Junction Chamber of Commerce Building to discuss Colorado River issues and build a platform for the proposed CWC. By this point several platforms had been proposed for the association. Western Slope representatives remained adamantly opposed to empowering the new organization to address controversial matters such as trans-basin diversions. In contrast, the Front Range delegates appeared open to discussing controversial matters.[44]

John Clayton of Greeley proposed a compromise between the two positions. A steering committee would be established with equal numbers of Western Slope and Eastern Slope members. Issues to be brought before the CWC would require the unanimous approval of the so-called steering committee, which became known as the Rules Committee. No subject would be brought before the congress that had not received the approval of at least thirteen members of the Rules Committee, composed of fifteen delegates, each representing an important region or drainage area. Seven members were from the Western Slope, with one delegate from the North Platte Basin and one from the Rio Grande Basin. Thus, it would only take three Western Slope Rules Committee members to prevent the consideration of matters they considered too controversial for the congress to entertain. With some basic agreement reached, it was hoped that the governor's call for a CWC would lead to an official organizational meeting as soon as early June 1958.[45]

Just a few weeks earlier, Barnard had updated the CRWCD on the progress of the water congress idea after attending several more meetings of the working group charged with forming the organization. More than ever and especially in the aftermath of the Saunders diatribe at Rocky Ford, Barnard believed the water congress should never discuss inflammatory issues such as trans-basin diversion. If such were done, "Western Colorado would soon be overwhelmingly outvoted." The "incident at Rocky Ford," as Barnard referred to it, had threatened to undermine the development of a platform for the Colorado Water Congress. Sensing that the statewide water organization had reached a breaking point, Governor Steve McNichols and his attorney general moved to provide money for the necessary water studies of the Colorado River long demanded by the Western Slope. However, the governor would not give full approval for the studies until a statewide platform for the CWC received general approval. Barnard believed the Western Slope should participate in the CWC to gain the Colorado River Basin study, funded by the state and carried out by engineers, hydrologists, and lawyers in Colorado representing local water entities such as the CRWCD. As a sign of good faith, Governor McNichols asked for $50,000 from the legislature for these special legal and engineering studies.[46]

McNichols invited water users, county commissioners, water attorneys, and conservation district board members to what would be an organizational meeting for the "Water Congress," as it was known, on June 4, 1958, at the Adams Hotel in Denver. The Colorado Water Congress was officially formed that day when its bylaws and a constitution were adopted. Most of the platform items were adopted unanimously. Some have called it the "single largest meeting" of water users ever held in Colorado, at least to that time. More than 500 attended the gathering. The Colorado Water Congress evolved out of the same feeling that produced the Eastern Slope–Western Slope final agreement to the Fryingpan-Arkansas controversy. A posture of state water unity was driven by the force of personalities like Congressman Aspinall and the rise of Felix Sparks to the leadership of the Colorado Water Conservation Board. The CWCB's period of drift had ceased. Sparks's leadership, though not without rancor at times, imparted a sense of fairness to the entire state, reminiscent of the Clifford Stone era. Colorado's newfound water unity also took root in what many viewed as the state's increasingly precarious position when measured against the water programs of neighboring states. The rise of new forces who demanded a place at the water decision-making table also forced Coloradans toward a more harmonious posture.[47]

Above all, Colorado faced a rise in significant threats to its water supply from outside its borders. These threats had existed during most of the twentieth century, but entering the 1960s Colorado needed to meet them. Led by the team of Aspinall, Sparks, and the Upper Colorado River Commission's Ival Goslin, the state focused more on developing and maintaining its compact water allotments. Above all, it hoped to protect its water resources from the new threats, which included the Lower Basin's bid to build large water projects—especially the long-dormant Central Arizona Project, which would spring to life in the early 1960s. Other emerging issues included the legal empowerment of Native American tribes, who would use a series of court victories to begin to realize their water rights.[48]

From the perspective of traditional Colorado water users, another complex issue emerged with the rise of the new environmental movement. Colorado and the Upper Basin had witnessed conservation and environmental groups' ability to flex their political muscle by stopping the Echo Park Dam and Reservoir in the mid-1950s. However, by the early to mid-1960s a surging national environmental movement was beginning to question "old truths" about western water politics. As the Colorado Water Congress phrased it in 1961, the organization existed because of a growing awareness that the state's internal water wars were damaging Colorado's ability to protect its "dwindling water supplies from demands by out of state interests, demands by the federal government, by fish and wildlife groups [the new environmental movement], and from other states."[49] In the 1960s, Colorado's tenuous unity would be tested time and again, but forces outside the state's borders would drive the formerly feuding parts of the state to assume greater unity.

NOTES

1. CRWCD Minutes, March 3, 1958, Colorado River Water Conservation District (hereafter CRWCD), Glenwood Springs.

2. As Clifford Stone remarked in a report to the Colorado Water Conservation Board in early 1938, "The Arkansas Valley water interests commenced an agitation for such a survey at the same time the Colorado–Big Thompson people attempted to secure a survey." See "Statement of Judge Clifford M. Stone, Counsel for the Colorado Water Conservation Board, January 15, 1938," Box 11, folder 3, Silmon Smith Papers, Colorado State Historical Society, Denver (hereafter CSHS).

3. Duane Vandenbusche and Duane A. Smith, *A Land Alone: Colorado's Western Slope* (Boulder: Pruett, 1981), 264.

4. Ibid., 264–65; Frank Delaney to Henry Lake Jr., February 18, 1938, Box 168, folder 2, Frank Delaney Papers, University of Colorado at Boulder Archives (hereafter (UCBA).

5. US Bureau of Reclamation, *The Colorado River: "A Natural Menace Becomes a Natural Resource": A Comprehensive Report on the Development of the Water of the Colorado River Basin for Irrigation, Power Production, and Other Beneficial Uses in Arizona, California, Colorado, Nevada, New Mexico, Utah, and Wyoming* (Washington, DC: Department of the Interior, 1946), 131–32; interview with Charles J. Biese, October 29, 1974, Box 74, folder "Statements-History of Fryingpan-Arkansas Project and Southeastern Colorado Water Conservancy District," J. Edgar Chenoweth Papers, UCBA.

6. *Official Comments and Recommendations of the State of Colorado on the Initial Development, Gunnison-Arkansas Project, Roaring Fork Division, Colorado,* Project

Planning Report no. 7–8a.49–1 (Washington, DC: Bureau of Reclamation, Department of the Interior, January 1950), 5–9; Colorado River Water Conservation District Minutes, February 19, 1951, Box 9, folder "CRWCD-Fryingpan-Arkansas Project—1955," John B. Barnard Papers, American Heritage Center, University of Wyoming (hereafter AHC), Laramie; Water Development Association of Southeast Colorado, *Operating Principles Governing Fryingpan-Arkansas Water Diversion Project* (Pueblo: Water Development Association of Southeast Colorado, n.d.), 3–9.

7. US Bureau of Reclamation, *Colorado River*, 131–32; interview with Charles J. Biese, October 29, 1974.

8. Steven C. Schulte, *Wayne Aspinall and the Shaping of the American West* (Boulder: University Press of Colorado, 2002), 100–101; Richard F. Fenno Jr., *Congressmen in Committees* (Boston: Little, Brown, 1973), 261.

9. For an overview of Saylor, see Thomas G. Smith, *Green Republican: John Saylor and the Preservation of America's Wilderness* (Pittsburgh: University of Pittsburgh Press, 2006); *Daily Sentinel* (Grand Junction, CO), October 29, 1954.

10. Aspinall quoted in *Daily Sentinel*, November 3, 1954; September 4, 1960; Stewart L. Udall, phone interview with Steven C. Schulte, November 10, 1997; Stewart L. Udall, interview with Steven C. Schulte, March 31 and April 1, 1998, Grand Junction, CO.; Schulte, *Wayne Aspinall*, 102. Ironically, Aspinall was also called out by southeastern Colorado project proponents, in 1954 and on several other occasions, when Fry-Ark legislation was under consideration by the House Committee on Interior and Insular Affairs. Pueblo's Harold Christy referred to Aspinall in March 1954 as "our so-called friend from Western Colorado on the [House Interior] Committee." See Harold Christy to Judge [J. Edgar] Chenoweth, March 1954, Box 74, folder 25, J. Edgar Chenoweth Papers, UCBA. Aspinall's other electioneering tactic, one he resorted to often in his career when water issues caused him political difficulty, was to argue that division of Colorado's water among sections of the state "is a question which is entirely in the hands of state officials." See *Daily Sentinel*, October 15, 1954. In a major advertisement for the campaign in the October 15, 1954, edition of Grand Junction's *Daily Sentinel*, Aspinall stated that Colorado officials—not Congress—"will decide whether or not there are waters surplus to the needs of Western Colorado."

11. Schulte, *Wayne Aspinall*, 101–2.

12. Frank Hoag Jr. to Senator Eugene D. Millikin, December 8, 1954, Box 74, folder 24, J. Edgar Chenoweth Papers, UCBA; Resolution of the CRWCD, January 25, 1955, Box 75, folder 21, J. Edgar Chenoweth Papers, UCBA. Third District congressman Chenoweth from southeastern Colorado expressed his disappointment at the CRWCD's resolution, arguing that the CRWCD Board of Directors had reached an accord with southeastern Colorado through the negotiation of the 1951

operating principles. Furthermore, he urged that each project be considered separately, since "there is no connection whatever between the Colorado River Storage Project and the Fryingpan project." Naturally, Chenoweth saw no reason why Fry-Ark should be delayed until after CRSP's construction. See J. Edgar Chenoweth to F. C. Merriell, January 31, 1955, Box 75, folder 21, J. Edgar Chenoweth Papers, UCBA.

13. Frank S. Hoag Jr. to Senator Eugene D. Millikin, December 8, 1954, Box 74, folder 24, J. Edgar Chenoweth Papers, UCBA; Fenno, *Congressmen in Committees*, 261; Carol Jean Drake Mehls, "Into the Frying Pan: J. Edgar Chenowith and the Fryingpan-Arkansas Reclamation Project" (PhD dissertation, University of Colorado–Boulder, 1986), 172; Schulte, *Wayne Aspinall*, 102–3.

14. Schulte, *Wayne Aspinall*, 103.

15. Special Meeting Minutes, December 10, 1956, Bureau of Reclamation, Colorado Water Conservation Board, Pitkin County Water Association, and Colorado River Water Conservation District, folder "CRWCD Minutes, 1956," CRWCD, Glenwood Springs.

16. Ibid.

17. CRWCD Minutes, July 16, 1957, folder "CRWCD Minutes, 1957," CRWCD, Glenwood Springs.

18. Ibid.

19. Schulte, *Wayne Aspinall*, 104; Executive Committee Minutes, December 22, 1958, folder "CRWCD Minutes, 1958," CRWCD, Glenwood Springs.

20. A new set of operating principles for Fryingpan-Arkansas was drafted in 1959 to take the place of the earlier guidelines that would have regulated the project when Aspen Reservoir was a part of it. The new principles, drafted in part by CRWCD counsel John B. Barnard, insisted that Ruedi Reservoir be completed before any water was diverted to the Eastern Slope. In addition, Barnard tried to stipulate that the decree to Fryingpan-Arkansas waters would be junior to other Western Slope decrees for in-basin use as well as to the waters of the hoped-for West Divide Project. See CRWCD Minutes, February 10, 1959, folder "CRWCD Minutes, 1959," CRWCD, Glenwood Springs; *Star-Journal* (Pueblo, CO), April 27, 1959. The Pueblo newspaper expressed the hope that the new operating principles, which it termed better for both slopes than the earlier edition, heralded a statewide unity that could result in expeditious enactment of the long-desired diversion bill.

21. Schulte, *Wayne Aspinall*, 104.

22. Ibid.; CRWCD Executive Committee Minutes, October 20, 1959, folder "CRWCD Minutes, 1959," CRWCD, Glenwood Springs.

23. *Denver Post*, January 1, 1961; Bureau of Reclamation News Release, May 3, 1961, Box 50, no file, Wayne N. Aspinall Papers, University of Denver Archives (hereafter UDA), Denver, CO; Udall quoted in Schulte, *Wayne Aspinall*, 104–5.

24. *Aspen (CO) Times*, May 26, June 9, 1961.

25. *Denver Post*, October 3, 1961; January 10, 1962; Claude Desautels to Larry O'Brien, April 11, 1962, Box 1, folder "Aspinall, Wayne," White House Staff Files, Lawrence O'Brien, John F. Kennedy Presidential Library, Boston, MA. The Kennedy administration offered help to pry the bill from a previously reluctant Rules Committee, but Aspinall believed the bill could be extricated without additional administration help. Aspinall reserved the right to call on administration support when the bill reached the House floor. Also see Mehls, "Into the Frying Pan," 218–20; *Colorado Water Congress Newsletter*, March 26, 1962, vol. 5, no. 3, Box 6, folder 4, William Nelson Papers, Colorado Mesa University Archives and Special Collections (hereafter CMUASC), Grand Junction; Wayne Aspinall to Colleagues, June 7, 1962; Wayne Aspinall, J. Edgar Chenoweth, Peter H. Dominick, and Byron Rogers to Colleagues, June 7, 1962, both in Box 20, folder "Fryingpan-Arkansas Project," Wayne N. Aspinall Papers, UDA.

26. Wayne Aspinall, "Capitol Comments," June 16, 1962, Box 102, folder 50, Wayne N. Aspinall Papers, UDA; Schulte, *Wayne Aspinall*, 107–8.

27. *Colorado Water Congress Newsletter*, June 29, 1962, vol. 5, no. 6, Box 6, folder 4, William Nelson Papers, CMUASC, Grand Junction; Mehls, "Into the Frying Pan," 251–52; Fenno, *Congressmen in Committees*, 262; Schulte, *Wayne Aspinall*, 108–9. The idea that Aspinall "quarterbacked" Fry-Ark to passage comes from several sources, including several editions of the *Colorado Water Congress Newsletter* in 1961–62 and from Colorado governor Steve McNichols. See Steve McNichols to Wayne N. Aspinall, August 10, 1962, Box 49, no file, Wayne N. Aspinall Papers, UDA.

28. See Obituary, Felix Sparks, *Denver Post*, September 28–30, 2007, accessed October 2, 2012, www.legacy.com/obituaries/denverpost/obituary.arpx?n=felix-spark &pid=9512492. Sparks helped organize the Colorado National Guard after World War II and rose to the rank of brigadier general. He died on September 25, 2007.

29. Executive Committee Minutes, December 22, 1958, folder "CRWCD Minutes, 1958," CRWCD, Glenwood Springs.

30. Johnson quoted in *Colorado Water Congress Newsletter*, September 25, 1961, vol. 4, no. 9, Box 6, folder 4, William Nelson Papers, CMUASC, Grand Junction. In 1960, Colorado senator Gordon Allott had said that "the more I witness the cooperative and constructive efforts of the Colorado Water Conservation Board and the Colorado Water Congress, the Bureau of Reclamation, and all members of the Colorado [congressional] delegation, the more optimistic I become." This is not a statement any Coloradan dealing with water issues could have made two years before. See Gordon Allott to Charles J. Beise, March 17, 1960, Box 73, folder "Public Works 1–Frying Pan, 1960," Gordon Allott Papers, UCBA; William Nelson to William R. Welsh Jr., August 20, 1956; William R. Welsh Jr. to William Nelson, August

22, 1956; F. M. Peterson to William Nelson, August 25, 1956, all in Box 6, folder 10, William Nelson Papers, CMUASC, Grand Junction.

31. *Denver Post*, July 3, 1957.

32. CRWCD Minutes, November 12, 1957, folder "CRD Minutes, 1957," CRWCD, Glenwood Springs.

33. CRWCD Executive Committee Minutes, December 19, 1957, folder "CRWCD Minutes, 1957," CRWCD, Glenwood Springs; John B. Barnard Jr., "The Early History of the Colorado Water Congress, 1957–58," author's possession.

34. Notes on State Water Conference, December 30, 1957, Box 12, folder "Colorado Water Congress," John B. Barnard Papers, AHC.

35. Silmon Smith to John B. Barnard, January 9, 1958; John B. Barnard, "Proposal for a Platform of a Colorado Water Congress," both in Box 5, folder 31, William Nelson Papers, CMUASC, Grand Junction.

36. Barnard, "Proposal for a Platform of a Colorado Water Congress."

37. CRWCD Minutes, January 21, 1958, folder "CRD Minutes, 1958," CRWCD, Glenwood Springs.

38. Ibid.

39. John B. Barnard to William H. Nelson, March 1, 1958, Box 7, folder "CRWCD–William Nelson Correspondence," John B. Barnard Papers, AHC; John B. Barnard to William Smith, January 8, 1958, Box 5, folder 31, William Nelson Papers, CMUASC, Grand Junction.

40. Meeting documented in John B. Barnard to Wiliam H. Nelson, March 1, 1958.

41. CRWCD Minutes, January 21, March 3, 1958, both in folder "CRWCD Minutes, 1958," CRWCD, Glenwood Springs.

42. John B. Barnard to William H. Nelson, March 1, 1958, Box 7, folder "CRWCD–William Nelson Correspondence," John B. Barnard Papers, AHC.

43. Glenn G. Saunders to Wayne N. Aspinall, March 31, 1958, Box 22, folder "1960 Personal," Wayne N. Aspinall Papers, UDA. Aspinall's short reply to Saunders indicated his willingness to help the state "pull together" on vital water questions. Water unity "has taken a long time and will take many years to complete, but if we speak frankly and understandingly we will do the job." See Aspinall to Saunders, April 3, 1958, Box 22, folder "1960 Personal," Wayne N. Aspinall Papers, UDA.

44. Notes on State Water Conference, May 3, 1958.

45. Ibid.; CRWCD Minutes, April 15, 1958, folder "CRWCD Minutes, 1958," CRWCD, Glenwood Springs.

46. CRWCD Minutes, March 3, 1958, folder "CRWCD Minutes, 1958," CRWCD, Glenwood Springs.

47. Stephen McNichols to Fellow Coloradans, May 21, 1958, Box 5, folder 31; *Colorado Water Congress Newsletter*, July 28, 1961, vol. 4, no. 7, Box 6, folder 4, both in William Nelson Papers, CMUASC, Grand Junction.

48. CRWCD counsel John B. Barnard commented on the Native American threat to Colorado's water supply. See CRWCD Minutes, December 19, 1957, folder "CRWCD Minutes, 1957," CRWCD, Glenwood Springs. Barnard correctly predicted in 1957 that a possible outcome of the ongoing litigation between Arizona and California could be the loss of up to 1 million more acre-feet of water. This development would impact all of the interstate compacts and agreements.

49. *Colorado Water Congress Newsletter*, July 28, 1961, vol. 4, no. 7, Box 6, folder 4, William Nelson Papers, CMUASC, Grand Junction.

7

A New Age of War and Peace

I don't care personally what people are going to say about me
at the present time. I am not going to put myself in a position
that 35 years hence it can be said of me by members of my family
or a constituent in my Congressional District or any members
of the State of Colorado that I gave away the birthright of the
water resources that legally belong to the State of Colorado.

Congressman Wayne N. Aspinall, September 7–8, 1967,
to the Colorado Water Conservation Board[1]

1960s STAGE SETTING

The 1960s heralded a new era in Colorado's twentieth-century water history.
The decade was a time of great political uncertainty, and the state confronted
the task of unifying itself to meet major challenges emanating from outside its borders. Perhaps the greatest challenge remained to hold its share
of the Colorado River at a time when Arizona began acting on its rights to

DOI: 10.5876/9781607325000.c007

2.8 million acre-feet of the river. In the post–World War II era, Arizona had grown exponentially, with Phoenix booming from a population of 65,000 in 1940 to 439,000 in 1960. When the Upper Colorado River Basin had started to receive water project benefits through the Colorado River Storage Project (CRSP), Arizona's population continued to expand, but its prodigious growth outstripped most of its short-term water supplies. After 1963, Arizona began to formulate water plans that would ultimately be called the Central Arizona Project (CAP).[2]

Another major hurdle to Colorado's water future emerged in the 1960s in the shape of the national environmental movement. Galvanized into action in the struggle against the proposed Echo Park Dam in the mid-1950s, environmentalism infused itself in the middle of debates over both authorized and proposed western dams. The new environmental movement gained strength from Rachel Carson's struggles against pesticides and chemicals documented in the 1962 best-seller *Silent Spring*. It also rallied around the movement to build a federal wilderness system while gaining strength from those advocating making federal land management more accountable to sustainable values. By the mid-1960s the massive reclamation program of the federal government came within the vision of groups like the Wilderness Society and the Sierra Club, which were asking the American people to rethink many of their traditional visions of what defined progress. Ted Steinberg remarked, "We may never know exactly what caused the birth of the environmental movement." However, it was likely a mixture, ranging from fear over the future of the planet to "a sharpening of the links between everyday life under consumerism and its ecological consequences."[3]

Colorado did not enter the 1960s without some advantages in meeting these challenges. Congressman Wayne N. Aspinall chaired the House Committee on Interior and Insular Affairs (Interior Committee), which dealt with the significant issues that impacted life in the American West, including reclamation, public lands, and mining issues. Felix L. Sparks of the Colorado Water Conservation Board (CWCB) had emerged as a skilled manager of water conflicts in the state. Ival V. Goslin, head of the Upper Colorado River Commission, was a reliable friend of Colorado and worked closely and well with both Sparks and Aspinall. Finally, Governor John Love, a Republican, ensured that his party remained committed to a bipartisan vision for state water policy. As has often been said about Colorado's political culture, partisan politics is adjourned when water is the main subject. Water even had a way of changing the minds of those who had supported environmental critics of water development before coming to office. Once in office, even politicians with strong environmental credentials like Richard Lamm, Tim Wirth, and Gary Hart all but tripped over themselves demonstrating their support for most Colorado water projects.[4]

Colorado faced all of these potential obstacles in the 1960s as the state moved to realize its full share of the Colorado River. The political world for water development by the late 1960s and beyond would be shaped not only by the perceived needs of western water states and developers but also through the strong assertion of environmental values. By the 1970s, soaring inflation and a national energy crisis caused the American West to confront an era of severe limits that led many people to question the old truths that had inspired an era of water project construction from the 1930s to the 1960s. The road to the post-1970 era of environmental limits began with the inflated hopes of Secretary of the Interior Stuart L. Udall's Pacific Southwest Water Plan (PSWWP).

"A COLORADO CHRISTMAS TREE": THE PACIFIC SOUTHWEST WATER PLAN

In 1963 the United States Supreme Court ruled in Arizona's favor in the decision *Arizona v. California*. As a young congressman in the 1920s, Arizona politician Carl Hayden had dreamed of a water project that would deliver water to the thirsty desert regions of central and southern Arizona. Hayden, who took a US Senate seat in 1927, introduced bills for a central Arizona water project on numerous occasions. Each time the bill would pass the Senate but fail in the House of Representatives. California's large House delegation, trying to protect that state's overuse of Colorado River water, overwhelmed Arizona's small congressional representation and defeated Hayden's legislation. Finally, in early 1952 a desperate Arizona filed suit to gain confirmation of its rights to Colorado River water. At that time, California was using in excess of 5 million acre-feet of the Colorado River a year.[5]

Arizona v. California proved to be, in historian Norris Hundley Jr.'s words, "among the most complicated and hotly debated [cases] in Supreme Court history." Several issues between the two states were at stake. Of course, the division of the water in the Lower Colorado River Basin was paramount.

In addition, the Court determined the status of the Gila River. California argued that the Gila's flow should be deducted from Arizona's total allotment. Arizona contended that since most of the river's flow was within Arizona, it should not be part of its court-determined totals. The Court's decision overjoyed Arizona. California, the Court determined, was entitled to 4.4 million acre-feet per year; Nevada's total was set at 300,000 acre-feet annually. Arizona received 2.8 million acre-feet, but the Court ruled that the Gila's flow would not be charged against Arizona's total allotment. From the perspective of Colorado and other western states, one of the most unsettling developments in the decision dealt with the federal government's overall involvement in the case. The federal government had intervened to protect the water rights of the more than twenty-five Indian reservations in the Colorado River Basin region. The government had largely ignored Indian water rights to this point in the twentieth century. Federal attorneys asked the Court to assure Indian tribes enough water to develop their irrigable lands and ensure a strong future reservation economy. While the Court's actual decision failed to quantify how much water Indian nations would have, it agreed with the findings of the 1908 *Winters v. U.S.* decision, which argued that when formed, "these reservations were not limited to land, but included waters as well."[6]

The Court also agreed with the findings of the special master appointed to the case, Simon H. Rifkind, who stated that the Indians possessed the right to about "enough water"—perhaps a million acre-feet—"to irrigate all the practicably irrigable acreage on the reservations." Significantly, Indian water allotments were to be charged against each state's apportionment with a priority dating to the time the reservation was created, which in most cases predated Anglo-American water uses. Since the Echo Park controversy of the mid-1950s, two new threats had appeared to challenge traditional river water users—the environmental movement and the region's American Indian community.[7]

On January 21, 1963, with Bureau of Reclamation commissioner Floyd Dominy at his side, Secretary of the Interior Stewart L. Udall unveiled his plan for an integrated, regional approach to the West's water problems, the Pacific Southwest Water Plan, which included a water delivery system for his home state of Arizona. By taking a regional approach, Udall separated himself from the strategy favored by most Arizona politicians, including the Senate's dean, Carl Hayden. Udall believed Arizona's best chance for a Central Arizona Project would be to make the project part of a large legislative package with water benefits distributed to all of the Colorado River states. California had initially reacted favorably to Udall's Pacific Southwest Water Plan, a vital development since the state, with thirty-eight members in the House of Representatives, controlled the political destiny of many reclamation projects. California also had five seats on the House Interior Committee to Arizona's one. Hayden and others believed an Arizona "go-it-alone" approach would now work, in the aftermath of the Supreme Court case. Udall favored the larger plan, which would allow most key western states to gain reclamation benefits and allow politically weak Arizona to tie its destiny to the interests of many western states.[8]

Udall's PSWWP proposed sandwiching Grand Canyon National Park with two dams—one at Marble Canyon at the top of the park and one at Bridge Canyon at the bottom. In addition to flooding some of the nation's most spectacular scenery in the canyon's bottom, the two dams were designed to produce electricity and the cash required to produce the pumping power to bring water to the populated regions of Arizona. California would get two high dams in the state's northern half, and water would be shuttled into the Sacramento River, eventually leading south to Los Angeles. New Mexico would get Hooker Dam, while Utah would gain the Central Utah Project. The "guarantee" of water availability, according to Udall, would be met through what he called the "salvage" or reuse of water that would otherwise go to waste and through the import of water from rivers "having surplus yields" in Northern California. The Sierra Club's David Brower summarized it this way: the Pacific Southwest Water Plan "was trying to have a little bit of everything in it for everybody, so that it was sort of a Colorado Christmas tree, with projects for all the states that could vote and possibly trade votes." However, Brower and, as it turned out, Secretary of the Interior Udall had forgotten one thing: there was little, if anything, in the plan for the state of Colorado, a fact that had not gone unnoticed by the politician who would control the plan's fate in the House of Representatives: Interior Committee chair Wayne Aspinall.[9]

Aspinall and Sparks Control the CAP Discussion

The two approaches—a regional water plan versus an Arizona "go-it-alone" approach—came into conflict time and again throughout 1964 and into 1965. Wayne Aspinall and western Colorado viewed the water discussion yet another way: as a possible avenue to obtain additional water projects for the Western Slope. As early as 1962, in anticipation of the Supreme Court decision, Aspinall had written a letter to Secretary of the Interior Udall indicating that the time had come to begin discussing the "broad parameters" that would guide discussions of the Lower Colorado River Basin question. Aspinall compared the situation facing the Lower Basin with the Upper Basin's problems prior to enactment of the Colorado River Storage Project. However, Aspinall did not believe the Lower Basin situation had reached the crisis point that precipitated the enactment of the CRSP in the mid-1950s. In other words, he would not be rushed into producing hasty or ill-conceived legislation. Yet Aspinall indicated to Udall that a comprehensive, basin-wide approach might well work for the Lower Basin, as it had in the Upper Basin in 1956. Toward that end, Aspinall suggested that Udall start formulating the studies necessary to move in that direction. In devising his Pacific Southwest Water Plan, Udall was in many ways carrying out the mandate suggested by the Colorado congressman. Aspinall had observed firsthand the efficacy of the basin-wide approach to reclamation lawmaking, and, in addition, he wanted to advance the interests of his state and the Western Slope.[10]

Heading into 1965, Wayne Aspinall began to actively shape the legislation that would bring water not only to Arizona but to several other states in the American West, including Colorado. In the process, he antagonized not only the Lower Basin states but also Front Range water officials. Yet Colorado managed to avoid a resumption of the full-scale water wars it had experienced from the 1930s through the 1950s. In part, this was a result of Aspinall's commanding position, which allowed him to bring both projects and funding to the entire state. By 1965, Aspinall, along with other Colorado water politicians, had begun to believe that the only way the CAP could provide needed water to Arizona would be at the expense of the Upper Colorado River Basin's water allotment. From 1965 to 1968, Aspinall aggressively pursued a strategy to strengthen Colorado and the Western Slope's reclamation future. Working in tandem with Felix L. Sparks, director of the Colorado Water Conservation Board, Aspinall asked Sparks to determine if enough water existed in the river system to build any of the projected Lower Colorado projects. During this era, Aspinall worked to build a political foundation for expanding water supplies on the Western Slope and in the Upper Colorado River Basin. He believed this could be accomplished in one of two ways. The most likely approach would be to weave additional storage reservoirs into the legislation. The other approach, discussed at great length in the mid-1960s, was to import water from outside the basin, most likely from the water-rich Pacific Northwest. By building water storage for western Colorado, the other southwestern states could be assured that the overall project enjoyed more general western political support, including Aspinall's crucial support.[11]

Following Senate and House hearings in 1964, Arizona, in conjunction with interior secretary Udall, modified its approach to the Southwest's water needs. By 1965 the Pacific Southwest Water Plan had been reborn as the Lower Colorado River Basin Project. Hayden's new bill, S. 75, resembled a trimmed-down version of the Pacific Southwest Water Plan but retained the CAP as its central feature. Hayden's new plan provided for a study by Udall of water importation into the region. Significantly, it also included both the Marble and Bridge Canyon Dams and a Southern Nevada Project to broaden the bill's political salability. Wayne Aspinall had also been encouraging the regional approach, not only to increase the bill's political chances but to allow the Upper Basin states, including Colorado, to add more reclamation features to the bill. After 1965, Aspinall emerged as the guardian of the Upper Colorado River Basin's water, attempting to ensure that any Lower Colorado legislation contained enough water to make the project viable and insurance that Colorado and the Upper Basin's water needs would be protected.[12]

Aspinall publicly articulated what he had been discussing with others since before the *Arizona v. California* Supreme Court decision: did enough water exist in the river to satisfy both Lower and Upper Basin plans for the stream? Would the CAP in any form (singularly or as a regional plan) undermine the plans of the Upper Basin states? To try to obtain answers to these questions, Aspinall addressed letters to all the governors of Colorado River Basin states. Aspinall's pro-Colorado and Upper Basin strategy was formulated with the close collaboration of Felix Sparks and Ival Goslin. By 1965 the three water leaders were fervently crafting a new strategy to gain additional water storage for Colorado, the Western Slope, and the Upper Colorado River Basin.[13]

Meanwhile, the threat from the Lower Basin seemed to grow continually more ominous. After protracted negotiations, Arizona and California appeared to settle their decades-old water war, agreeing to bills with substantially the same language that would enact a CAP and give California an annual guarantee of 4.4 million acre-feet of Colorado River water. From Colorado's perspective, the Lower Basin Project seemed dangerously close to enactment with the sudden support of California's large and powerful House of Representatives delegation. The agreement contained the provision that any CAP legislation must first pass the House of Representatives. The California-Arizona accord thus placed the pressure to act squarely on Wayne Aspinall and his House Interior Committee. Arizona's water leaders, including Secretary of the Interior Udall, tried to nudge Aspinall to schedule House hearings on the Lower Colorado bill. Above all, Arizona's politicians hoped Aspinall would begin to move and not resort to stalling tactics or parliamentary tricks to delay action.[14]

On May 22, 1965, Aspinall appeared to resort to stalling, sending the aforementioned letter to the governors of the Colorado River Basin states asking them to provide data on their projected water needs and available supplies under the Colorado River Compact. This tactic would buy Aspinall and the Upper Basin valuable time, forcing each state to calculate how much water remained available for current and future water projects. More important to Colorado, it would allow the state to argue that not enough water existed to build a CAP without seriously infringing on the Colorado River Compact allotment of the Upper Basin states. The evidence suggests that Aspinall, Sparks, and Goslin were indeed trying to slow the congressional pace. By 1964–65, Colorado seemed more unified on water questions than ever in the state's history, a development likely inspired by stronger state water leadership and the threat to the state's water supply posed by the Lower Basin.[15]

Aspinall's demand to the Colorado River governors inspired Colorado governor John Love to commission a state water engineering study by Denver water consultants Tipton and Kalmbach. While Tipton and Kalmbach were widely respected, they also understood that their study would need to conclude that Colorado and the Upper Basin states would suffer greatly if a CAP were authorized. The avowed public purpose of Aspinall's demands to the Colorado River state governors was to determine how much water each state was using; in addition, they were to measure what their water needs were and then, above all, calculate how much remained to be used in the gargantuan Central Arizona Project. In words that likely chilled Arizona's water community, Aspinall declared that no state had a right to "expect to develop its sectional potentialities at the expense of any other part." He also again reminded Arizona that he would refuse to be "stampeded" into a fast scheduling of House hearings without obtaining the information he had requested from the governors.[16]

Arizona's powerful senator, Carl Hayden, responded by applying his own brand of pressure on Aspinall and the House Interior Committee to schedule hearings on the CAP and to act on the legislation in a timely manner. In a letter to reclamation commissioner Floyd Dominy, Hayden noted that he took issue with Aspinall on the all-important topic of Colorado River water availability. The Colorado, Hayden thundered, had enough water for the next fifty or sixty years. However, if Aspinall was correct and a water shortage occurred, Hayden, in his position as chair of the Senate Committee on Appropriations, indicated that the ongoing financial feasibility of both the Colorado River Storage Project and the Fryingpan-Arkansas Project— pet pieces of Aspinall's legislation—might be threatened. This not-so-veiled threat was not lost on Aspinall, as the two congressional titans seemed to be on a collision course as early as 1965.[17]

Aspinall and Sparks had closely consulted with each other in devising this particular legislative strategy in the hope that it would eventually lead to dividends for Colorado's water community. In a memorandum written to Colorado Water Conservation Board members and copied to Ival Goslin and Aspinall, Sparks admitted that Arizona needed to develop its water. Furthermore, Arizona had been a steady supporter of Upper Basin water development over the decades, hoping to have this favor returned at an appropriate time. Several issues, however, clouded the future of the Lower Basin's reclamation efforts.[18]

The Mexican Water Treaty of 1944 threatened the Upper Basin's future water supplies. In addition, the *Arizona v. California* Supreme Court decision ruled that Arizona would not have to count the Gila River toward its Colorado River Compact allotment of 2.8 million acre-feet. Sparks also believed the agreement between Arizona and California that allowed California an annual guarantee of the first 4.4 million acre-feet posed a grave danger to the Upper Basin's water planning. Sparks had reached a conclusion that would constitute the bedrock of Colorado's mid-1960s interstate water strategy: insufficient water was available for the Central Arizona Project unless water was imported into the region.[19]

An emphasis on Colorado's vulnerability to any sizable Lower Basin reclamation projects became the Sparks-Aspinall mantra over the next several years. In a memo to the Colorado Water Conservation Board in June 1965, Sparks elaborated on this theme. The Central Arizona Project's construction would occur largely at the expense of Colorado's compact allocation. The rapid population growth of both California and Arizona would allow more political pressure to be applied against Colorado to relent in its opposition. Colorado, Sparks remarked, found itself in a crisis. If it opposed the CAP, Colorado could reasonably expect its planned reclamation projects to be opposed by other states. By supporting CAP as a stand-alone project, it was signing its own death warrant for future water projects. By supporting a large-scale regional solution, complete with water importation, it risked losing the support of areas like the Pacific Northwest, the principal target source of the importation schemes. Western Slope newspapers like Grand Junction's *Daily Sentinel* also weighed in on Colorado's fears over a Central Arizona Project, noting that Arizona and Colorado were "edging toward a red-hot water battle over Colorado River water." Arizona, the newspaper noted, feared that Aspinall was using the purported water shortage to question the CAP's overall efficacy. Aspinall's tactics were viewed in the Lower Basin as a stalling strategy, and the Grand Junction newspaper noted with some irony that Aspinall had succeeded in doing the formerly impossible: driving Arizona and California closer together.[20]

In July 1965 the CWCB-commissioned Tipton Report appeared, adding further fuel to the Central Arizona Project fire. Most observers believed that in 1922, the framers of the Colorado River Compact had seriously overestimated the amount of water in the river system. The annual average figure of 17.5 million acre-feet, however, was not first seriously questioned until the Hill Report in 1953. Hill had pointed out that since 1930 the river had averaged only 11.7 million acre-feet per year. Needless to say, with the seven Colorado River Basin states counting on a flow of 17.5 million acre-feet per year and in particular the Upper Basin required to deliver 75 million acre-feet on a ten-year basis, all of the basin states had started to feel pressure to develop their share of a river that seemed smaller in flow than ever. In 1956 the Colorado River Storage Act passed, which essentially ignored any evidence that the compact's optimistic water estimates were wrong. Yet by the mid-1960s many western water planners were beginning to rethink the earlier optimistic water estimates. Maybe Hill was more correct than many of his early 1950s critics had thought.[21]

While Tipton's water estimate was more optimistic than Hill's had been, his overall conclusion still caused panic among water officials in the Upper Basin: the proposed CAP and Pacific Southwest Water Plan posed great risks for the states of the Upper Basin. Much of the water used in the Lower Colorado River Basin was available only "because of unused flows in the Upper Basin passing Lees Ferry." Tipton made several bold claims in his study that reinforced some of the arguments Aspinall and Sparks had been making about the threat the CAP posed to the Upper Basin's water supply. Tipton pointed out that the total amount of water available to the Upper Basin on an annual basis was actually closer to 6.3 million acre-feet per year than to the compact division of 7.5 million acre-feet. Tipton's report concluded that for both basins to get their water and satisfy other pending obligations (including still unquantified Native American claims), water importation projects would need to be built. Without importation on a massive scale, Tipton reasoned, beneficial consumptive use in the Upper Basin states might be limited to as little as 4.8 million acre-feet per year—a fearful prospect for many Coloradans.[22]

By August 1965 most Colorado water officials and interested observers had done something dozens of governors' appeals, statewide conferences, and hundreds of passionate editorials had failed to accomplish—move the state toward unity over the water issue. Colorado's official position, expressed at the August 1, 1965, meeting of the Colorado Water Conservation Board, favored the enactment of a Central Arizona Project, but only if it allowed the Upper Basin to utilize its full compact allotment. The state water board qualified its support, but only if some guarantees were woven into the authorizing legislation. The first guarantee specified that the Upper Basin would not be required to deliver more than 75 million acre-feet to the Lower Basin in any ten-year period. The CWCB also stipulated that any bill must contain a provision for the importation of 2.5 million acre-feet of water annually into the Colorado River Basin. Colorado particularly feared that if the favored Lower Basin bill passed into law, the Upper Basin would lose 1.2 million acre-feet per year to the Lower Basin. Former Colorado senator and governor Ed Johnson, then serving as the state's commissioner to the Upper Colorado River Commission, stated that the Colorado River Compact would be "mutilated" beyond recognition if the bill passed without provisions for water importation. Worse yet, Colorado and other Upper Basin states would be unable to build additional water projects.[23]

During the House Subcommittee on Irrigation and Reclamation's August 1965 hearings, several issues became apparent that threatened to undermine the drive for the Central Arizona Project. The notion of out-of-basin importation, or what was termed "water augmentation," continued to be argued. Politicians from the Pacific Northwest denounced the scheme and would continue to, especially Senator Henry "Scoop" Jackson and Representative Tom Foley, both Washington Democrats. Another issue that began to gain momentum centered on the construction of dams in or near the Grand Canyon. The growing environmental movement challenged the dams and gained great national strength from its role in determining the final shape of the Central Arizona Project. Secretary of the Interior Stewart Udall, who had originally favored two Grand Canyon dams, had capitulated to changing political conditions and now favored only one. Opponents of two dams in the Grand Canyon had raised the same objections that "we quarreled over in the upper Colorado river program at Echo Park," Aspinall observed. It is evident that Aspinall had begun to fear the impact the environmentalist critics of the Lower Basin plan might have on the political resolve of other supporters of federal reclamation. Finally, the Native American water rights issue erupted during the hearings, threatening to disrupt all of the Colorado River states' claims.[24]

When questioning Udall, Aspinall asked if he believed the CAP was more significant than the Animas–La Plata and Dolores Projects planned in Aspinall's Western Slope congressional district. Udall did not hesitate to say that Arizona's rapid groundwater depletion made the Arizona project more important at that time. However, Udall did tell Aspinall that the Department of the Interior had recently compiled long-awaited feasibility projects on both Colorado projects and would be sending them on to Congress. Aspinall had at least gotten his point across—other projects needed to be folded into the Lower Basin Project, preferably some that would benefit his Western Slope congressional district.[25]

David Brower and other environmentalist leaders offered strong testimony against the Grand Canyon dams during the 1965 hearings, setting the stage for a reconfiguration of the project over the next couple of years. At least twenty-five witnesses offered testimony against the Marble and Bridge Canyon Dams in the Grand Canyon. Brower's testimony got right to the point of what would be his steady mantra for several years: "We do not believe the American people would tolerate such an invasion of the Grand

Canyon and the national park system if they knew what was being proposed and what the alternatives are."[26]

In the immediate aftermath of the 1965 House hearings, Arizona congressman Morris Udall wrote a memorandum discussing what issues had been addressed and perhaps agreed to by representatives of the two basins during the hearings. Udall summarized his ideas and carried them personally to Congressman Wayne Aspinall for the latter's consideration. Udall believed information presented at the hearings illustrated that the Upper Basin must be able to fully use its allotted compact share. He also agreed that both basins would benefit in the long run if 2.5 million acre-feet of water were imported into the Colorado River by 1980. Most important from Colorado's perspective was the apparent agreement by both basins that three of the Upper Basin's "ready" projects be authorized as part of the CAP legislation and that the remaining CRSP projects be authorized upon the interior secretary's findings of feasibility. The House hearings, as well as Aspinall's pre-hearing setting of guidelines for water availability, had convinced the Lower Basin that the bill that would be eventually agreed to needed to include tangible benefits for all seven Colorado River states.[27]

Following the House hearings, the CWCB formed a Colorado River Advisory Committee to advise the state on sentiments in Colorado and suggest changes to the bill that would enhance Colorado's position in the legislation. By this time Colorado, largely through the efforts of Sparks, Aspinall, and Goslin, had managed to insert into the draft bill provisions for several Western Slope water projects including West Divide, Animas–La Plata, and Dolores. Alternative plans were considered by the Colorado River Advisory Committee, which included adding specific protective wording provisions and water importation plans into the Colorado River Basin. The committee discussed which projects it should request be inserted in the CAP legislation. To Colorado water officials this had been the underlying strategy all along— to add several projects to the state's water infrastructure.[28]

Colorado Water Conservation Board director Sparks, with input from the Colorado River Advisory Committee, Aspinall, and Goslin, added five western Colorado water projects to the CWCB's proposed draft of a revised HR 4671. This would be Colorado's price for constructively cooperating on Arizona's water project. Rumors had floated for several months over how many and which projects Colorado would try to add to the CAP bill. The five added were all located in Aspinall's Western Slope congressional district: Animas–La Plata, Dallas Creek, Dolores, San Miguel, and West Divide. All of these projects had been studied for years—decades in some cases—and were at varying stages in the Bureau of Reclamation's review process. Some had been authorized for study as Participating Projects in the 1956 CRSP. Colorado's water leaders, especially those from western Colorado, believed the time had arrived to secure the state's water future. As Sparks succinctly phrased it, "The main object in all of the [recent] discussions and work on this legislation was to build projects in Colorado." Western Colorado's agenda for the Lower Colorado–CAP had emerged from the shadows.[29]

The opportunity to add more western Colorado water projects to the growing Colorado River Basin bill would have other, unintended impacts. Within Colorado the five added Western Slope projects had the effect of kindling the fires of another possible intrastate water war. Denver-area congressman Byron G. Rogers was particularly incensed at the addition of the five projects. Perhaps predictably, the Denver Board of Water Commissioners believed western Colorado was "getting too much." The board feared that by building the five Western Slope projects, Colorado would use its entire Colorado River Compact allotment. As a result, the time would come "when there would be no more water for Denver." The Denver Board of Water Commissioners saw the Sparks-Aspinall action as a "radical departure" from previous CWCB positions toward the CAP. The board maintained that construction of five Western Slope water projects could significantly affect Denver's plans for future trans-mountain diversions. The always controversial Blue River diversion's operation might be particularly compromised because the 1955 Blue River stipulation made it clear that if a deficiency occurred in the Upper Basin's water deliveries to Lees Ferry, the Blue River diversion would be shut down prior to the Colorado–Big Thompson or any other Western Slope diversion. Because of this possibility, the Denver Board of Water Commissioners had been lobbying the CWCB to insist upon large-scale water importations to the Colorado River.[30]

In a letter to Sparks, Wayne Aspinall recognized the importance of state unity but also stressed the need for haste in making Colorado's project selections. Upper Basin states like Colorado, Aspinall asserted, had a small window of opportunity to secure some water guarantees in the form of new projects while the Lower Colorado legislation was taking shape. In what was surely something of an understatement, Aspinall said he had no "set personal position" on which projects to include, but he also understood that whatever was done, some conflict was inevitable between eastern and western Colorado and among the Upper Basin states.[31]

At the Colorado River Water Conservation District's (CRWCD) October 1965 board of directors meeting, Felix Sparks addressed the course of action being pursued by the state. Sounding like Wayne Aspinall, Sparks insisted that Colorado needed to strike immediately and add what projects it could to the CAP mix. Colorado had its best political opportunity to ensure its full compact allocation at this exact moment. Arizona was "desperate" for the CAP; California concluded the same about Arizona and had received its 4.4 million acre-foot annual guarantee. All the states except Colorado and Wyoming were slated to receive something from the Central Arizona Project legislation. The 1956 Colorado River Storage Project remained Colorado's unsteady and sole path to its water future. The various CRSP Participating Projects were subject to more feasibility studies and uneven congressional budget allocations. Colorado no longer felt optimistic that any of those projects would ever see the light of day. No guarantee existed that any of the other Upper Basin states would support Colorado's bid to realize its CRSP projects. Sparks concluded that the other states scheduled to gain benefits from the CAP (Arizona the Central Arizona Project, Utah the Dixie Project, Nevada the Southern Nevada Water Supply Project, New Mexico the Hooker Dam Project, to name several) might be less likely to support Colorado in the future. Following this lengthy preface, Sparks finally stated why he had inserted the five Western Slope projects into the CAP bill: he had started to worry that even if Colorado placed all the protective language it could into the bill and if all of the Colorado River Compact water was being used, Colorado would be on the end of a "monstrous deception." Sparks concluded, "I considered that the best possible protection for Colorado was to authorize the remaining projects that we have in Colorado simultaneously with the CAP."[32]

Most CRWCD board members wholeheartedly endorsed Sparks's logic and actions. However, veteran Western Slope water advocate Frank Delaney believed that by inserting five Western Slope projects into bill drafts, the possibility of fomenting another round of water conflicts with the Front Range appeared likely. Yet board member John Hughes reasoned that with Wayne Aspinall as chair of the House Interior Committee, "We enjoy [a] position of some stature," but "we have no guarantee this situation will be of long duration. We should make every effort to get these projects authorized while Wayne Aspinall is in office."[33]

WESTERN COLORADO AND THE CAP, 1966–1968

With the threat of another Colorado water war looming over the possible inclusion of the five Western Slope projects in the CAP, Aspinall appeared on Denver's KLZ television station on January 28, 1966, to try to reduce the renewed statewide tensions. Aspinall argued that Denver had no need to worry—it had enough water to take it well into the twenty-first century (at least to 2040). In fact, Denver had so much water in the mid-1960s that it hoped to market its surplus to eastern Colorado's agricultural interests. Under Colorado state law, however, it was prohibited from doing so if the Western Slope objected to any of the proposed transactions. Aspinall offered a white flag to the escalating inter-slope tensions: Denver should encourage and support the construction of the five western Colorado projects "so that she [sic] can get a hold of those later on because she can always stay within her own borders" and get water. Once the water leaves the state's borders, "I don't think there is any way to recall it."[34]

The Colorado River Advisory Committee continued to meet through the fall and winter of 1965–66, soliciting feedback from the various major water conservancy districts like the CRWCD and the Northern Colorado Water Conservancy District. After passing its recommendations along to the CWCB, Colorado's official water agency continued to fine-tune its CAP draft recommendations. Ever since Aspinall's August 1965 hearings, many Colorado River Basin water officials had hoped to amend HR 4671 into something that would be acceptable to all seven Colorado River states. The re-drafting of the bill had been the principal task of Felix Sparks, who had not only been gathering input from throughout Colorado but been in close touch with officials from other states. A seven-state meeting convened in Los Angeles in January 1966 to consider the Sparks re-drafts. The meeting led to considerable agreement among the states, but coming out of the conclave, serious issues continued to pose obstacles to the CAP's passage. The issue of river augmentation continued to hover over the proceedings, with the Pacific Northwest states striking a dour pose at even a slight mention of a raid on the Columbia River and its tributaries. The latest approved draft also retained one Grand Canyon dam at Bridge Canyon. Not surprisingly, by retaining even one dam that impacted the Grand Canyon, Colorado River state water planners incurred the growing wrath of an alerted environmental movement that had been planning to mount a national public relations campaign against the CAP if any Grand Canyon dams were included.[35]

A final threat to the revised CAP emerged from Colorado itself. Even though Colorado, under the Sparks-Aspinall leadership tandem, had taken the lead in retooling the bill, Aspinall still feared the five Western Slope projects would not be favorably received by the Department of the Interior's review process. On March 9, 1966, Arizona congressmen Morris Udall and John J. Rhodes met with Congressman Aspinall in the latter's office to discuss the Coloradan's plans for moving the revised HR 4671 through the Interior Committee. Aspinall indicated that he hoped to convene hearings on April 18 but would only do so if favorable interior department and Bureau of the Budget reports on the five Colorado water projects were in his hands. Without those reports, according to Rhodes, Aspinall would withdraw Colorado's support for the entire CAP bill. Though Aspinall was too good a politician to say it outright, "the implication was very clear that if Colorado did this, the whole affair would grind to a complete halt" as far as the House Committee on Interior and Insular Affairs was concerned. The question of contemporaneous Senate action was also discussed at the meeting. Aspinall told the Arizonans that the Senate could act on the revised HR 4671 as long as it did not move in a new direction from the revised House bill. If the Senate moved away from HR 4671, Aspinall indicated that his honor would be compromised and he would likely drop the bill.[36]

That same day, Assistant Secretary of the Interior Orren Beaty, Stewart Udall's chief confidant and fellow Arizonan, referred to the actions of Sparks, Aspinall, and Colorado as "Operations Blackmail." There is little doubt that from the perspective of the spring of 1966, Colorado, through Wayne Aspinall, controlled the pace and timing of congressional deliberations on the bill. Roy Elson, Arizona senator Carl Hayden's most trusted lieutenant, agreed with Beaty that "everyone was trying to blackmail us[, especially those] from the Upper Basin—it was just a nightmare going on all the time."[37]

Ironically, in 1966 water importation and Grand Canyon dams posed hurdles to the project, but the biggest obstacle may have been Aspinall's demand for positive Department of the Interior and Bureau of the Budget action on his five western Colorado projects. Although each had acceptable cost-benefit ratios, several of the Western Slope projects had ridiculously high development costs, ranging from $1,400 to $1,600 per acre. Interior secretary Udall's rule was never to endorse a project with development costs above $1,000 per acre. Beaty and Congressman Mo Udall of Arizona continued to push for favorable Colorado project reports from the interior department. Both officials regarded positive reports as "imperative if there are to be hearings this year in the House." Rules and time frames would need to be broken to meet Aspinall's imperious demands. Arizona's water brain trust, desperate for action, convinced Aspinall to try to expedite favorable Colorado project reports from the Bureau of the Budget. In a forceful letter to President Lyndon B. Johnson's budget director, Charles L. Schultze, Aspinall indicated that "we are nearly ready to bring peace among the Colorado River states with regard to the use and development of the water resources of the Colorado River."[38]

For several months, Aspinall had scheduled 1966 House hearings to commence on April 18. As if to underscore his serious intent, lacking a full complement of favorable executive branch reports, Aspinall decided to postpone the hearings for three more weeks. Aspinall's demand for the western Colorado project reports, first made in February, was viewed by some as outrageous; few water policy experts believed that five major reclamation project reports could be concluded in such a short time span. Yet the Department of the Interior, familiar with Aspinall's dilettante ways, dropped other projects and focused on providing the House interior chair with the reports he needed. Initially, the Bureau of the Budget failed to approve the Animas–La Plata Project. Aspinall responded by calling for approval of all five Colorado water projects. Because he had not received a full array of positive project reports, Aspinall delayed the start of the hearings until May 9.[39]

Both the Bureau of the Budget and the Department of the Interior suffered under an avalanche of political pressure to prepare positive reports on Aspinall's five Colorado projects. Many observers believed the entire American Southwest's water future depended on these studies. On April 30, the Budget of the Bureau released its hastily cobbled report. Unfortunately for Colorado and the West, the report did not say what Aspinall wanted it to say, leaving the status of the projects in a muddled state. While it did not reject the five projects outright, it did not endorse them either. The Bureau of the Budget noted that the Colorado projects would require a huge subsidy to all irrigation farmers. As a result, the bureau report questioned "the desirability in areas of critically short water supply of federal [project] sponsorship without further consideration of both alternative uses and of supplemental water sources." The Animas–La Plata Project in particular was singled out for critical comments. Water users' repayments would not be strong, and the federal investment per farm would be $157,000. Project cost per acre was $840, and the project had a disadvantageously low cost-benefit ratio. As a group, the five Colorado projects were not endorsed or rejected. The Bureau of the Budget's negative comments would hover like a dark shadow over Aspinall's five projects.[40]

After a several-week delay, on May 9, 1966, Aspinall convened the House hearings on the revised HR 4671 legislation. From Aspinall and Colorado's perspective, two issues needed to be dealt with: a fast affirmation of the revised bill that included the western Colorado water projects and a short-circuiting of the national environmental movement's growing influence. Despite his wishes for only a few pro-Colorado project witnesses to testify, seventy-three witnesses demanded to be heard, with fourteen appearing to give anti–Grand Canyon dam testimony. The less-than-enthusiastic executive branch reports on behalf of the Colorado projects all but guaranteed that the hearings would not proceed smoothly. On the first day, Colorado governor John Love and Felix L. Sparks appeared to give strong and complete support for the revised bill. At the conclusion of Love's testimony, Chairman Aspinall seized an opportunity to summarize Colorado's position on the revised bill. Colorado would favor the new HR 4671 provided it included a river augmentation study and the five Western Slope water projects. Colorado would withdraw its support for the legislation, Aspinall warned, if either of these requirements was omitted from the bill. In effect, the Interior Committee chair had thumbed his nose at the executive branch for failing to produce a full slate of favorable reports on the five projects. As for importation, Aspinall believed it remained a key bill requirement. It would ensure that enough water would be available when the Upper Basin states were ready to realize their share of the Colorado River.[41]

Aspinall ensured that many of the May hearing witnesses came to give strong testimony for the five Colorado projects. The congressman was clearly concerned with creating a strong hearing record favoring the Western Slope projects. For example, the West Divide Project had a strong cadre of supporters present. In January 1966 the West Divide Project's feasibility report appeared. The study recommended enactment of the project because of its cost-to-benefit ratio and its importance to the infant oil shale industry. West Divide would be located in the heart of shale country, a region laden with "some of the largest known oil shale deposits in the world," an area with eight times more than the world's "presently known supplies of liquid petroleum." West Divide's fortunes would always be linked to oil shale's shifting fortunes. Edward Morrill, president of the Colony Development Company, argued that enough water existed for the oil shale industry's short-term needs. However, any long-range planning and industry expansion required additional water storage on the scope of the proposed West Divide Project.[42]

A notable showdown occurred during the hearings that had the potential to impede progress toward a legislative solution. Assistant Secretary of the Interior Kenneth Holum appeared to add support for the Bureau of the Budget's recommendation to defer the Bridge Canyon Dam and build only two of the five western Colorado projects. He supported the dam at Marble Canyon and agreed that California should receive its 4.4 million acre-feet of water annual priority. Holum gave positive testimony about only two of five of Aspinall's pet projects, Animas–La Plata and Dolores, as both had unit costs "within defensible limits." Secretary Udall, Holum added, favored the immediate enactment of both projects. Development of all five Colorado projects, Holum remarked, would "almost fully utilize the remaining portions of the assured entitlements of Colorado and New Mexico to Colorado River water." Much to Aspinall and the Colorado contingent's chagrin, the Department of the Interior was unprepared to offer a recommendation on the other three Colorado water projects.[43]

Before the House Subcommittee on Irrigation and Reclamation could meet to mark up and vote on the revised bill, Aspinall declared that the proposed Grand Canyon dams remained a vital source of project power and income. As an "exponent" of the outdoors, Aspinall argued that more people would be able to enjoy the canyon, not just the able few. The two dams would make the hard-to-reach place accessible to many without substantially damaging the canyon's natural integrity. But before HR 4671 could be voted out of subcommittee, three key motions that revealed the depth of the controversies surrounding the bill had to be dealt with. One, introduced by Representative Thomas Foley (D-WA), asked to curtail all discussion of water importation. Another motion tried to delete both Grand Canyon dams from HR 4671. A third motion, introduced by Congressman John P. Saylor (R-PA), attempted to eliminate both Grand Canyon dams and Aspinall's five Western Slope water projects. While all three motions were easily defeated, they revealed the scope of the controversy surrounding the bill.[44]

With the possibility looming of a House bill that would authorize the construction of two dams in the Grand Canyon, the Sierra Club and other national environmental organizations began to mobilize nationally in an effort to modify or kill the bill. Employing arguably the most radical yet innovative tactics in the history of American conservation activism, on June 9, 1966, the Sierra Club placed expensive full-page ads opposing the dams in the *New York Times, Los Angeles Times, Washington Post,* and *San Francisco Examiner.* The ads proclaimed: "Now Only You Can Save the Grand Canyon from Being Flooded . . . for Profit." The advertising copy vividly described the horrible disfiguration awaiting America's premier scenic masterpiece while urging members of the public to write to their congressmen and the president of the United States. The ad concluded with a stirring emotional flourish: "Remember, with all the complexities of Washington politics and Arizona politics, and the ins and outs of committees and procedures, there is only one simple, incredible issue here: This time it's the Grand Canyon they want to flood. The Grand Canyon."[45]

With the Grand Canyon issue echoing as loud as the Colorado River's rushing waters, the House Subcommittee on Irrigation and Reclamation voted the revised HR 4671 over for consideration by the full Interior Committee. As committee members deliberated, the bill had become increasingly complex, cumbersome, and expensive. Other Colorado River Basin states wanted to emulate Colorado and insert their own water projects into the mix. Debates also centered on the transfer of water from the Pacific Northwest. For the time being, a water basin transfer study remained in the bill, as did the National Water Commission provision to conduct a reconnaissance of possible water transfer options by 1969. More than a dozen committee votes were taken on various bill provisions, including the Grand Canyon dams. Saylor lost an 18 to 8 vote to eliminate both dams from the bill, although he came closer (losing 16 to 13) in a bid to eliminate only the Bridge Canyon Dam. On

July 28, the controversial bill passed the committee by a 22 to 10 margin. The bill's fate in 1966 was now in the hands of the House Committee on Rules, which, feeling pressure from House members who wanted to return to their home districts to begin fall reelection campaigns, bottled up the measure. Further action on the bill would await a new Congress in early 1967.[46]

Congressman Wayne Aspinall did not wait long to introduce his latest version of the Lower Colorado River Basin bill in the new 90th Congress. The Aspinall proposal contained, among other features, a Central Arizona Project, the five western Colorado projects, and a dam in Bridge Canyon outside the Grand Canyon National Park border. Aspinall also proposed shifting the park's western boundary to the east, thus undercutting antici-pated charges that the Bridge Canyon or Hualapai Dams would back water far into the national park. To perhaps encourage support from the Pacific Northwest, Aspinall called for only a preliminary study of the water impor-tation question. Aspinall had also begun to surmise that until the CAP issue was resolved, Colorado and other western states could expect little in the way of reclamation legislation. Action on the CAP had become impera-tive. The haste of the Lower Basin states, notably Arizona, to have a CAP at all costs had led to a classic Old West High Noon showdown between Colorado and Arizona—and the near death for all forms of Central Arizona Project legislation.[47]

The Senate strategy in 1967 appeared to be based on a proposal by Sec-retary of the Interior Udall, who had revealed a new approach to the issue in a report dated February 1, 1967. Udall had separated the National Water Commission from the bill, but the legislation still contained a CAP authori-zation, although with only two western Colorado projects. The other three would be left to the findings of the National Water Commission. Udall sur-prised many observers and delighted environmentalists by scrapping the hydroelectric dams in the Grand Canyon in favor of privately built coal-fired plants to be constructed in the Four Corners region.[48]

The first notable legislative action toward a CAP in the 90th Congress in early 1967 occurred in the House of Representatives. The House Subcom-mittee on Irrigation and Reclamation had held hearings in March 1967 on a set of bills closely modeled after Aspinall's HR 3300, which appeared dia-metrically opposed to Secretary Udall's new 1967 proposal. Colorado gov-ernor John Love and CWCB director Felix Sparks appeared once again to give Aspinall's bill strong support. The Colorado contingent endorsed the five western Colorado projects, noting that all five had been authorized for feasibility studies in the 1956 CRSP. Each had been carefully planned and analyzed for more than twenty years. Up to this point, Love asserted, Colorado, which contributed more than 70 percent of the Colorado River's overall flow, had only been able to realize a small portion of its Colorado River Compact allotment. Love indicated that he and other Colorado officials believed the Centennial State had been in effect "singled out" by Secretary Udall by having three of its projects made subject to the whims of a National Water Commission study. "To suggest that a National Water Commission should determine the internal allocation of water within a state is to perpetuate a cruel hoax upon our people," Love exclaimed. Aspinall joined in to second Love's assertion. He had also been angry that Secretary Udall had apparently caved in to environmentalist pressure by removing both Grand Canyon dams. In a stern rebuke to Udall, Aspinall indicated that as far as he was concerned, "there won't be any legislation if we don't have Hualapai [formerly Bridge Canyon] Dam in the bill."[49]

By early June 1967, most Coloradans realized that for all intents and purposes, any version of the CAP was virtually dead for the year. In a memorandum to the CWCB board, the Colorado River Advisory Committee, and the state's congressional delegation, Felix Sparks announced that the Colorado River Basin Project "has no chance of passage during the 90th Congress." From Colorado's official perspective, two roadblocks to passage had been erected: the move to delete the Bridge (Hualapai) Dam and the controversy over water importation. In a statement that foreshadowed some of Aspinall's later 1967 comments, Sparks indicated that Colorado and the other basin states (except for Arizona) had been abandoned by President Johnson, the Bureau of the Budget, and Secretary of the Interior Udall.[50]

In the summer of 1967 the Senate passed its version of the CAP by a 70 to 12 margin. The Senate bill contained no hydroelectric dams in the Grand Canyon and remained free of water importation provisions. After hearing of the Senate's action, Aspinall announced that the Senate bill had destroyed the possibility of a CAP "for the session" of Congress. While the Senate bill retained Aspinall's five Colorado projects, the Coloradan did not believe the CAP could remain feasible without hydroelectric dams to generate both power and income to offset immense project costs. Perhaps more important, he resented the appearance of another congressional capitulation, in the manner of Echo Park, to the growing environmentalist movement. Finally, he objected to the absence of water importation provisions. Without at least one Grand Canyon dam or provisions for water importation, Aspinall believed the project lacked feasibility. "This then, is the death knell for the basin project," Aspinall declared, "and I am saddened to hear about it. I denounce this [the Senate's action]. I reject it. I will fight against it." After the House Interior Committee adjourned on August 28, Aspinall returned to Colorado with no intention of calling his committee back into session in 1967.[51]

Aspinall's action or lack thereof would lead to one of the most embarrassing moments in his legendary political career while ironically setting the stage for the final push toward CAP legislation. When it became apparent that Aspinall actually was going to adjourn his committee and return to Colorado, Arizona water strategists began urging Senator Carl Hayden, not a vituperative man by nature, to use his immense legislative reach to try to force the House Interior Committee chair back to his post in the nation's capital. Pressure on Aspinall to hold his committee in session also emanated from House speaker John McCormack (D-MA) and the chair of the House Committee on Public Works, Mike Kirwan (D-OH). Both leaders could undermine appropriations deemed vital to Aspinall and Colorado's reclamation projects, including Fryingpan-Arkansas and several of Colorado's CRSP projects.[52]

Aspinall was finally pressured to return to Washington, DC, through an unusual parliamentary maneuver. Ironically, this procedure was suggested to Arizona congressman John J. Rhodes by Bureau of Reclamation commissioner Floyd Dominy—normally an Aspinall ally. Dominy informed Rhodes that the CAP could be authorized as part of an appropriation bill. While Rhodes questioned whether this tactic was legal, Dominy assured the Arizonan that it had been done with many reclamation projects over the years. The Arizona congressional delegation convinced Hayden to attach a CAP rider to a Senate public works appropriation bill by amendment. In a House-Senate Conference Committee session, all the House conferees needed to do was adopt the Senate amendment, then take the bill to the House floor where it had the votes to pass. In this way, Aspinall's committee could be bypassed. Hayden admitted that "I don't like to do things like that," but Arizona's other congressional members convinced him to take this course of action. Interestingly, the Colorado–Big Thompson Project had been authorized by a similar technique.[53]

In a fall 1967 appearance before the Colorado Water Conservation Board, Aspinall explained his recent actions, indicating that he believed he had been carrying out the wishes of Colorado's citizens, expressed through the CWCB and state water conservation districts. Aspinall indicated that his long career in Congress was likely nearing its end, and it was doubtful that any Colorado politician would hold as commanding a position over water legislation for many years. As a result, Colorado and the Upper Basin needed to play their cards carefully at this time: "I do not personally desire to support a project [the CAP in the Senate bill] that does not have an assured water supply or must depend for its water supply on water that belongs legally to somebody else." Acutely aware that his legacy and historical reputation might be at stake, Aspinall remarked: "I don't care personally what people are going to say about me at the present time. I am not going to put myself in a position that 35 years hence it can be said of me by members of my family or a constituent in my Congressional District or any members of the State of Colorado that I gave away the birthright of the water resources which legally belong to the State of Colorado."[54] Aspinall's impassioned conclusion, which in many respects could stand as an epithet for his rapidly concluding congressional career, brought the CWCB board, its staff, and the audience to a loud standing ovation.

Back in Colorado, Aspinall got wind of Hayden's action and decided to make an expeditious return to Washington, DC, to limit the political damage. After meeting with Hayden, Aspinall called his committee briefly back into session on October 10 and agreed to take up the CAP legislation in January or February 1968. For Aspinall, two overarching concerns remained: the fate of the five western Colorado projects and a guarantee that the Colorado River water-supply question would be taken seriously. With the possibility of a CAP project again a reality, western Colorado officials began discussing what final shape the bill might take. At the quarterly meeting of the CRWCD on October 17, 1967, Secretary-engineer Phillip Smith noted that new plans for pumping water from the Colorado River to supply the CAP, as a substitute for the Grand Canyon dams, were under way. In addition, Smith reported that Aspinall remained adamant that any form of a CAP must include the five Western Slope projects. Less than a week later, Aspinall sounded optimistic that when Congress resumed its business in early 1968, an "equitable" bill, fair to both the Upper and Lower Basins, could be agreed upon.[55]

1968: WATER FOR COLORADO AND THE SOUTHWEST

Wayne Aspinall prepared for 1968 by consulting closely with Ival Goslin, director of the Upper Colorado River Commission. Goslin prepared an academic article with Aspinall that dealt with the CAP and the problem of water supply in the Colorado River system. Calling the Colorado the "most controversial stream in modern history," Aspinall, with input from Goslin, noted that the Colorado River Compact had originally overestimated the amount of water in the river. Aspinall maintained that approval of the CAP should only occur if Congress "simultaneously" provides for a "definite and realistic water augmentation program." Though Aspinall had agreed to consider the Central Arizona Project bill in early 1968, the article is proof that his position still differed widely from the conventional wisdom circulating in the Lower Basin.[56]

The Colorado Water Conservation Board also reexamined the CAP legislation in late 1967 and early 1968, with an eye to redrafting the House version. At its December 13, 1967, meeting, the CWCB affirmed its previous policies in support of Aspinall's CAP bill, HR 3300, subject to any changes made by Director Sparks, the board's staff, and the state's Colorado River Advisory Committee. Those changes included a recommendation that the National Water Resources Council (and later the National Water Commission) give "highest priority" to preparation of a program "to relieve water shortages on the Colorado River." This represented a significant departure and scaling back for Colorado's water politicians, who had been insisting on a program to tap the water-rich Pacific Northwest.[57]

The CWCB also advised that the interior secretary not make a recommendation regarding water importation without first gaining approval from the state of water origin. These provisions would go a long way toward making peace with the northwestern states and perhaps toward gaining their support. The CWCB also supported California's priority for 4.4 million acre-feet per year until such time as a working water importation plan was in place to supplement the Colorado River's flow. The CWCB's draft asked for construction of the five western Colorado water projects but, in a significant change, called for their construction to be "concurrent with construction of the Central Arizona Project." It appeared that this new Colorado-prepared draft of HR 3300 would guide Aspinall's House committee during the upcoming months. Sparks, who likely did most of the work on the re-draft, had sent the bill to the other Colorado River Basin states; as of January 1, 1968, no states had registered any serious objection.[58]

The Subcommittee on Irrigation and Reclamation of the House Interior Committee's hearings on the CAP legislation lasted from January 30 to February 2, 1968. In its first item of business, Chair Harold "Bizz" Johnson of California recognized Congressman Aspinall who placed in the committee record a letter he had written to Secretary of the Interior Stewart Udall that indicated the strategy the House Interior Committee would employ to consider the Colorado River Basin Project bill. Aspinall's letter to Udall, dated December 29, 1967, outlined the issues that remained to be considered before a bill could be passed. With the likelihood of no Grand Canyon dams to power and finance the project, Aspinall indicated that funding to build the massive and expensive project still needed to be found. Other remaining issues Aspinall identified included the need for reliable data on the available water supply, a matter that continued to trouble Colorado water officials.[59]

The Bureau of Reclamation and, by implication, Arizona water boosters favored generous basin water availability estimates that would take into account stream flow records prior to 1922—some of the wettest years of the century. Aspinall called the use of those records "unrealistic," believing the Upper Colorado River Commission's estimates of stream flow were far more accurate. Aspinall also circled back around to the tricky political question of river augmentation. However, this time he steered clear of inter-basin transfer from the Pacific Northwest, confining his comments and questions to the interior department's recent studies of augmentation through desalinization of sea water and weather modification. While Aspinall made it clear to Udall that he would no longer be an obstacle, the Colorado congressman indicated that CAP advocates still had to provide answers to lingering questions before he would advance the bill. In testimony delivered on January 31, Udall tried to answer Aspinall's concerns and those of the state of Colorado and the Upper Basin. Udall made it clear that the administration and Arizona's water interests had embraced new sources of power for the project, notably coal-fired power plants in the Four Corners region.[60]

The House hearings ended after three days. The Interior Committee's next task was to revise HR 3300 to reflect concerns raised during the hearings. After a week of bill markups, the House Subcommittee on Irrigation and Reclamation passed the legislation by a 17 to 5 vote. The re-drafted HR 3300 harmonized more closely with S. 1004. Gone were the Grand Canyon dams, replaced by the coal-fired power plants. No mention was made of a National Water Commission that might have recommended water transfers from the Pacific Northwest. Aspinall included a carefully worded section on the need for feasibility studies to ultimately augment the river by 2.5 million acre-feet annually. Inter-basin water transfers, in Aspinall's re-drafted bill, would only be allowed with the interior secretary's recommendation and the approval of the affected states. Needless to say, Aspinall's legislation included both California's annual 4.4 million acre-foot guarantee and the five western Colorado projects.[61]

The House Interior Committee reported Aspinall's HR 3300 bill by a 22 to 10 margin in mid-April 1968. The bill had no difficulty escaping the grasp of the House Committee on Rules. An Arizona observer counted the late April arrival of the CWCB's Felix Sparks in Washington, DC, to help corral votes as a positive portent. The bill could now move to the House floor and be debated and voted on. Preliminary vote counts had started to turn in favor of the bill, with the number of commitments rising daily.[62]

In testimony on the House floor, Wayne Aspinall traced the history of the bill alongside a history of legislative attempts to develop the Colorado River. The Colorado River, Aspinall asserted, "has been a river of trouble and controversy from the beginnings of its development. It has been undependable, unruly, and wasteful because of the vagaries of nature." When the House speaker called for a voice vote on May 15, 1968, HR 3300 passed by overwhelming acclamation. The bill now moved on to the House and Senate Conference Committee. Colorado was well represented on the committee by both Aspinall and Senator Gordon Allott. Arizona was equally well represented by Morris Udall from the House of Representatives and Senator Carl Hayden.[63]

After seven negotiating sessions, on August 1 an agreement was reached between House and Senate conferees by a 14 to 1 margin on what was being called S. 1004, likely in deference to the Senate's dean, Carl Hayden. The bill's final language stepped delicately around the issue of northwestern water importation, which occupied the majority of the Conference Committee's time. The committee authorized the interior secretary to make a full reconnaissance study for the purpose of creating a general plan to meet the future water needs of the American West. A ten-year moratorium was also imposed on importation studies to assuage the fears of the northwestern states. For Colorado, the Conference Committee affirmed the authorization of the Animas–La Plata, Dolores, Dallas Creek, West Divide, and San Miguel Projects, to be "constructed concurrently with the Central Arizona Project." Other provisions were also included, including California's 4.4. million acre-feet annual priority right, which would remain in effect until the interior secretary believed enough water had augmented the river's flow to satisfy the Lower Basin's annual consumptive use of 7.5 million acre-feet. The five Western Slope projects carried a collective price tag of $391,760,000, though the bill did not specify an appropriation to start construction on any of the authorized projects.[64]

Grand Junction's *Daily Sentinel* praised Congressman Aspinall's role in shaping the final bill, now known as the Colorado River Basin Project (CRBP). Aspinall had delayed the bill and suffered a withering barrage of national criticism, but he had played his legislative hand to gain the best possible results for western Colorado under the "political circumstances." The *Sentinel* also warned that the aftermath of the bill's passage continued to hold little promise for expedited construction of reclamation projects. The mounting costs of the Vietnam War and the need for the Bureau of Reclamation to prepare planning reports for the five western Colorado projects would surely delay their construction starts by several years. Other issues would also come into play, including decisions to be made by the CWCB and Colorado water users about which western Colorado projects to prioritize. Finally, continuing potential conflicts between the Eastern and Western Slopes could, as always, impede state water planning.[65]

Inaccurate interpretations of a segment of the CRBP law over Senate Document 80's continued importance demonstrated how easily the state's two halves could resume verbal warfare. A Denver newspaper editorial stated that the CRBP repealed Senate Document 80. Naturally, western Colorado took umbrage at this assertion, noting that Senate Document 80 had been affirmed in the new law at the insistence of Western Slope water officials. The *Daily Sentinel* noted: "Farmers in the Grand Valley are using water released from the [Green Mountain] reservoir at this time" and would continue to be protected by Senate Document 80, included as part of the Colorado–Big Thompson Project's authorization.[66]

FIGURE 7.1. Dallas Creek Project, groundbreaking, 1978. Dallas Creek was one of five western Colorado projects authorized under the Colorado River Basin Project, along with the Central Arizona Project. Only three of the five Colorado projects have been built: Dallas Creek, Dolores, and Animas–La Plata. *Courtesy*, Colorado Mesa University Archives and Special Collections, Grand Junction.

THE NEW ERA OF THE 1970S: CAP'S CLOUDY AFTERMATH

In the aftermath of the Lower Colorado River struggles, Colorado, almost predictably, resumed its internal bickering over water allotment. At almost the exact moment the CAP was finalized, the Central Colorado Water Conservancy District sought the endorsement of the Colorado Water Conservation Board for the massive Central–South Platte Project, based largely on the old Blue River–South Platte Project, which dated back to Bureau of Reclamation designs in the late 1930s. The 1955 Blue River diversion constituted only a small part of this projected, more than 700,000 acre-feet diversion. A spokesman for the project noted that existing components of the Blue River diversion—such as Dillon Reservoir, the Roberts Tunnel, and other integral water management structures on the Front Range including the Cherry Creek and Chatfield Dams—would be incorporated into the overall structure of the project. The updated plan would also include the Narrows Project on Colorado's eastern plains near Fort Morgan and the long-discussed Two Forks Reservoir on the South Platte, west of Denver. The project would build ten new reservoirs on the Eastern Slope, storing almost 4 million acre-feet.[67]

CWCB director Felix Sparks tried to quickly quash talk of another controversial diversion by noting that water did not exist for a project of that magnitude; thus CWCB approval "would be a foolish and futile gesture." In his report at a CWCB meeting in Alamosa, Colorado, in late summer 1968, Sparks "assailed" the Central–South Platte Project as "infeasible" and "based on monumental inaccuracies." If any water in the state remained available, it was only temporarily available until authorized projects were constructed. For example, the Blue River system could be used on an interim basis to provide agricultural water to eastern Colorado. However, Sparks quickly noted that the Blue River decree limited Denver's water use to municipal purposes only. Attorneys for the Central Colorado Water Conservancy District, according to Sparks, had overestimated the amount of water available for diversion. Central Colorado Water Conservancy District attorney Mills E. Bunger estimated Colorado's annual share of Colorado River water at 3.83 million acre-feet. This stood in sharp contrast with the Hill Report total of 3.1 million acre-feet and the 1965 Tipton and Kalmbach estimate of 3.23 million acre-feet. Sparks maintained that no matter how the river could be measured, it was now completely appropriated.[68]

Sparks added an insightful footnote in assessing Colorado's 1960s intra-mural and external water wars. "The past bitter interstate battles among the seven states of the basin have not been predicated upon the knowledge that there is a surplus of water in the river," Sparks asserted, "but rather upon the firm conviction that there will be a great deficit." The looming water deficit underscored why the most controversial aspect of the CAP struggle was the search for basin augmentation. One question in this era that often jumped to the fore of conversations about Colorado's twentieth-century water program revolved around the impact of the state's volatile east-west political struggles on the state's overall ability to use its compact allotments. Colorado's twen-tieth-century water wars undoubtedly acted as a brake on the state's ability to utilize its full Colorado River Compact and Upper Colorado River Basin Compact allotments. In some cases, the state's water fights also delayed the utilization of expected water allotments.[69]

Felix Sparks positively bristled whenever anyone suggested that Colorado could have done more to develop its water, especially considering his direct involvement from the late 1950s. He asserted that in the last ten years, Colorado's authorized and constructed water projects had "far exceeded the total cumulative efforts" of the preceding eighty-two years since statehood was achieved in 1876. Yet it is clear that the state's preoccupation with its east versus west water politics distracted it from taking a more unified stance characteristic of some other Colorado River Basin states.[70]

The Colorado River Basin Project Act had overcome what at times had seemed daunting odds to be passed by the US Congress. In a news confer-ence held ten days before President Lyndon B. Johnson signed the bill into law, Secretary of the Interior Stewart Udall termed the struggle leading to the bill's passage "the oldest and most bitter water rights controversy in the country." Arizona congressman John Rhodes believed the bill had slipped through "a very narrow window" that was about to close. The era of mas-sive river basin projects, launched by both the New Deal and the post–World War II era of unmatched American economic prosperity, was fast coming to an end. Some visionaries still harbored big reclamation dreams, but political realities were changing fast. Inflation was rising, the economic toll of the Vietnam War was leading to calls to curtail domestic spending, and by the early 1970s the soaring costs of energy and energy production would soon lead to the end of America's love affair with massive public works projects like dam construction. A new generation of environmental activists would convince Congress to enact legislation that would enable anti-reclamation crusaders to delay, downsize, or halt many water projects. No new significant reclamation projects on a grand scale were authorized by Congress after the Colorado River Basin Project Act of 1968. It also proved difficult, if not nearly impossible, to enact all of the parts of this large and expensive bill as it became caught in the tide of rising inflation and a lack of national commitment to grand water solutions.

NOTES

1. Colorado Water Conservation Board Minutes, September 7–8, 1967, Box 178, folder 5, Frank Delaney Collection, University of Colorado at Boulder Archives (hereafter UCBA).

2. Marc Reisner, *Cadillac Desert: The American West and Its Disappearing Water*, rev. ed. (New York: Penguin Books, 1993), 259–61.

3. Ted Steinberg, *Down to Earth: Nature's Role in American History* (New York: Oxford University Press, 2002), 249–51; Hal K. Rothman, *The Greening of a Nation: Environmentalism in the United States since 1945* (Fort Worth: Harcourt Brace, 1998), 84–90.

4. See Reisner, *Cadillac Desert*, 415–19. Reisner quotes Alan Merson, a regional administrator of the Environmental Protection Agency who had beaten Wayne Aspinall in the 1972 Democratic congressional primary and lost the general election. Merson argues that all elected congressional and state officials in Colorado were "on the run" from water developers. Richard Lamm, Gary Hart, Floyd Haskell, and Tim Wirth were "scared to death of not liking water enough." When the state boomed in the 1970s, "they're for any water project—they don't care how bad it is."

5. *Arizona v. California*, 373 U.S. 546 (1963); Byron E. Pearson, *Still the Wild River Runs: Congress, the Sierra Club, and the Fight to Save the Grand Canyon* (Tucson: University of Arizona Press, 2002), 46–47; Norris Hundley Jr., *Water and the West: The Colorado River Compact and the Politics of Water in the American West*, 2nd ed. (Berkeley: University of California Press, 2009), 302–6.

6. Hundley, *Water and the West*, 302–6.

7. Ibid.

8. Pearson, *Still the Wild River Runs*, 35–57; Carl Hayden to Stewart L. Udall, December 19, 1963, Box 167, folder "December 1963," Stewart L. Udall Papers, Special Collections, University of Arizona Library (hereafter SCUAL), Tucson.

9. Pearson, *Still the Wild River Runs*, 47–50; Reisner, *Cadillac Desert*, 273–77; Susan Schrepfer, *David Brower: Environmental Activist, Publicist, and Prophet* (Berkeley: Regional Oral History Office, Bancroft Library, University of California, 1974–78), 143–44; Stewart L. Udall to President Lyndon B. Johnson, February 14, 1964, Box 476, folder "1964–65," Morris K. Udall Papers, SCUAL, Tucson. Marc Reisner in *Cadillac Desert* (275–76) argues that even though the early drafts of the Pacific Southwest Water Plan (PSWWP) did not say it, the plan was a "smokescreen" to tap the water of the Columbia River Basin. Long afterward, Morris Udall characterized the PSWWP as "the reclamation equivalent of [Ronald Reagan's] Star Wars plan." Udall remarked, "Ronald Reagan wants to unfurl a peace-shield umbrella over North America; the bureau [of Reclamation] wanted to unroll a hose three thousand miles long." See Morris K. Udall, *Too Funny to Be President* (New York: Henry Holt, 1988), 49–50.

10. Wayne Aspinall to Stewart L. Udall, November 27, 1962, Box 141, folder "L-11-b," Wayne N. Aspinall Papers, University of Denver Archives (hereafter UDA).

11. See the *Denver Post*'s veteran writer Bert Hanna's discussion of this topic in "Aspinall Vows to Guard Upper Basin Water Rights," an early 1965 *Denver Post* article in Box 196, folder "L-11-b-1-A," Wayne N. Aspinall Papers, UDA.

12. Rich Johnson, *The Central Arizona Project: 1918–1968* (Tucson: University of Arizona Press, 1977), 150–51; Steven C. Schulte, *Wayne Aspinall and the Shaping of the American West* (Boulder: University Press of Colorado, 2002), 185.

13. Hanna, "Aspinall Vows to Guard Upper Basin Water Rights"; Schulte, *Wayne Aspinall*, 185–86.

14. Carl Hayden to Wayne Aspinall, June 10, 1965, Box 184, folder "39 G," Wayne N. Aspinall Papers, UDA. Hayden made it clear that if a lack of available water to make projects feasible occurred, he would halt construction on both the CRSP and Fryingpan-Arkansas to "minimize risks of loss of federal investment in them." To illustrate his serious intent, Hayden asked Dominy to advise him as to which project appropriations should be omitted by the committee, which could be reduced, and the "extent of such reduction." Word of Hayden's political gamesmanship quickly reached Aspinall.

15. Johnson, *Central Arizona Project*, 158; Schulte, *Wayne Aspinall*, 187; Carl Hayden to Wayne Aspinall, May 18, 1965, Box 5, folder 22, Carl Hayden Papers, Arizona State University, Special Collections Department (hereafter ASUSCD), Tempe.

16. Hanna, "Aspinall Vows to Guard Upper Basin Water Rights."

17. Carl Hayden to Floyd E. Dominy, June 10, 1965, Box 5, folder 12, Carl Hayden Papers, ASUSCD; Carl Hayden to Wayne Aspinall, June 10, 1965, Box 184, folder "39 G," Wayne N. Aspinall Papers, UDA.

18. Felix L. Sparks to Colorado Water Conservation Board, June 2, 1965, Box 113, folder 15, Frank Delaney Papers.

19. Ibid. California's guarantee would last until 2.5 million acre-feet of additional water were imported into the Colorado River system from outside the region. Sparks noted that the most likely source of the water would be the Columbia River region, but he correctly predicted that the states of that area "would not eagerly accede to diversion of water from the Columbia."

20. Sparks to Water Conservation Board, June 2, 1965; *Daily Sentinel* (Grand Junction, CO), June 1, 1965.

21. Reisner, *Cadillac Desert*, 262–63.

22. Upper Colorado River Commission, *Water Supplies of the Colorado River, Available for Use by the States of the Upper Division and for the Use from the Main Stem by the States of Arizona, California, and Nevada on the Lower Basin* (Denver: Tipton and Kalmbach, July 1965), 5–21.

23. Edwin Johnson, "Upper Basin Rights, Lower Basin Water," Box 196, folder "L-11-b1-A," Wayne N. Aspinall Papers, UDA; *Rocky Mountain News* (Denver), August 12, 1965.

24. Lower Colorado River Basin Project, Hearings, Subcommittee on Irrigation and Reclamation, House Interior and Insular Affairs Committee, 89th Congress, 1st Session, on HR 4671 et al., 1965, 166, 202–3, 232; Johnson, *Central Arizona Project*, 163–65; Wayne N. Aspinall to Edwin C. Johnson, July 30, 1965, Box 196, folder "L-11-b-1-A," Wayne N. Aspinall Papers, UDA; Schulte, *Wayne Aspinall*, 188–89.

25. Lower Colorado River Basin Project, Hearings (1965), 165–66, 232, 245, 767; Jared Farmer, *Glen Canyon Dammed: Inventing Lake Powell* (Tucson: University of Arizona Press, 1999), 149.

26. Lower Colorado River Basin Project, Hearings (1965), 245, 767.

27. Morris K. Udall to Wayne Aspinall, September 21, 1965, Box 89, folder "3/2," John Rhodes Papers, ASUSCD, Tempe.

28. Schulte, *Wayne Aspinall*, 192.

29. Ibid.; Sparks quoted in Colorado River Advisory Committee Minutes, September 28, 1965, Box 3, folder "Colorado River Advisory Committee," William Nelson Papers, Colorado Mesa University Archives and Special Collections (hereafter CMUASC), Grand Junction.

30. Jack Ross and Robert Fischer to Members of the [Denver] Board of Water Commissioners and Executive Staff, October 8, 1965, Box 17, folder 3, Edwin C. Johnson Papers, UDA; Schulte, *Wayne Aspinall*, 193.

31. Felix L. Sparks to Wayne N. Aspinall, October 11, 1965, and Wayne N. Aspinall to Felix L. Sparks, October 13, 1965, both in Box 184, folder "39-H," Wayne N. Aspinall Papers, UDA; Schulte, *Wayne Aspinall*, 193.

32. Colorado River Water Conservation District Minutes, October 11, 1965, folder "CRWCD Minutes, 1964–66," Colorado River Water Conservation District (hereafter CRWCD), Glenwood Springs.

33. CRWCD Minutes, October 18, 1965, January 18, 1966, folder "CRWCD Minutes, 1964–66," CRWCD, Glenwood Springs.

34. Taped on January 28, 1966, KLZ TV, Wayne Aspinall, transcript of interview, Box 94, folder "Central Arizona Misc., 1/1/66," Byron Rogers Papers, UDA.

35. Johnson, *Central Arizona Project*, 175–79; Pearson, *Still the Wild River Runs*, 102–24; Minutes, Colorado River Advisory Committee, January 10, 1966, Box 3, folder "Colorado River Advisory Committee," William Nelson Papers, CMUASC, Grand Junction.

36. John J. Rhodes, Memorandum for the Files, March 9, 1966, Box 476, folder "January–March 1966," Morris K. Udall Papers, SCUAL, Tucson.

37. Roy Elson, interview by US Senate Historical Office, Washington, DC, ASUSCD, April 27–August 21, 1990.

38. Wayne N. Aspinall to Charles L. Schultze, March 14, 1966, Box 89, folder "3:/4," John Rhodes Papers, ASUSCD, Tempe; "Notes on March 15, Conference," Box 476, folder "January–March 1966," Morris K. Udall Papers, SCUAL, Tucson; Orren Beaty to Stewart L. Udall, March 9, 1966, Box 127, folder 1, Stewart L. Udall Papers, SCUAL, Tucson.

39. *Durango (CO) Herald*, April 11, 1966; Johnson, *Central Arizona Project*, 183–84; Helen Ingram, *Water Politics: Continuity and Change* (Albuquerque: University of New Mexico Press, 1990), 77.

40. Ingram, *Water Politics*, 77–78.

41. Lower Colorado River Basin Project, Hearings, Subcommittee on Irrigation and Reclamation, House Interior and Insular Affairs Committee, 89th Congress, 2nd session, on HR 4671 et al., May 9, 1966, 1071–73, 1082–83; Pearson, *Still the Wild River Runs*, 125–27; Schulte, *Wayne Aspinall*, 195.

42. Lower Colorado River Basin Project, Hearings (1966), 1262.

43. Ibid. 1337–39, 1362–63.

44. Ibid.

45. *New York Times*, June 9 and 19, 1966; Pearson, *Still the Wild River Runs*, 139–43; Schulte, *Wayne Aspinall*, 197.

46. *Congressional Quarterly*, "Committee Roundup," August 5, 1966, 1697–98, Box 215, no file, Wayne N. Aspinall Papers, UDA; Schulte, *Wayne Aspinall*, 198–99.

47. See Aspinall's bill in Box 275, folder "1967 Legislation, Interior and Insular Affairs, Colorado River Basin, Bills, Reports, Etc.," Wayne N. Aspinall Papers, UDA; Pearson, *Still the Wild River Runs*, 165. Also see Felix L. Sparks to Members,

Colorado Water Conservation Board and Colorado River Advisory Committee, November 25, 1966, Box 10, folder 5, Edwin C. Johnson Papers, UDA.

48. Ingram, *Water Politics*, 60–61; Schulte, *Wayne Aspinall*, 204–8.

49. Love and Aspinall quoted in Lower Colorado River Basin Project, Hearings, 1966, 525–26; *New York Times*, March 14, 1967.

50. Felix L. Sparks, Memorandum to Members of the Colorado Water Conservation Board, Colorado River Advisory Committee, and Colorado Congressional Delegation, June 6, 1967, Box 10, folder 6, Edwin C. Johnson Papers, UDA; *Colorado Water Congress Newsletter*, vol. 10, no. 6, June 1, 1967, Box 6, folder 5, William Nelson Papers, CMUASC, Grand Junction.

51. Ingram, *Water Politics*, 61; Schulte, *Wayne Aspinall*, 209; *Denver Post*, June 26, 1967. Wayne Aspinall seemed to believe that most of the water-shortage issues in the Colorado River Basin could be solved through importation. For Aspinall, importation from the Pacific Northwest would be expensive on an acre-foot basis but was more reliable and less expensive overall than other methods discussed at the time—ocean desalinization and weather modification. See Wayne N. Aspinall to Phillip Smith, June 28, 1967, Box 11, folder 2, Edwin C. Johnson Papers, UDA.

52. Schulte, *Wayne Aspinall*, 210–11; Morris Udall to John McCormack, August 11, 1967, Box 90, folder "1/3," John Rhodes Papers, ASUSCD, Tempe; Ingram, *Water Politics*, 61; Carl Hayden to Michael J. Kirwan, August 10, 1967, Box 5, folder 12, Carl Hayden Papers, ASUSCD, Tempe; Wayne N. Aspinall to Michael J. Kirwan, August 18, 1967, Box 274, folder "Legislation, Interior and Insular Affairs, Colorado River Basin Project," Wayne N. Aspinall Papers, UDA.

53. John Rhodes interview with Ross R. Rice, December 6, 1973, folder 96, Ross R. Rice Papers, ASUSCD, Tempe; Roy Elson interview, April 27–August 21, 1990; Wallace Duncan, confidential letter to Roy Elson, September 27, 1967, Box 15, folder 5, Carl Hayden Papers, ASUSCD, Tempe; Schulte, *Wayne Aspinall*, 211–12.

54. Colorado Water Conservation Board Minutes, September 7–8, 1967, Box 178, folder 5, Frank Delaney Papers, UCBA.

55. CRWCD Minutes, October 17, 1967, folder "CRWCD Minutes, 1967–68," CRWCD, Glenwood Springs; *Daily Sentinel*, October 15 and 17, 1967.

56. Honorable Wayne N. Aspinall, "The Colorado River Water Supply," Box 308, folder "L 11b (1)," Wayne N. Aspinall Papers, UDA.

57. *Colorado Water Congress Newsletter*, January 1, 1968, vol. 11, no. 1, Box 8, folder 8, Edwin C. Johnson Papers, UDA.

58. Ibid.

59. Wayne N. Aspinall to Stewart L. Udall, December 29, 1967, in Colorado River Basin Project, Part 2, Hearings, Subcommittee on Irrigation and Reclamation,

House Committee on Interior and Insular Affairs, 90th Congress, 2nd session, on HR 3300 and S. 1004, January 30–February 2, 1968, 692–93.

60. Ibid.

61. Wayne Aspinall, "Statement on Aspinall Substitute," February 8, 1968, Box 15, folder 5, Carl Hayden Papers, ASUSCD, Tempe; Central Arizona Project Association, "Situation Report," March 8, 1968, Box 15, folder 3, Carl Hayden Papers, ASUSCD, Tempe; Schulte, *Wayne Aspinall*, 214–15.

62. Schulte, *Wayne Aspinall*, 215–16.

63. Ibid.

64. Ival Goslin to Upper Colorado River Commissioners et al., August 5, 1968, Box 3, folder 20, William Nelson Papers, CMUASC, Grand Junction; "Text of Language Agreed upon by Conferees on S. 1004," 90th Congress, 2nd session, House of Representatives, July 31, 1968, Box 309, folder "S.1004, Colorado River," Wayne N. Aspinall Papers, UDA; *Colorado Water Congress Newsletter*, vol. 11, no. 9, September 1, 1968, Box 8, folder 8, Edwin C. Johnson Papers, UDA; "Remarks of the President at the Signing of S. 1004, the Colorado River Project Bill," September 30, 1968, Box 308, folder "L11b (1)," Wayne N. Aspinall Papers, UDA; *Daily Sentinel*, September 30, 1968. The law was "An Act to authorize the construction, operation, and maintenance of the Colorado River Basin Project, and for other purposes," Public Law 90–537, 90th Congress, S. 1005.

65. *Daily Sentinel*, October 3, 1968.

66. Editorial cited in ibid.

67. *Colorado Water Congress Newsletter*, vol. 11, no. 10, October 1, 1968, Box 6, folder 5, William Nelson Papers, CMUASC, Grand Junction.

68. Felix L. Sparks to Colorado Water Conservation Board, August 30, 1968, Box 11, folder 2, Edwin C. Johnson Papers, UDA; Sparks quoted in *Colorado Water Congress Newsletter*, October 1, 1968.

69. Felix L. Sparks to Colorado Water Conservation Board, August 30, 1968.

70. Ibid.

Epilogue

The View from Western Colorado

Colorado's water wars did not end in the 1970s. From the 1970s to the dawn of the twenty-first century, round after round of sparring occurred in the state's water wars. The issues had the ring of familiarity, but changing social, economic, and political circumstances introduced new variables to the water battlefields. Colorado and the American West's political culture underwent a rapid change in the 1970s. While the state hoped to continue its breakneck pace of water development in the decades after 1970, a combination of new political variables conspired to constrain and undermine the fondest hopes of Colorado's water establishment.

Nationally, an energized environmental movement continued to interject itself into reclamation policy. A host of new laws at the federal level made it possible to challenge or delay reclamation projects on the grounds of new environmental values codified into law. Legislation like the National Environmental Policy Act (1969) and the actions of the Environmental Protection Agency could be used to stifle or suffocate water projects indefinitely. At the state level, in 1973 the Colorado Water Conservation Board

DOI: 10.5876/9781607325000.c008

(CWCB) gained the power to appropriate "sufficient water to preserve the natural environment to a reasonable degree."[1] The 1970s and beyond introduced a new milieu for Colorado water planners; the era, one of distinct limits, would cause a great deal of frustration and lead to few of the grand legislative successes of earlier decades.

Colorado's political culture changed in other ways as well. The environmental movement began to attract a large following as Coloradans began to rethink the social costs of continuous economic expansion. Part of this calculation included damming wild streams to increase water supplies. The state became a haven for displaced urbanites from other regions and for retirees who demanded pristine views and unfettered access to outdoor recreation. A burgeoning ski industry, access to gold-medal fishing waters, and the popularity of river rafting all spoke to a changing attitude toward water and its uses in post-1970s Colorado. In 1972, Coloradans rejected state funding to support the 1976 Winter Olympic Games. The group that organized the opposition to the games, Citizens for Colorado's Future, crafted a deliberate anti-growth and pro-environmental image to rally its base of support. Colorado's political culture had indeed changed.[2]

In 1968, Colorado rejoiced when President Lyndon B. Johnson signed the Colorado River Basin Project into law, a bill that contained the five Western Slope water projects Congressman Wayne N. Aspinall and CWCB director Felix L. Sparks had labored diligently to include. By the 1970s it had become apparent that all five projects, while authorized, remained a long way from being funded or constructed. As early as 1969, Sparks charged Secretary of the Interior Stewart Udall with "double-crossing" Colorado. In the 1969 federal budget, both the Central Arizona Project (CAP) and Utah's Dixie Project received considerable project planning money. Colorado's five projects did not receive "a dime." In early 1969 Colorado senator Gordon Allott wrote to President Richard M. Nixon requesting money for the five Colorado projects while protesting the nearly $1 million in planning monies appropriated for the Central Arizona Project. "This [budgetary] recommendation is in direct contravention of the provisions of Section 501b of this law," Allott fumed. Section 501b directed the interior secretary to proceed with construction of the five western Colorado projects concurrent with construction of the CAP. It was later revealed that Arizona representative John Rhodes had written to President Nixon insisting that while all Colorado River Basin projects were supposed to be built in concert, the CAP deserved higher priority because for Arizona and the nation it constituted "an emergency measure."[3]

As early as 1969, Rolland (Rollie) C. Fischer, director of the Colorado River Water Conservation District, detected the development of a "significant change in national attitudes toward water resources development." Fischer blamed the new environmental movement but also the many members of Congress who had been warming to its agenda. The national emphasis on wilderness, water pollution control, wild and scenic rivers, wildlife habitat, and outdoor recreation worked against the traditional water project planning environment. Fischer had also observed more public questioning of water projects and attitudes considered critical of reclamation. What should Colorado's water proponents do? Fischer believed they needed to engage in more energetic public relations and be "more aggressive in emphasizing public benefits" of water project construction.[4]

By 1970, Fischer's prediction of a "Brave New World" for water politics had arrived with the appointment of a new Bureau of Reclamation commissioner, Ellis W. Armstrong. Armstrong's message was that the Bureau of Reclamation needed to take a "broader" role in resource development. While dam and reservoir construction remained important, the bureau was trying to fit its traditional mission into a society that had started to recognize that water resources were limited and that valued the aesthetics and permanent health of the ecosystems. In words that must have chilled traditional Colorado water advocates, Armstrong noted that the maintenance and enhancement of "environmental quality become . . . equal partner[s] in the multipurpose concept." Armstrong, too, understood the need to communicate water resource development's significance to the broader public. His bureau, he maintained, needed to sell to a "bold, young, intellectual society the proposition that we are making the best possible use of the available water resources in Colorado [and the] West." This, he candidly admitted, would be "no easy job," since many Americans were questioning "our historic mission." Statements like Armstrong's, coming especially from the top Bureau of Reclamation official, would have been unthinkable five years before.[5]

Into this new water universe, in 1970 Colorado repeated its request for appropriations to plan its five Western Slope projects. The state had once again struggled to speak with one voice in its bid for project appropriations. Appearing before the Executive Committee of the Colorado Legislative

Council on Water, Colorado state senator Dan Noble (R-Norwood [Western Slope]) emphasized the need for all parts of the state to unify to gain federal support. With support and planning, Noble believed, construction of the five projects could begin by 1975. However, as this vignette makes clear, as early as 1970 some Coloradans appeared to see the opportunity to build the five western Colorado projects slipping away. By 1972 all of the Colorado projects except West Divide had received some planning monies, yet no construction of any of the Colorado River Basin Project's features had begun.[6]

To compound problems, in 1972 Colorado's most reliable water delivery boy, Wayne Aspinall, lost his reelection bid in the Democratic primary to Alan Merson, an eastern Colorado environmentalist and college professor. During the campaign, Merson attacked Aspinall as a tool of special interests, including those who consistently fed the state's constant growth by building unnecessary water projects, and as having failed to recognize the arrival of a new era of environmental limits. Aspinall underestimated Merson's appeal in a state growing more sensitized to environmental concerns. Aspinall also had to run for reelection in a reconfigured congressional district; the Colorado General Assembly had redrawn congressional districts, forcing Aspinall to represent a large amount of territory in the fast-growing region north of Denver. This area, which included several large college towns, provided Merson with a comfortable margin of victory in the primary election against Aspinall. Merson went on to lose the general election to Republican James P. Johnson. Aspinall's defeat was, in Arizona's Morris Udall's words, "the end of an era."[7]

For Colorado, this assessment rang especially true. While small reclamation projects would be authorized from time to time after 1972, no new water projects of any size would be built for a long time. Those already authorized, as part of the Colorado River Storage Project or the Colorado River Basin Project, would have a difficult time being funded or built in upcoming years. Of the five Western Slope projects so crucial for Colorado's support of the Central Arizona Project, only three have been constructed; in the case of the Animas–La Plata Project, it was built at a much smaller configuration than its original planners had intended. The three projects were also built long after most of the CAP features had been constructed. The West Divide and San Miguel Projects have not seen the light of day. This is especially ironic in the case of West Divide, which had been justified as crucial for the Colorado oil shale industry's water supply.

Even in Arizona, the Central Arizona Project struggled and lurched toward completion over a twenty-year period. Obtaining appropriations to proceed with construction became a painstaking ritual for Arizona politicians. As late as 1985 the project was only 50 percent complete, though some water finally flowed through parts of the system by 1986. In the mid-1980s the Reagan administration instituted new cost-sharing regulations for water projects that added financial burdens for participating states. Coupled with the plethora of environmental regulations, water project authorization and construction had become a difficult process. Henceforth, fewer projects would be proposed and they tended to be smaller, with a multitude of beneficiaries who would help with cost sharing. The new policies forced Arizona to climb onboard the "cost-sharing bandwagon" or face an even greater construction slowdown. As it was, the CAP was not completed until 1993–94.

In the twenty-five years after passage of the Colorado River Basin Project, the era of big water projects came to a crashing halt. In an age of growing environmental sensitivity, many Americans began frowning upon the old western political approach of constructing massive water projects. This approach struck an increasing number of Americans as both a waste of money and destructive to the environment. Finally, many Americans were openly questioning the damage massive reclamation had done to the pristine landscapes and ecology of Colorado and the West. Older projects were riddled with silt; salinity problems abounded; and riparian habits had been altered beyond recognition, contributing to the growing numbers of organisms added to the new Endangered Species Act (1973) listings.[8]

Ironically, even if they were personally and politically drawn to some of the era's new environmental values, many of Colorado's 1970s–80s political leaders still gave strong political public lip service to neo-Aspinall water development strategies. Being opposed to water development or even to a specific water project continued to spell a fast end to a political career in Colorado. No one demonstrates this dilemma better than Colorado Democratic senator Gary Hart. Elected to the Senate during the Democratic Watergate tide in 1974, Hart struggled to balance a fundamentally liberal environmental ideology with traditional western desires for water and energy development. Hart stretched his worldview to its breaking point to win the support of Colorado's water establishment, which did not trust or "warm" to him. Whenever possible, Hart attempted to raise his profile on water development issues. Joining with his fellow Colorado senator, the conservative Republican Bill Armstrong, Hart urged the funding of several water projects originally authorized but not yet on the path to construction, including Animas–La Plata[9] and eastern Colorado's Narrows Project. Colorado governor Richard Lamm (in office from 1975 to 1987) faced a similar dilemma.[10]

Lamm, according to former Aspinall foe Alan Merson, "got religion rather late in life." Merson's definition of "religion" was a more traditional and supportive attitude toward water development. Once a strong environmentalist who had criticized Wayne Aspinall's shaping of the Colorado River Basin Project, Lamm had won the governor's office in part for his successful opposition to Colorado's bid to host the 1976 Winter Olympics. In office, however, Lamm faced the reality of maintaining power in a state where the water community continued to exert great influence over public policy agendas. With the state believing it would need every drop of water it could get in the future, "politicians," according to Merson, "tend to go blind in office. They're for any water project. They don't care how bad it is."[11]

More recently, the Eastern and Western Slopes have continued to struggle over water projects that are smaller than those built in previous decades. Yet as both the Windy Gap Project (completed in 1985) and Wolford Mountain Reservoir (finished in 1996) indicate, cooperation between the two slopes is possible.[12] Yet the conflict scenarios between the Eastern and Western Slopes essentially follow the same script written in previous decades: the population-rich Front Range has continued to seek access to Western Slope water supplies. The Western Slope has fought back using many of the same well-rehearsed arguments it used in previous decades. Arguments emphasize that the region remains in its relative population and economic infancy, and, above all, it will soon realize its calling as the nation's chief natural resource and energy provider with the certain maturation of the oil shale industry. In addition, the Western Slope has continued to employ other time-tested, historical lines of reasoning: calls for additional water projects, more compensatory storage, delaying project planning and construction, and, in recent decades, using alliances with environmental organizations to call for reassessments of ecologically damaging trans-mountain diversions. However, one tool in the Western Slope's water protection toolbox no longer exists: no federal-level politician occupies a position of power like Edward T. Taylor and Wayne N. Aspinall enjoyed in earlier eras.

In 2014, water remained an ultra-sensitive topic on Colorado's Western Slope. Eastern Colorado's attempts to access more trans-mountain water continued, despite the calls for goodwill in the recent Colorado River Cooperative Agreement, ratified in 2013.[13] The Front Range Water Council told a group writing a new Colorado State Water Plan that the state's water future "needs to contain an assurance rather than just a hope" for future trans-mountain diversions. Western Colorado's reaction to such statements has varied, ranging from outright refusal to guarded consideration as long as protection for the Western Slope existed in dry years. Western Slope sensitivity even extended to official state historical representations. A 2014 display at the History Colorado Center in Denver called *Living West*, sponsored by the Gates Foundation and the Denver Water Board (DWB), proclaimed that the "Western Slope has water, but a small population. To eastern Colorado, this is a waste; shouldn't water go where the people are?" This and other exhibit messages incurred the immediate wrath of the Western Slope, with one Mesa County commissioner alleging that the DWB was using public monies to indoctrinate the public "to view water the way the Front Range does."[14]

Colorado's water wars are of long-standing origin, with roots in early territorial and statehood settlement patterns and in Colorado's unique geography that separates the state into halves. Open struggles over water between east and west Colorado began in the 1920s when the American Southwest began dividing its water supply among Colorado River states. In the 1920s, Denver and the Front Range made the first significant step toward reaching across the mountains to tap the waters of the Colorado River Basin. The Western Slope's reactions were designed to safeguard a regional water supply for a later era when population and economic growth needed it. The Colorado–Big Thompson Project, the struggles for the Colorado River Storage Project, the Blue River diversion, and the Fryingpan-Arkansas controversy all provided battlegrounds for Colorado's water wars. In the 1960s, under the state leadership of Felix Sparks, Governor John Love, Upper Colorado River Commission director Ival Goslin, and the immense federal political power of Wayne Aspinall, Colorado entered a new era characterized by more statewide cooperation inspired by threats to its water supply emanating from outside the state. In recent decades, open and loud intrastate water struggles are more rare, but they continue to occur. All of the variables remain in place for a continuation of Colorado's water wars in the decades ahead.

NOTES

1. Steven C. Schulte, *Wayne Aspinall and the Shaping of the American West* (Boulder: University Press of Colorado, 2002), 290.

2. Carl Abbott, Stephen J. Leonard, and Thomas J. Noel, *Colorado: A History of the Centennial State*, 4th ed. (Boulder: University Press of Colorado, 2005), 367–68.

3. See the undated reports from the Grand Junction *Daily Sentinel*'s Washington Bureau from this time period in Box 3, folder 20, William Nelson Papers, Colorado Mesa University Archives and Special Collections (hereafter CMUASC), Grand Junction; Gordon Allott to Richard M. Nixon, February 24, 1969, Box 131, folder 26, Frank Delaney Papers, University of Colorado at Boulder Archives (hereafter UCBA); Helen Monberg, "Colorado River Problems," March 6, 1969, Frank Delaney Papers, UCBA; Linda C. McGehee and John Newman, *Guide to the Ival Goslin Water Resources Collection*, rev. ed. (Fort Collins: Colorado State University Water Resources Archive, 2007).

4. CRWCD Minutes, October 30, 1969, folder "Minutes of the CRWCD, 1969–70," Colorado River Water Conservation District (hereafter CRWCD), Glenwood Springs; George Sibley, *Water Wranglers: The 75-Year History of the Colorado River District—a Story about the Embattled Colorado River and the Growth of the West* (Glenwood Springs: Colorado River District, 2012), 284–86.

5. CRWCD Minutes, January 20, 1970, folder "CRWCD Minutes, 1969–70," CRWCD, Glenwood Springs.

6. *Colorado Water Congress Newsletter*, vol. 13, no. 11, November 1, 1970, Box 6, folder 5, William Nelson Papers, CMUASC, Grand Junction.

7. Schulte, *Wayne Aspinall*, summarizes the 1972 Aspinall primary campaign. See Aspinall's own assessment of his primary defeat in a letter to constituent Leo Bouret, September 21, 1972, Box 463, folder "Pol-1a," Wayne N. Aspinall Papers, University of Denver Archives (hereafter UDA). Aspinall blamed the loss on "redistricting . . . environmental issues, and age." Udall's assessment is from the *Congressional Record*, October 18, 1972, 10423.

8. Donald Worster, *Rivers of Empire: Water, Aridity and the Growth of the American West* (New York: Pantheon Books, 1985), 291; John Opie, *Nature's Nation: An Environmental History of the United States* (Fort Worth: Harcourt, Brace, 1998), 337, 342.

9. Since the original 1968 legislation, the Animas–La Plata Project had been deemed unfeasible and had come under close scrutiny for a range of issues, from its original cost to many alleged destructive environmental impacts. See Helen Ingram, *Water Politics: Continuity and Change* (Albuquerque: University of New Mexico Press, 1990), 127–28.

10. Marc Reisner, *Cadillac Desert: The American West and Its Disappearing Water*, rev. ed. (New York: Penguin Books, 1993), 418.

11. Ibid.

12. Wolford Mountain in particular showcased the possibilities of Eastern-Western Slope cooperation. The DWB contributed most of the cost of constructing the reservoir for the Western Slope, and in return Denver received about 40 percent of the water. Denver believed it needed this arrangement after the demise of its Two Forks plans. See Patricia Nelson Limerick with Jason Hanson, *A Ditch in Time: The City, the West, and Water* (Golden, CO: Fulcrum, 2012), 232–33; Sibley, *Water Wranglers*, 335–36, 391–92. Daniel Tyler, *W. D. Farr: Cowboy in the Boardroom* (Norman: University of Oklahoma Press, 2011), contains an extended discussion of both Windy Gap and Wolford Mountain and features the role played by W. D. Farr in fostering these agreements and his role as a water leader in northern Colorado.

13. The 2013 Colorado River Cooperative Agreement, though not fully ratified by all parties (and more than forty parties were a part of it), appears to be a breakthrough in recent east-west Colorado water relations. Colorado governor John Hickenlooper hailed it as evidence of Colorado's "cooperative spirit," while Senator Mark Udall could not resist the obvious metaphor that the pact represented a "high water mark for collaboration." The agreement allows the DWB to expand several reservoirs as well as to develop more water supplies from Western Slope areas. Western Colorado interests pledged to not contest these actions. In return it received assurances that Denver would limit future diversions, work harder to keep Dillon Reservoir full for recreational activities, and help to finance Western Slope municipal water plants. See *Daily Sentinel*, September 17, 2010; Colorado River Water Conservation District, Colorado River Cooperative Agreement, accessed April 25, 2013, www.coloradoriverdistrict.org; *Denver Post*, April 25, 2011; May 2, 2012; Limerick and Hanson, *A Ditch in Time*.

14. *Daily Sentinel*, March 20, April 20, April 29, May 4 (quote about the exhibit), May 6, May 8, 2014. In a May 6, 2014, editorial, the *Daily Sentinel* proclaimed: "No Wonder Water Is Such a Thorny Issue," arguing that in an attempt to educate the public, especially children, to the complexities of the water issue, the exhibit creates a "first impression that many young Coloradans will carry into adulthood." With the DWB as an exhibit sponsor, "people wonder why we don't trust them," remarked Grand Junction area Chamber of Commerce president Diane Schewenke.

Glossary

This is a compilation of water terms frequently referenced in the book. Many of the terms are based on definitions in Gregory J. Hobbs Jr., *Citizen's Guide to Colorado Water Law* (Denver: Colorado Foundation for Water Education, 2004) and Colorado State University Extension, "Glossary of Water Terminology," accessed June 25, 2015, http://extension.colostate.edu/topic-areas/agriculture/glossary-of-water-terminology-4-717/.

Acre-feet. The amount of water required to cover one acre of land to a depth of one foot (325,851 gallons).

Beneficial use. A lawful appropriation of water that uses reasonably efficient practices to put water to use without waste. Some common beneficial uses include agriculture, municipal, mining, wildlife, and recreation uses.

Call. A request by a water appropriator for water to which the person is entitled. A call forces users with a junior water right to cease or diminish using their water to allow it to flow downstream to the holder of a senior water right.

CAP. Central Arizona Project, also known as the Colorado River Basin Project Act of 1968.

C-BT. Colorado–Big Thompson Project of 1937.

CFPS (cubic feet per second). A rate of water flow amounting to a volume of one cubic foot for each second of time.

Colorado River Compact of 1922. Also known as the "Law of the River," a compact negotiated among the seven Colorado River states to divide the river's waters into the Upper and Lower Basins.

Compensatory storage. A response by the Western Slope to the Colorado–Big Thompson Project in the 1930s. Compensatory storage would have compensated the basin of origin, the Western Slope, for water diverted to the Front Range region.

CRSP. Colorado River Storage Project of 1956.

CRWCD. Colorado River Water Conservation District, often referred to as the River District. Established by statute in 1937, the organization's mission is to protect and develop the waters of the Colorado River Basin within Colorado.

CWCB. Colorado Water Conservation Board, established by the state of Colorado in 1937 to provide central direction and to aid in the protection and development of the state's waters.

Doctrine of Prior Appropriation. This doctrine is the water law system used in most western states. It is based on the idea that the earliest diversion is superior to later diversions. The water must also be applied to beneficial use.

DWB. The Denver Water Board, also referred to as the Denver Board of Water Commissioners or Denver Water, was established in 1918 when the city of Denver purchased the Denver Union Water Company. The five-person board oversees Denver's water management.

Fryingpan-Arkansas Project. Also known as Fry-Ark, this is a trans-basin water diversion project in Colorado that carries water from the Fryingpan River and other tributaries of the Roaring Fork River on the Western Slope to the Arkansas River Basin on the Eastern Slope.

PSWWP. The Pacific Southwest Water Plan was a precursor of the Central Arizona Project.

Senate Document 80. A fundamental legal protective document for Western Slope water, derived from the authorization of the Colorado–Big Thompson Project.

Trans-mountain diversion. The moving of water from one drainage basin to another basin across the Continental Divide; also referred to as trans-basin diversion.

Upper Colorado River Basin Compact of 1949. The five states of the Upper Colorado River Basin divided their share of the Colorado River (7.5 million acre-feet) among themselves.

WCPA. The Western Colorado Protective Association was formed to negotiate on behalf of the Western Slope during the Colorado–Big Thompson controversy in the mid-1930s. It is a precursor organization to the Colorado River Water Conservation District.

Sources Consulted

MANUSCRIPT COLLECTIONS

American Heritage Center, University of Wyoming, Laramie
  John B. Barnard Papers
Arizona State University, Special Collections Department, Tempe
  Carl Hayden Papers
  John Rhodes Papers
  Ross R. Rice Papers
Colorado Mesa University Archives and Special Collections, Grand Junction
  Minutes and Records of the Colorado River Commission Negotiating the
    Colorado River Compact of 1922
  William Nelson Papers
  Vivian Passer Papers
Colorado River Water Conservation District, Glenwood Springs
  Larry Brown, Colorado River Water Conservation District History
  East-West Position, CWCB-TMD Collection

DOI: 10.5876/9781607325000.c009

Colorado River Water Conservation District Minutes

River District/WCPA Basin States, etc., Collection

Source Material, CWCB Minutes, RE: TMDCRD Collection

Colorado State Historical Society, Denver (now known as History Colorado)

Ralph Carr Papers

Glenn Saunders Papers

Silmon Smith Papers

Edward T. Taylor Papers

Denver Public Library, Western History Collection, Denver, CO

Papers of the Wilderness Society

Vertical File: Water Supply–Colorado

Vertical File: Water-Tunnels-Roberts

John F. Kennedy Presidential Library, Boston, MA

White House Staff Files

Lyndon B. Johnson Presidential Library, Austin, TX

Lyndon B. Johnson Presidential Papers

Name Files

Museum of the West, Loyd Files Research Library, Grand Junction, CO

D. W. Aupperle File

Oral History Files

John Page File

Silmon Smith File

National Archives, Washington, DC

US House Interior and Insular Affairs Committee Papers, Center for Legislative Archives

Special Collections, University of Arizona Library, Tucson

Morris K. Udall Papers

Stewart L. Udall Papers

University of Colorado at Boulder Archives

Gordon Allott Papers

Wayne N. Aspinall Papers

George M. Bull Papers

J. Edgar Chenoweth Papers

Frank Delaney Papers

Gary Hart Papers

Ray Kogovsek Papers
E. Grosvenor Plowman Papers
George A. and James M. Pughe Papers
Edward T. Taylor Papers
University of Denver Archives
Wayne N. Aspinall Papers
Edwin C. Johnson Papers
John Love Papers
Byron Rogers Papers

NEWSPAPERS

Albuquerque (NM) Tribune
Aspen (CO) Times
Bingham (UT) Bullet
Daily Press (Montrose, CO)
Daily Sentinel (Grand Junction, CO)
Denver News
Denver Post
Durango (CO) Herald
Glenwood (Glenwood Springs, CO) Post
Fort Lupton (CO) Press
Free Press (Grand Junction, CO)
Gunnison (CO) News-Champion
New York Times
Rocky Mountain News (Denver, CO)
Salt Lake City Tribune
Star-Chieftain (Pueblo, CO)
Star-Journal (Pueblo, CO)

ORAL INTERVIEWS

Aspinall, Wayne N. Interview by Nancy Whistler, Association of Former
   Members of Congress Project. Library of Congress, Washington DC.
   February 15, 1979.

Aspinall, Wayne. Interview by Helen Hansen, Mesa County Oral History Project (MC-OH-473). Part One. Museum of the West, Grand Junction, CO. August 10, 1981.

Brower, David R. "Environmental Activist, Publicist, and Prophet." Oral history conducted by Susan R. Schrepfer. Regional Oral History Office, Bancroft Library, University of California at Berkeley. 1974–78.

Elson, Roy. Interview by US Senate Historical Office, Washington, DC. Arizona State University, Special Collections Department, Tempe. April 27–August 21, 1990.

Neal, Tommy. Interview by Steven C. Schulte. Grand Junction, CO. January 4, 1997. Transcript in author's possession.

Rhodes, John. Interview by Ross R. Rice. Folder 96, Ross R. Rice Papers, Special Collections, Arizona State University Library, Tempe. December 6, 1973.

Udall, Stewart L. Interview by Steven C. Schulte. Grand Junction, CO. March 31 and April 1, 1998.

Udall, Stewart L. Phone interview by Steven C. Schulte. November 10, 1997.

GOVERNMENT DOCUMENTS

An Act to Authorize the Secretary of the Interior to Construct, Operate, and Maintain the Colorado River Storage Project and Participating Projects, and for Other Purposes. Public Law 485. 84th Congress, 2nd Session. Chapter 203. S. 500. April 11, 1956.

Boulder Canyon Project Act. HR 5733. 70th Congress. December 21, 1928.

Colorado River Basin Project. Hearings. Subcommittee on Irrigation and Reclamation, House Committee on Interior and Insular Affairs. 90th Congress, 1st Session, on HR 3300 et al. 1967.

Colorado River Basin Project. Part Two. Hearings. Subcommittee on Irrigation and Reclamation, House Committee on Interior and Insular Affairs. 90th Congress, 2nd Session, on HR 3300 and S. 1004. January 30–February 2, 1968.

Colorado River Storage Project. Hearings. Subcommittee on Irrigation and Reclamation, House Committee on Interior and Insular Affairs. 83rd Congress, 2nd Session, on HR 4449 et al. January 1954.

Colorado River Storage Project. Part One. Hearings. Subcommittee on
Irrigation and Reclamation, House Committee on Interior and Insular
Affairs. 84th Congress, 1st Session, on HR 270 et al. 1955.

Session Laws of Colorado. 1937. Water Conservation Districts (CRS 37-45-101).

Congressional Directory. 73rd Congress, 2nd Session. Washington, DC:
Government Printing Office, 1936.

Congressional Quarterly Fact Sheet. January 23, 1959.

Congressional Record. Various dates.

Lower Colorado River Basin Project. Hearings. Subcommittee on Irrigation
and Reclamation, House Interior and Insular Affairs Committee. 89th
Congress, 1st Session, on HR 4671 et al. 1965.

Lower Colorado River Basin Project. Hearings. Subcommittee on Irrigation
and Reclamation, House Interior and Insular Affairs Committee. 89th
Congress, 2nd Session, on HR 4671 et al. 1966.

Official Comments and Recommendations of the State of Colorado on the
Initial Development, Gunnison-Arkansas Project, Roaring Fork Division,
Colorado. Project Planning Report no. 7-8a.49-1. Washington, DC: Bureau
of Reclamation, Department of the Interior. January 1950.

Upper Colorado River Basin Compact. Hearings. Subcommittee on Irrigation
and Reclamation, Committee on Public Lands, House of Representatives.
81st Congress, 1st Session, on HR 2325–34. March 14–18, 1946.

Upper Colorado River Commission. Water Supplies of the Colorado River,
Available for Use by the States of the Upper Division and for the Use from
the Main Stem by the States of Arizona, California, and Nevada on the
Lower Basin. Denver: Tipton and Kalmbach, July 1965.

US Bureau of Reclamation. The Colorado River: "A Natural Menace Becomes
a Natural Resource": A Comprehensive Report on the Development of the
Water of the Colorado River Basin for Irrigation, Power Production, and
Other Beneficial Uses in Arizona, California, Colorado, Nevada, New Mexico,
Utah, and Wyoming. Washington, DC: Department of the Interior, 1946.

US Department of the Interior. A Survey of Recreational Resources of the
Colorado River Basin. Washington, DC: US Government Printing Office,
Department of the Interior, 1950.

US Senate, 75th Congress, 1st Session. Senate Document 80. Colorado–Big
Thompson Project. Synopsis of Report on Colorado–Big Thompson

Project, Plan of Development and Cost Estimate Prepared by the Bureau of Reclamation, Department of the Interior, June 15, 1937. Washington, DC: Government Printing Office, 1937.

US Statutes at Large. 14 (1865–67), 253.

Water Development Association of Southeast Colorado. Operating Principles Governing Fryingpan-Arkansas Diversion Project. Pueblo: Water Development Association of Southeast Colorado, n.d.

LEGAL CASES

Arizona v. California. 373 U.S. 546 (1963).

City and County of Denver et al. v. the Colorado River Water Conservation District et al. 276 P.2d 992 (1954).

Coffin v. Left Hand Ditch Company. 6 Colo. 443 (1882).

Denver v. Northern Colorado Water Conservation District. 130 Colo. 375, 276 P.2d 992 (1954).

Kansas v. Colorado. 185 U.S. 125 (1902).

Wyoming v. Colorado. 259 U.S. 419 (1922).

BOOKS

Abbott, Carl. *Colorado: A History of the Centennial State.* Boulder: Colorado Associated University Press, 1976.

Abbott, Carl. "The Federal Presence." In *Oxford History of the American West*, ed. Clyde A. Milner II, Carol O'Connor, and Martha A. Sandweiss, 469–99. New York: Oxford University Press, 1994.

Abbott, Carl, Stephen J. Leonard, and Thomas J. Noel. *Colorado: A History of the Centennial State,* 4th ed. Boulder: University Press of Colorado, 2005.

Baker, Richard Allan. *Conservation Politics: The Senate Career of Clinton P. Anderson.* Albuquerque: University of New Mexico Press, 1985.

Broadhead, Michael. *David J. Brewer: The Life of a Supreme Court Justice, 1837–1919.* Carbondale: Southern Illinois University Press, 1994.

Cosco, Jon M. *Echo Park: Struggle for Preservation.* Boulder: Johnson Books, 1995.

Crawford, Ivan C. *Water Resources Planning in Colorado.* Denver: Colorado Water Conservation Board, 1957.

Davis, Laurena. *125 Years, 125 People: The Grand Junction Story.* Grand Junction: Museum of Western Colorado, 2007.

Davis, Sandra K. "Water Politics in Colorado: Change, or Business as Usual?" In *Politics in the Postwar American West*, ed. Richard Lowitt, 64–81. Norman: University of Oklahoma Press, 1995.

deBuys, William. *A Great Aridness: Climate Change and the Future of the American Southwest*. New York: Oxford University Press, 2011.

Decker, Peter R. *Old Fences, New Neighbors*. Golden, CO: Fulcrum, 1998.

Delaney, Robert W. *The Ute Mountain Utes*. Albuquerque: University of New Mexico Press, 1988.

Dunbar, Robert G. *Forging New Rights in Western Waters*. Lincoln: University of Nebraska Press, 1983.

Farmer, Jared. *Glen Canyon Dammed: Inventing Lake Powell*. Tucson: University of Arizona Press, 1999.

Fenno, Richard F., Jr. *Congressmen in Committees*. Boston: Little, Brown, 1973.

Fradkin, Phillip. *A River No More: The Colorado River and the West*. Expanded and updated. Berkeley: University of California Press, 1996.

Gottlieb, Robert. *A Life of Its Own: The Politics and Power of Water*. New York: Harcourt Brace Jovanovich, 1988.

Gottlieb, Robert, and Peter Wiley. *Empires in the Sun: The Rise of the New American West*. New York: Putnam, 1982.

Guice, John D.W. *The Rocky Mountain Bench: The Territorial Supreme Courts of Colorado, Montana, and Wyoming, 1861–1890*. New Haven, CT: Yale University Press, 1972.

Harvey, Mark W.T. "Loving the Wild in Postwar America." In *American Wilderness: A New History*, ed. Michael Lewis, 187–204. New York: Oxford University Press, 2007.

Harvey, Mark W.T. *A Symbol of Wilderness: Echo Park and the American Conservation Movement*. Seattle: University of Washington Press, 1994.

Hobbs, Gregory J., Jr. *Citizens Guide to Colorado Water Law*. Denver: Colorado Foundation for Water Education, 2004.

Hoffman, Abraham. *Vision or Villainy: Origins of the Owens Valley–Los Angeles Water Controversy*. College Station: Texas A&M Press, 1981.

Hundley, Norris, Jr. *The Great Thirst: Californians and Water, 1770s–1990s*. Berkeley: University of California Press, 1992.

Hundley, Norris, Jr. *Water and the West: The Colorado River Compact and the Politics of Water in the American West*, 2nd ed. Berkeley: University of California Press, 2009.

Hundley, Norris, Jr. "The West against Itself: The Colorado River—an Institutional History." In *New Courses for the Colorado River: Major Issues for the Next Century*, ed. Gary D. Weatherford and F. Lee Brown, 9–49. Albuquerque: University of New Mexico Press, 1986.

Ingram, Helen. *Water Politics: Continuity and Change*. Albuquerque: University of New Mexico Press, 1990.

Iverson, Peter. "The Cultural Politics of Water in Arizona." In *Politics in the Postwar American West*, ed. Richard Lowitt, 22–41. Norman: University of Oklahoma Press, 1995.

Johnson, Rich. *The Central Arizona Project: 1918–1968*. Tucson: University of Arizona Press, 1977.

Kahrl, William L. *Water and Power: The Conflict over Los Angeles' Water Supply in the Owens Valley*. Berkeley: University of California Press, 1982.

Kupel, Douglas. *Fuel for Growth: Water and Arizona's Urban Environment*. Tucson: University of Arizona Press, 2003.

Leonard, Stephen J., and Thomas J. Noel. *Denver: From Mining Camp to Metropolis*. Niwot: University Press of Colorado, 1990.

Leuchtenburg, William E. *Franklin D. Roosevelt and the New Deal, 1932–40*. New York: Harper and Row, 1963.

Limerick, Patricia Nelson, with Jason Hanson. *A Ditch in Time: The City, the West, and Water*. Golden, CO: Fulcrum, 2012.

McCarthy, Michael G. *Hour of Trial: The Conservation Conflict in Colorado and the West*. Norman: University of Oklahoma Press, 1977.

McGehee, Linda C., and John Newman. *Guide to the Ival Goslin Water Resources Collection*, rev. ed. Fort Collins: Colorado State University Water Resources Archive, 2007.

Mulholland, William, Lippincott, and Parker. "Report on Water Supply." In *Annual Report of the Board of Water Commissioners of the Domestic Water Works System of the City of Los Angeles for the Fiscal Year Ending November 30, 1902*, 79. Los Angeles: Press of the Out West Company, 1902.

Nash, Gerald D. *The American West Transformed: The Impact of the Second World War*. Lincoln: University of Nebraska Press, 1985.

Neel, Susan Rhoades. "A Place of Extremes: Nature, History, and the American West." In *A New Significance: Re-Envisioning the History of the American West*, ed. Clyde Milner II, 105–26. New York: Oxford University Press, 1996.

Noel, Thomas J., Paul F. Mahoney, and Richard E. Stevens. *Historical Atlas of Colorado*. Norman: University of Oklahoma Press, 1993.

Opie, John. *Nature's Nation: An Environmental History of the United States*. Fort Worth: Harcourt Brace, 1998.

Pearson, Byron E. *Still the Wild River Runs: Congress, the Sierra Club, and the Fight to Save the Grand Canyon*. Tucson: University of Arizona Press, 2002.

Pisani, Donald J. "State versus Nation: Federal Reclamation and Water Rights in the West: The Progressive Era." In *Water, Land, and Law in the West: The Limits of Public Policy, 1850–1920*, ed. Donald J. Pisani, 38–49. Lawrence: University of Kansas Press, 1996.

Pisani, Donald J. *To Reclaim a Divided West: Water, Law, and Public Policy, 1848–1902*. Albuquerque: University of New Mexico Press, 1992.

Pisani, Donald J. *Water and American Government: The Reclamation Bureau, National Water Policy, and the West, 1902–1935.* Berkeley: University of California Press, 2002. http://dx.doi.org/10.1525/california/9780520230309.001.0001.

Pisani, Donald J., ed. *Water, Land, and Law in the West: The Limits of Public Policy, 1850–1920.* Lawrence: University of Kansas Press, 1996.

Radosevich, G. E., K. C. Nobe, D. Allardice, and C. Kirkwood. *Evolution and Administration of Colorado Water Law: 1876–1976.* Fort Collins, CO: Water Resources Publications, 1976.

Reisner, Marc. *Cadillac Desert: The American West and Its Disappearing Water,* rev. ed. New York: Penguin Books, 1993.

Richardson, Elmo R. *Dams, Parks, and Politics: Resource Development and Preservation in the Truman-Eisenhower Era.* Lexington: University Press of Kentucky, 1973.

Righter, Robert W. *The Battle over Hetch Hetchy: America's Most Controversial Dam and the Birth of Modern Environmentalism.* New York: Oxford University Press, 2005. http://dx.doi.org/10.1093/acprof:oso/9780195149470.001.0001.

Rothman, Hal K. *The Greening of a Nation: Environmentalism in the United States since 1945.* Fort Worth: Harcourt Brace, 1998.

Saunders, Glenn G. "Reflections on Sixty Years of Water Law Practice." Natural Resources Law Center, Occasional Papers Series. Boulder: University of Colorado School of Law, 1989.

Schlesinger, Arthur, Jr. *The Coming of the New Deal.* Boston: Houghton Mifflin, 1959.

Schorr, David. *The Colorado Doctrine: Water Rights, Corporations, and Distributive Justice on the American Frontier.* New Haven, CT: Yale University Press, 2012. http://dx.doi.org/10.12987/yale/9780300134476.001.0001.

Schrepfer, Susan. *David Brower: Environmental Activist, Publicist, and Prophet.* Berkeley: Regional Oral History Office, Bancroft Library, University of California, 1974–78.

Schulte, Steven C. *Wayne Aspinall and the Shaping of the American West.* Boulder: University Press of Colorado, 2002.

Sherow, James Earl. *Watering the Valley: Development along the High Plains Arkansas River, 1870–1950.* Lawrence: University of Kansas Press, 1990.

Sibley, George. *Water Wranglers: The 75-Year History of the Colorado River District—a Story about the Embattled Colorado River and the Growth of the West.* Glenwood Springs: Colorado River District, 2012.

Smith, Duane A. *Henry M. Teller: Colorado's Grand Old Man.* Boulder: University Press of Colorado, 2002.

Smith, Duane A. *Rocky Mountain West: Colorado, Wyoming, and Montana.* Albuquerque: University of New Mexico Press, 1992.

Smith, Thomas G. *Green Republican: John Saylor and the Preservation of America's Wilderness.* Pittsburgh: University of Pittsburgh Press, 2006.

Stegner, Wallace. *Beyond the Hundredth Meridian: John Wesley Powell and the Second Opening of the West.* Boston: Houghton Mifflin, 1954.

Steinberg, Ted. *Down to Earth: Nature's Role in American History*. New York: Oxford University Press, 2002.

Stenzel. Dick. "An Irrigated Legacy: The Union Colony." In *Citizen's Guide to Colorado's Water Heritage*, ed. Karla Brown, 19–23. Denver: Colorado Foundation for Water Education, 2004.

Tyler, Daniel. *The Last Water Hole in the West: The Colorado–Big Thompson Project and the Northern Colorado Water Conservancy District*. Niwot: University Press of Colorado, 1992.

Tyler, Daniel. *Silver Fox of the Rockies: Delphus E. Carpenter and Western Water Compacts*. Norman: University of Oklahoma Press, 2003.

Tyler, Daniel. *W. D. Farr: Cowboy in the Boardroom*. Norman: University of Oklahoma Press, 2011.

Ubbelohde, Carl, Maxine Benson, and Duane A. Smith. *A Colorado History*, 9th ed. Boulder: Pruett, 2006.

Udall, Morris K. *Too Funny to Be President*. New York: Henry Holt, 1988.

Underwood, Kathleen. *Town Building on the Colorado Frontier*. Albuquerque: University of New Mexico Press, 1987.

Vandenbusche, Duane, and Duane A. Smith. *A Land Alone: Colorado's Western Slope*. Boulder: Pruett, 1981.

Walton, John. *Western Times and Water Wars: State, Culture, and Rebellion in California*. Berkeley: University of California Press, 1993.

White, Richard. *It's Your Misfortune and None of My Own: A New History of the American West*. Norman: University of Oklahoma Press, 1991.

Wickens, James F. *Colorado in the Great Depression*. New York: Garland, 1979.

Wilkinson, Charles E. *Crossing the Next Meridian: Land, Water, and the Future of the West*. Washington, DC: Island, 1992.

Wilkinson, Charles E. "To Settle a New Land: An Historical Essay on Water Law and Policy in the American West and Colorado." In *Water and the American West—Essays in Honor of Raphael J. Moses*, ed. David H. Getches, 1–17. Boulder: Natural Resources Law Center, University of Colorado, 1988.

Worster, Donald. *Rivers of Empire: Water, Aridity and the Growth of the American West*. New York: Pantheon Books, 1985.

Wyckoff, William. *Creating Colorado: The Making of a Western American Landscape, 1860–1940*. New Haven, CT: Yale University Press, 1999.

PERIODICALS

Brietenstein, Jean. "The Upper Colorado River Basin Compact." *State Government* 22 (1949): 214–16, 225.

DeVoto, Bernard. "Sacred Cows and Public Lands." *Harper's Magazine* (July 1948): 44–45.

Gibbard, Frank. "*Wyoming v. Colorado*: A 'Watershed' Decision." *Colorado Lawyer* 34, no. 3 (2005): 37.

Grigg, Neil S. "A History of Colorado Water by the Decades." *Colorado Water* 27, no. 2 (March-April 2010): 12–14.

Hobbs, Gregory J., Jr. "Colorado Water Law: An Historical Overview." *Water Law Review* 1, no. 1 (Fall 1997): 1–160.

Hundley, Norris, Jr. "Water and the West in the Historical Imagination." *Western Historical Quarterly* 27, no. 1 (Spring 1996): 4–31. http://dx.doi.org/10.2307/969919.

Sherow, James E. "The Contest for the Nile of America, *Kansas v. Colorado* (1907)." *Great Plains Quarterly* 10 (1990): 48–61.

Smith, Duane A. "A Land unto Itself: The Western Slope." *Colorado Magazine* 55 (1978): 181–204.

THESES AND DISSERTATIONS

Ellison, Brian Adrian. "The Denver Water Board: Bureaucratic Power and Autonomy in Local Natural Resource Agencies." PhD dissertation, Colorado State University, Fort Collins, 1993.

Hildner, Matthew. "Fight for the Faucet: The Denver Water Board, the Blue River, and Metropolitan Water Supply." MA thesis, Colorado State University, Fort Collins, 1999.

Mehls, Carol Jean Drake. "Into the Frying Pan: J. Edgar Chenoweth and the Fryingpan-Arkansas Reclamation Project." PhD dissertation, University of Colorado–Boulder, 1986.

LECTURES/PRESENTATIONS

Hobbs, Gregory. "History of Colorado River Law, Development, and Use: A Primer and Look Forward." Paper presented at the Conference Hard Times on the Colorado River: Drought, Growth, and the Future of the Compact. Natural Resources Law Center, University of Colorado School of Law, Boulder, June 8–10, 2005.

Raley, Bradley F. "Irrigation, Land Speculation, and the History of Grand Junction, Colorado." Paper presented at the Western History Association Meeting, St. Paul, MN, October 17, 1996.

ELECTRONIC SOURCES

Barnard, John B., Jr. "The Early History of the Colorado Water Congress, 1957–58." Source in author's possession.

Biography of John Page, Commissioner, Bureau of Reclamation. http://www.usbr.gov/history/CommissBios/page.html.

Colorado River District History. http://www.coloradoriverdistrict.org.

Colorado River Water Conservation District. Colorado River Cooperative Agreement. Accessed April 25, 2013. www.coloradoriverdistrict.org.

Constitution of the State of Colorado. Accessed March 8, 2011. www.michie.com/colorado/lpext.dll?f=templates&fn=main-h.htm&cp=.

Denver Water for Today and Tomorrow: An Integrated Water Resource Plan—Water Supply Planning, Appendix. 1997. Accessed June 8, 2011. www.nwo.usace.army.mil/html/od-t/eis/moffat.deis.tech.rpt.DW-1997-IRP-Appendix-Water-Supply-Planning.pdf.

Economics Summit and the Adams Group. *Water and Colorado's Economy.* December 2009. http://summiteconomics.com/FRWP_Econ_Final_2011910.pdf.

"Front Range Counties to Dominate Colorado's Population and Politics." *Ciruli Associates,* March 23, 2011. http://fciruli.blogspot.com/2011/03/front-range-counties-to-dominate.html.

History and Description of the Fryingpan-Arkansas Project. Accessed August 20, 2009. www.secwcd.org/content/fryingpan-arkansas-project-history.

Obituary, Felix Sparks. Accessed October 2, 2012. www.legacy.com/obituaries/denverpost/obituary.arpx?n=felix-spark&pid=9512492.

Online Archive of California. Accessed June 12, 2011. http://oac.cdlib.org/.

Proceedings of the Public Lands Convention, Held in Denver, Colorado, June 18–20, 1907 by the States and Territories Containing the Public Lands of the United States and Lying West of the Missouri River. Copied and published by authority of the convention, Fred C. Johnson, secretary, Denver, CO. Accessed February 10, 2013. http://memory.loc.gov/cgi-bin/query/r?ammem/consrv:@field(DOCID+Alit(amrvgvg56)#vg56023.

Quillen, Ed. "Courts and Conservancy." *Colorado Central Magazine* (April 2001). Accessed June 24, 2016. http://cozine.com/2001-april/courts-and-conservancy/.

Quillen, Ed. "The War on the West." *High Country News Online,* February 15, 2011. Accessed November 10, 2012. http://www.hcn.org/articles/the-latest-war-on-the-west.

Quillen, Martha, ed. "Trust the Experts." *Colorado Central Magazine* (April 2006). Accessed February 17, 2012. http://cozine.com/2006-april/trust-the-experts/.

Simonds, William Joe. *The Grand Valley Project.* Washington, DC: Bureau of Reclamation, 1994. Accessed April 20, 2015. http://www.usbr.gov/projects/ImageServer?imgName=Doc_1305042485344.pdf.

Winchester, John N. "A Historical View: Transmountain Diversion Development in Colorado." Hydrosphere Resource Consultants, Inc. Accessed February 29, 2012. https://dspace.library.colostate.edu/bitstream/handle/10217/46354/116_Proceedings%202001%20USCID%20Water%20Management%20-%20Transbasin%20Water%20Transfers%20Winchester.pdf?sequence=15&isAllowed=y.

Index